AESTHETIC INDIVIDUALISM AND PRACTICAL INTELLECT

Aesthetic Individualism and Practical Intellect

AMERICAN ALLEGORY IN
EMERSON, THOREAU, ADAMS,
AND JAMES

OLAF HANSEN

PRINCETON UNIVERSITY PRESS
PRINCETON, NEW JERSEY

Published by Princeton University Press,
41 William Street, Princeton, New Jersey 08540
In the United Kingdom:
Princeton University Press, Oxford

Library of Congress Cataloging-in-Publication Data

Hansen, Olaf, 1943–
Aesthetic individualism and practical intellect:
American allegory in Emerson, Thoreau, Adams, and James/Olaf Hansen.
p. cm.
Bibliography: p.
Includes index.
ISBN 0-691-06823-2 (alk. paper)
1. American literature—19th century—History and criticism.
2. Allegory. 3. Individualism in literature. 4. Emerson, Ralph Waldo, 1803–1882—Criticism and interpretation. 5. Thoreau, Henry David, 1817–1862—Criticism and interpretation. 6. Adams, Henry, 1838–1918—Criticism and interpretation. 7. James, Williams, 1842–1910. I. Title.
PS217.A46H3 1990
810'.9'15—dc19 89-3841

This book has been composed in Linotron Baskerville

Princeton University Press books are printed on acid-free paper, and meet the guidelines for permanence and durability of the Committee on Production Guidelines for Book Longevity of the Council on Library Resources

Printed in the United States of America by
Princeton University Press,
Princeton, New Jersey

1 3 5 7 9 10 8 6 4 2

For

Daniel Aaron

and

Martin Christadler

Teachers and Friends

CONTENTS

PREFACE

Between so many possible beginnings, middles, and endings, we always identify aspects of a moral culture which we would like to call our past, our tradition. We have to make a choice and must face what William James, in a brief essay published in 1906, called "a certain ultimate hardihood, a certain willingness to live without assurances or guarantees." The existence of a moral culture, in other words, always depends upon the conscious act of making sense, knowing well enough, as William James put it, that we all "live on some inclined plane of credulity." To claim the right to the inheritance of a moral culture means to admit a specific history of both selfhood and knowledge. In fact, the title which William James gave to his essay, "The Absolute and the Strenuous Life," can be read today like a summary of all the possible fates selfhood and knowledge could have chosen as paths towards their own history out of the nineteenth century into modernity.

Broadly speaking, in this book my only concern is to unfold one particular strand within the complex history of both selfhood and knowledge in the American nineteenth century. The history in question refers to the kind of selfhood and knowledge which have tried to resist what Max Weber called the inevitable course of the disenchanted world towards a closed, bureaucratized system of rationality. Men like Emerson, Thoreau, Adams, and James knew that in order to make sense they had to accept the limits of preliminary selfhood and knowledge. It was a kind of acceptance, however, which had its rewards. To the degree that since the beginning of the nineteenth century the amount of possible choices offering themselves to the self increased so rapidly that the fear of social anomie became a widespread obsession, the preliminary self defied its integration into the order of social structures. Also, the kind of self-choice which preferred to confront "the whole body and drift of all the truths in sight," to refer once more to William James, was not only unable to "let loose quietistic raptures," it also invented a specific language and genre to express the seriousness of making sense as part of a general aesthetic endeavor. The aesthetic endeavor was a way of creating a morally practical unity of life knowing that the creative will would always remain a quest. So, from the very beginning, the conception of the self we are talking about and the kind of knowledge it helped to preserve and to produce were both oriented towards transcendence and towards practicality. Aesthetic individualism and practical intellect, in the American nineteenth century, had become the essential elements of a philosophical style which promised a kind of morality which would be generalized without destroying particularity and individualism.

Out of this genuine American philosophical style, a mode of thought which basically tried to negate the difference between life and art, the form of allegorical expression arose as the most suitable one for the purpose of making sense by preferring the fragment to the system. The language of allegory was subversive, it did not avoid hermeticism or paradox, it frequently was meant to be understood by only a few and always made heavy demands on those who cared to listen. Undoubtedly the American allegory of the nineteenth century revealed definite gnostic aspects as well. The American allegory was the perfect expression for a mode of thought which had to be philosophical within a tradition which quickly moved from secularization to professionalization. In short, the American allegory, simply because as an intellectual and artistic style it allowed the expression of conflicts and contradictions, kept a sense of tradition alive, when it was most threatened, by the old dilemma of having to choose between absolute subjectivity on the one hand and absolute objectivity on the other. Emerson, Thoreau, Adams, and James refused to make a choice. In a letter to his friend Charles Milner Gaskell, in 1891, Henry Adams presented his own position in a way which could easily serve as a categorical imperative for society in general: "The moral seems to be that every man should write his own life, to prevent some other fellow from taking it. The moral is always worse than the vicious alternative, and after all, the sacrifice would not ensure safety." A working tradition will have to live without the idea of its own biography. The American allegory drawing upon the past as much as it pointed towards the future, simply by insisting on the sensibility of keeping questions open and alive, has managed to make that part of our own tradition accessible to us which we are most likely to forget: in order to live our lives within a moral culture we have to remake it again and again. There is no other choice if we want to make sense.

Many individuals and institutions have given invaluable help in the process of writing this book. The American Council of Learned Societies first provided a generous fellowship that allowed me to start this project, which was finally finished during a year at the magnificent National Humanities center, North Carolina. The generosity and help which I have experienced at the Center cannot be praised enough. I want to express my profound gratitude to both the staff and to my wonderful cofellows. From among the many colleagues and friends who have helped me through their criticism and reassurance I can name only a few:

Daniel Aaron, Sacvan Bercovitch, Warner Berthoff, Nina Birnbaum, William Bouwsma, Timothy Breen, Scott Carson, Jules Chametzky, Martin Christadler, Gisela Dietz-Hansen, William Dray, Everett Emerson, Philip Fisher, Franklin Ford, Bettina and Herwig Friedl, Melvin Friedman, Alex Gelley, Mick Gidley, Timothy Gilmore, Eugene Goodheart, Anne Halley, Jack Hexter, Jasper Hopkins, Heinz Ickstadt, Linda Kauffman, Anne Koenen, Alice Kuzniar, Hans-Joachim Lang, Kurt and Gladys Lang, Blanche Linden, Leo Marx, Martin Meisel, Barbara Novak, Ortrun O'Connor, Barbara Packer, Robert Phelps, Richard Poirier, Joel Porte, John Shelton Reed, Paul Ricoeur, William Rorabaugh, Elaine Scarry, Richard Schiff, John Seelye, Werner Sollors, Gisela Stahl, Alan Trachtenberg, Jörg Villwock, Ronald Witt, and Leonora Woodman. Finally, I want to thank my editor Robert Brown, for both his patience and for his good advice.

If in writing this book I have managed to pay back some of the debts which I owe to individuals, institutions, and a culture from which I have profited so greatly, I am willing to consider the writing of this book, whatever its shortcomings, a small but significant success.

Frankfurt am Main

December 1987

AESTHETIC INDIVIDUALISM AND PRACTICAL INTELLECT

INTRODUCTION

Vision precedes language. The cultural process of transforming time into history reflects this order of precedence. In fact, it is the tension between vision and language which provides the elementary energy which it takes to create meaning. The true *epoché*, therefore, often produces forms of expression, which by means of intricate and highly configurative rhetoric try to recapture, as Francis Bacon put it, the "volume of creation."

Within the context of the American Renaissance, it was Emerson's theory of vision and language which more than anything else served to radicalize the idea of the epochal moment as one of reflection and redefinition. It is true, of course, that for the historian whose task it is to demonstrate continuities, it is the event which marks the period it helped to create. But even at its most accessible level of historiographical narrative, the representation of events frequently turns into the kind of discourse which points to itself as a reminder of its origin.

It is not surprising, then, that Thomas Wentworth Higginson, the reliable though not philosophically inclined chronicler of New England events, has given us one of the most perceptive accounts of the epochal qualities of the year 1836. Drawing upon the whole arsenal of visual metaphors which informed the era of transcendentalism as a culturally specific period in the American intellectual history Higginson puts the year into a double perspective, thus emphasizing the mythical function of the historically decisive *epoché.*

> What is called the Transcendental movement amounted essentially to this: that about the year 1836 a number of young people in America made the discovery that, in whatever quarter of the globe they happened to be, it was possible for them to take a look at the stars for themselves. This discovery no doubt led to extrav-

> agances and follies; the experimentalists at first went stumbling about, like the astrologer in the fable with their eyes on the heavens; and at Brook Farm they, like him, fell into a ditch. No matter![1]

"Looking at the stars for themselves" is the quintessential expression of asserted selfhood; it represents the evidence of man's ability and will to make sense in clear view of what he will never reach. The tragic potential of such self-consciousness would always be a reminder of what young H. D. Thoreau identified as man's fate. "How alone must our life be lived! We dwell on the seashore, and none between us and the sea . . . The weakest child is exposed to the fates henceforth as barely as its parents. Parents and relations but entertain the youth; they cannot stand between him and his destiny. This is the one bare side of every man. There is no fence; it is clear before him to the bounds of space."[2]

The clear view of the unattainable lends identity to our existence in this world *because* we cannot integrate the cosmos. So then, whatever shape each individual's existence will have, its identity is derivative of a purity of vision which can only be defined in terms of its unworldliness. Hence the worldly, practical consequences of our quest for identity.

Higginson is drawn in by his first line about taking "a look at the stars for themselves" and must reveal its pagan substance by quoting a fable, which itself has served in the course of time as a commentary on the worldly fate of vision.[3] Whether we think of Plato's version of the fable, or of its original content within the Aesopian context or remember Bacon's comments on the astronomer's fall: the transcendental movement, in Higginson's words is firmly placed as a beginning which clearly has its own tradition. The fact that Higginson picked this particular anecdote to illustrate what he thought to be characteristic of the transcendentalist movement attests to more than the mere durability of the fable itself. It is the way in which the sense of the fable is produced which allows Higginson to shed some light on how the transcendentalist movement was perceived. By linking the subjective

[1] Thomas Wentworth Higginson, *Margaret Fuller Ossoli* (New York, 1968), p. 133. All quotations from Higginson are from the 1968 reprint. The book was first published in 1884.

[2] Henry David Thoreau, *The Journal of Henry David Thoreau* (New York, 1962) 1: 239. All quotations from Thoreau's *Journal* are taken from the Dover edition, a reprint of the fourteen-volume Houghton Mifflin edition of 1906.

[3] Hans Blumenberg, "Der Sturz des Protophilosophen," *Poetik und Hermeneutik* 7 (1977): 11–64.

traces of transcendentalism to its political background, his densely packed statement opens a clear vista on the transcendentalist movement and its self-conception; on its peculiar blend of Enlightenment and romanticism, of subjectivity and of the function of the objective reality it kept probing.

Even if Higginson does not exploit his material to its full extent, he manages to outline its potential. Ingeniously he gives credit to the transcendentalist's originality, by discarding the importance of the failure of Brook Farm.

> There were plenty of people to make a stand in behalf of conventionalism in those very days; the thing most needed was a few fresh thinkers, a few apostles of the ideal; and they soon made their appearance in good earnest. The first impulse, no doubt, was in the line of philosophic and theological speculation; but the primary aim announced on the very first page of the "Dial" was "to make new demands on literature." It is in this aspect that the movement must especially be treated here.[4]

One would expect, after such self-exhortation, that Higginson should move on to a description of literary theories or at least to some preferences of artistic taste as advanced in the *Dial*. But there is no easy escape from the metaphysical content of his beginning. In a circular movement he returns to his primary image and then adds to its meaning. As a result, he also enhances the meaning of the fable mentioned earlier.

> The moment they made the discovery that they could see the universe with their own eyes, they ceased to be provincial. . . . After all, narrowness or enlargement are in the mind. Mr. Henry James, turning on Thoreau the reverse end of a remarkable good telescope, pronounces him "parochial" because he made the woods and waters of Concord, Massachusetts, his chief theme. The epithet is consciously felicitous. To be parochial is to turn away from the great and look at the little; the daily newspapers of Paris afford the best illustration of this fault.[5]

The idea of Henry James reversing the telescope demonstrates the ambivalence of progress. The original version of Emerson or Thoreau could not have been reversed. Instead they desperately tried to maintain the validity of a personal, technically unmediated interaction with

[4] Higginson, *Ossoli*, p. 133.

[5] Ibid., p. 34.

the world around them. Thus they not only accepted without program or ideology the limitations of the mind's place in nature, they also faced the dilemma of having lost faith in the substance of idealism without being able to replace it with some kind of acceptable realism. The awareness of man's uncertain position in a world of seemingly unlimited varieties of reality which Emerson and Thoreau shared with both Henry Adams and William James can hardly be overestimated.

At the same time, however, it was the very fact of these men's acceptance of a limitation as to what kind of truth one could possibly expect from personal vision as a basis of experience which allowed the introduction, and as a logical result, the reversal of the telescope as a reality-constructing tool of the intellect by their opponents.

Even if the time sequences between the fable of Thales of Miletus and the reminder of the *querelle des anciens et des modernes* in Higginson's placing of the transcendentalists will eventually confirm our suspicion that the American Renaissance owed more of its characteristics to the legacy of the Enlightenment than to romanticism, we have to admit that by mere force of protest, Higginson admits an interesting defeat. The machinery of refined vision, the telescope or microscope, is indeed an indicator of a hope of improvement. The defeat in question begins with Thoreau, on whom, according to Higginson, the telescope is reversed. Emerson after all, would hardly have liked to admit that an optical device could fundamentally change the meaningful and sensible relation between the eye and the horizon. If, then, Higginson tries to aid Thoreau, it is in the spirit of Emerson. But the spirit has become abstract, for Emerson would have denied the primary importance of the telescope as a means of improved vision. He saw himself much more naturally in the role of the observer than Thoreau would.[6] His mild and yet clear remarks on the faculties of the naturalist in his journal and in his lectures demonstrate this aptly. Higginson's final defense goes to Thoreau—and, in the end, to Margaret Fuller Ossoli, when he writes: "It is not parochial, but the contrary, when Dr. Gould spends his life in watching the stars from his lonely observatory in Paraguay; or when Lafargue erects his isolated studio among the Paradise Rocks near Newport; or when Thoreau studies birds and bees, Iliads and Vedas, in his little cottage by Lake Walden. To look out of the little world into the great, that is enlargement; all else is parochialism."[7]

As the passage from Higginson's book on Margaret Fuller Ossoli

[6] Thoreau repeatedly referred to the activities of observing and recording as naming.
[7] Higginson, *Ossoli*, p. 134.

shows, it was not that simple; even a very brief account of what made the year 1836 so special had to work with a variety of layers of meaning. The influence of the available contemporary knowledge does not suffice in order to explain the specific quality of a disruptive beginning within an ongoing tradition. As Higginson correctly observes: "The sources of intellectual influence then most powerful in England, France, and Germany, were accessible and potent in America also . . . thanks to this general fact, that the best literature is transportable and carries the same weight everywhere, these American innovators, living in Boston and Cambridge and Concord, had for literary purposes a cosmopolitan training. This advantage would, however, have been of little worth to them unless combined with the consciousness that they were living in a new world and were part of a self-governing nation."[8]

Once more, Higginson, by way of quoting from the young Robert Bartlett's "Master of Arts oration" held in 1839, demonstrates how the national consciousness which he mentioned earlier on would have to invent a particular language of self-reference.

> Let us come and live, and know in living a high philosophy and faith, so shall we find now, here, the elements, and in our own good souls the fire. Of every stories bay and cliff and plain, we will make something infinitely nobler than Salamis or Marathon. This pale Massachusetts sky, this sandy soil and raw wind, all shall nurture us, . . . Rich skies, fair fields shall come to us, suffused with the immortal hues of spirit, of beauteous act and thought. Unlike all the word before us, our own age and land shall be classic to ourselves.[9]

In its final turn of temporal structure, the move is made, from an appeal to the future to the rhetoric of allegory. The desire to "be classic to ourselves" will never be fulfilled, and it is the very statement of such a wish, which implies the realization of its impossibility. We can go one step further than this. The appeal to the future establishes the future as an authoritative and authentic fact of history's progression, whereas the temporal impossibility of being classical to oneself acknowledges the fact of infinite nonidentity. The language of the American allegory has legitimized the transition from the insight into the fundamental impossibility of becoming classical to oneself—that is, an authority over one's own existence in time—to the formalized ex-

[8] Ibid., pp. 134, 136.
[9] Ibid., p. 139.

pression of the insistence that the pursuit of the unattainable literally *makes sense*.

The claims of intellectual history must be modest: for the sake of its authenticity it has to work by exclusion. Any argument, then, made within the limits of the mind at work creates an enormous, sometimes an overwhelming, background. The obvious question is: how can one not talk about the social, political, and economical dimensions of whatever we think history is all about? If we want to avoid the fray of metadisciplinary discourse concerned with defining the method and scope of intellectual history, the answer to the question raised will have to be given in the form of a simple proposition. We assume that an advanced, complex, and self-conscious mode of thought exists which addresses itself to comprehensive problems of humankind. Max Weber, who has tried to outline the characteristics of the intellectual in his *Economy and Society*, has coined the phrase of the intellectual's "soteriological" disposition. What he meant was, quite simply, that an unbiased analysis of society will have to account for the existence of a kind of individual who becomes preoccupied with metaphysical problems and questions concerning the idea of a sensible world as a whole, without being forced to do so by external pressures. These people do not look for a way out of a desperate situation—they desperately try to understand the larger design. If there is any specific disposition which we can call their very own, it is the desire to understand the sense and the order of a world which they find elusive, puzzling, enigmatic, and often quite chaotic. It is these people's way of dealing with the world which is under scrutiny here—under scrutiny in its particular form as it has been produced in the second half of the nineteenth century in America.

All we have said so far helps to distinguish the "man of letters" from the intellectual in the modern sense of the word. It is, in fact, one of the disturbing findings with which we have to come to terms, that the modern intellectual, emerging as a social type in America after the turn of the century reacted very strongly to outside social, political, or ideological pressures, whereas it is the man of letters who is driven by the "soteriological" desire which Max Weber talks about. His wish to order the world in such modes of thought which recognizes, identifies, and interprets problems which go beyond particular or special-interest groups is by its very nature the primary subject matter of intellectual history. The rest follows.

Man thinking, to borrow a phrase from Ralph Waldo Emerson, is the center of intellectual history. We are dealing with active minds creating a tradition, claiming the right to do so from an independent point of view and fully aware of the fact that others who do not participate in the making of both culture and tradition will have to live within the boundaries which such making necessitates. If we look at the four men who represent what is the allegorical tradition in American culture, Emerson, Thoreau, Henry Adams, and William James, we are struck immediately by the fact that they "represent" in a strange way. They are certainly not part of what Raymond Williams would have called the "dominant culture" of their time, and yet, if we look for the larger questions raised within the turmoil of the American nineteenth century, we turn to them and follow their discussion of the issues at stake. If we want to appreciate the full body of their intellectual substance, we will have to acknowledge that all four allowed themselves a certain aloofness from pressing social matters of the day. They were, all of them in significantly different ways, masters of distantiation. Occasionally this attitude of non-involvement has embarrassed historians of culture to such an extent that they have felt obliged to take it upon themselves to concentrate on social and economic as well as political matters, which they thought to have been unduly neglected. Such noble labor has produced fine, historically detailed accounts of the material emergence of American society.[10] But as a reaction to the suspicious detachment from vital social problems which Emerson, Thoreau, Adams, and James seem to display, it misses the point. Intellectual distance was their only way to *make sense*! The making of sense was their true business and it is, of course, this effort which constitutes the allegorical tradition.

The particular blend of practical intellect and aesthetic individualism which we find represented in their endeavor to create a reasonably controlled plurality of coherent links of meaning in a fundamentally indeterminate, chaotic universe is the main characteristic of the American tradition of allegory. It is a *mode of thought* which sees itself as practical action *in essence*. If we look at the works of Emerson, Thoreau, Adams, and James in this light as expressions of the tension which such self-conception creates, we will have to admit that it is the fate of any theoretical conceptualization to be too late, when confronted with original thought. It would be a mistake, then, to impose upon the driving force of the allegorical tradition such theoretical constraints as we find in the theory of "symbolic action" or in a theory of alienation. The framework of such discourse would plainly destroy the

[10] See Alan Trachtenberg, *The Incorporation of America* (New York, 1982). Trachtenberg also provides a useful and extensive bibliographical essay on related works.

very substance of the allegorical tradition: its counterfactual promise that there is meaning in man's paradoxical struggle with nature. The knowledge that the struggle must be fought—and will be lost—is an essential part of the allegorical tradition, a fact which we find confirmed if we pay attention to the sudden disappearance of this awareness at the turn of the century. A final glimpse of what had been a tradition at work before its replacement can be caught in Randolph Bourne's fall from Deweyite optimism into bitter but helpless despair.[11]

To the generation of young intellectuals at the turn of the century the world seemed full of possibilities. The profound knowledge about the hard facts of limitation had disappeared as a visible part of the public, collective consciousness. Hardly anyone cared to point out the limitations of professionalization. If we fail to be amazed by the questions which the generation of 1910 did *not* ask, when we look at them from the perspective of the nineteenth century, we can hardly miss the tone of certainty and purpose in the prose of someone like Van Wyck Brooks in his essays on American culture and its discontents. What we find is an almost technologically organized blueprint of how things *must* be, were they to be well—what we miss is the skeptical quality of the allegorical sense of history. Gone is the noetic quality which puts the reader's ability to think an argument through to a severe but wholesome test, and gone is the quality which Angus Fletcher holds up as an essential element of allegory: its tendency toward "a human reconstitution of divinely inspired messages, a revealed transcendental language which tries to preserve the remoteness of a properly godhead."[12]

There is little sensitivity for all that is so typical of allegorical prose to be found in the cultural criticism of Van Wyck Brooks.[13]

Allegory as a mode of representation had been safely delegated to the realms of poetry and fiction. In fact, there was no use for the allegorical mode of thought that men of letters like Emerson, Thoreau, Adams, and James represented. With the establishment of philosophy, with the establishment that is of departments of philosophy and of sociology in the universities, the process of professionalization had reached a point which made the kind of discourse which had created

[11] Olaf Hansen, ed., *The Radical Will: Randolph Bourne, Selected Writings* (New York, 1977).

[12] Angus Fletcher, *Allegory: The Theory of a Symbolic Mode* (Ithaca, N.Y., 1964), p. 221.

[13] Van Wyck Brooks's early cultural criticism is extremely straightforward and causal in its analysis of what he perceived to be the roots of the alleged American cultural poverty.

the allegorical tradition obsolete. But what if this kind of obsolescence has to be seen as a symptom rather than as a solution? What if we need to know what allegory tells us: That the *provisional making* of sense will continue and must?

The following chapters, to a large extent, will address problems and fundamental issues which the function of the American allegory raises. Their problems are more or less clearly defined by the emergence of American allegory out of a Puritan tradition. I say "more or less," in order to avoid the erroneous assumption that there is one particular and specific point of origin from which we can safely depart. The opposite is the case: we not only lack any kind of primary matrix which could be outlined as a well-defined birthplace of tradition, but we have to take into account further considerations which press the issue that whatever we call the Puritan tradition is already a result rather than a beginning. Whenever we call something, by title or denotation, of "Puritan" origin, we must admit at once that we refer to a visible segment of a larger, partly invisible whole. Therefore, the Puritan tradition we talk about and which we see as an active force in the formation of the American allegory is a tradition which at the beginning of the nineteenth century had become part of a highly complex social process.

The main characteristic of this social development was an increasing modernization of the social system expressing itself above all in an acceleration of secularized social subsystems. The rapid emergence of extremely differentiated and functionally interdependent subsystems within a growing and cohesive society as a whole created both private and collective worlds of everyday life and of not so quotidian vision which had to compete and to coexist at the same time. Such issues cannot be simplified.

If the term culture in this context is often used with a certain capaciousness, it is done so with the idea in mind that those interdependent subsystems which we arrange under the rubric of culture, in order to be functionally interrelated at all, had to necessarily maintain a specific amount of autonomy. When allegory emerges as a mode of thought, it is in order to acknowledge this Janus-faced quality of what we call the cultural experience. In this sense, then, the seemingly private intellectual worlds created by Emerson, Thoreau, Adams, and William James were in a genuine dialectical way part of the collective American cultural history as it unfolded throughout the nineteenth century.

The second major concern of our argument about the role of the American allegory in the transformation of the American cultural tradition is the particular nature of this tradition itself and the peculiar process of its formation. Once again the concession must be made that the use of the word *tradition*, here, applies to a rather large segment of accessible history. If the use of such terms as *culture* and *tradition* seems to be rather loose and encompassing, that use is limited to a manageable size by our working hypothesis that the allegorical mode of thought articulates only a small part of the cultural history under discussion. It expresses, and here lies the limitation, precisely those otherwise latent energies in the making of a cultural tradition which the overt culture has tried to repress, to ignore, or to replace. The overt culture, the visible and, last but not least, the practical side of it, prefers manifestations of absolute truths, broken down into neat bits and pieces yielding to an impatient mind. Thus the movement of cultural history is explained in terms of class struggle, of generational conflict, in the name of progress or manifest destiny and other, similar concepts. Naturally all these concepts serve a purpose and have a certain, though somewhat reductivist, explanatory value. But as William James has pointed out, quoting the Danish philosopher Kierkegaard: "We live forward but we understand backward." The mere fact, therefore, that we can always ask another sensible question about our past indicates that the transformation within the flow of tradition works according to a pattern of forgetting and remembrance which we must try to decipher, even though, or rather *because*, we are part of this pattern.

We are, in other words, always part of an invisible sector of tradition, a fact which we can only discuss in a terminology of nonidentity. The American man of letters in the nineteenth century was aware of this fact, often to the point of despair. If we look at the work of the men we have chosen to discuss, or if we take the example of historians like Prescott and his colleagues, we never cease to be amazed to what an extent extreme self-doubt and overwhelming productivity seemed to coexist. The answer to our amazement lies of course exactly in the quality of the self-doubt from which the man of letters seems to suffer, a kind of self-doubt which is radically different from what a later generation would describe in terms of an identity crisis. Henry Adams, in his own inimitable style of self-reference, has sketched for us the quality in question in *The Education*, and to the extent that his observation is made from hindsight we may safely assume that it can be generalized, applying to a whole generation of hearty self-doubters.

> As it happened, he never got to the point of playing the game at all; he lost himself in the study of it, watching the errors of the

> players; . . . The habit of doubt; of distrusting his own judgement and of totally rejecting the judgement of the world; the tendency to regard every question as open; the hesitation to act except as a choice of evils; the shirking of responsibility; the love of line, form, quality, the horror of ennui; the passion for companionship and the antipathy to society—all these are well-known qualities of New England character in no way peculiar to individuals.[14]

The last, of course, is not true, even if Henry Adams in order to justify *his* generalization, evokes the familiar topos of the climate as the great generalizing force to which, after all, all men are exposed.

> New England was harshness of contrast and extremes of sensibility—a cold that froze the blood, and a heat that boiled it—so that the pleasure of hating—oneself if no better victim offered—was not its rarest amusement; but the charm was a true and natural child of the soil, not a cultivated weed of the ancients. The violence of the contrast was real and made the strongest motive of education. The double exterior nature gave life its relative values. Winter and summer, cold and heat, town and country, force and freedom, marked two modes of life and thought, balanced like lobes of the brain.[15]

Suffice it to say here that not everybody is equally susceptible to the weather and that the next generation of city intellectuals would inhabit a totally different climate of their own making. What Henry Adams really tells us in the brief passage just quoted is that such qualities of self-doubt as he playfully ascribes to everybody are in fact a rare gift in need of defense. Self-hatred, to utilize his own phrase, is hardly everyone's pleasure—and again, in the language of theory, we might say that seeing the world in terms of nonidentity was the gift of those men of letters, who adopted the allegorical mode of thought as their way of expressing a fear about the future. The self, then, which so productively doubted acted out the fear of self-loss. Self-doubt, to put it differently, was in many ways an act of anticipation and resistance.

Anticipations of the kind which we find represented in the works of Emerson, Thoreau, Adams, and William James only become a visible part of tradition, if they are "successful," the measure of success being the degree to which the object of their anxiety would become itself

[14] Henry Adams, *The Education of Henry Adams* (Boston, 1973), p. 4. All subsequent quotations from *The Education* come from the Riverside edition, edited by Ernest Samuels.

[15] Adams, *Education*, p. 7.

part of reality. If it is true, then, that the allegorical mode of thought as adopted by Emerson and those who would become the carriers of the transcendentalist's legacy, represented among other motives a choice, we must raise and answer the question whether this choice, by the standards of success mentioned above, was a reasonable one.

Our answer, by way of introduction, must necessarily be brief. It may, at first glance, seem like an odd choice on our part to place someone like William James, and with him, of course, large parts of pragmatism into an allegorical tradition which began with Emerson's version of transcendentalism. But the author of *The Pluralistic Universe* defended exactly the same qualities of self-doubt which Henry Adams had described in such a different fashion. Together with Emerson and Thoreau the insistence of their defense is on the legitimacy of pretheoretical experience—which is not the same as random subjectivity! Their fear was that the right to self-doubt would become obsolete in a social context which did not allow for doubt, and consequently not for choice either. The sociological blueprint as envisioned by Lester Ward's idea of "social telesis" would indeed leave little room for qualified doubting. After the turn of the century, with the rise of a new class of intellectuals, the arrival of which, ironically enough, James himself would proudly proclaim in the pages of the *New Republic*, the question asked demanded an answer. The freedom which the idea of self-doubt had helped to establish a few decades earlier was irrevocably gone. Even if Dewey's optimism and the spirit of the New proved the point of pessimists of the nineteenth century only in so far as they confirmed the innermost anxieties which Emerson, Thoreau, Adams, and William James expressed in their allegorical defense of the self, we can hardly avoid listening to the voices of such minor figures as Isaac Rosenfeld. Rosenfeld, a few decades later, once again confronted with a different reality, would in a manner of despair not unfamiliar to the student of the nineteenth century confirm that age's worst fears as expressed in the allegorical tradition: self-doubt as a condition of freedom had become obsolete, like the self which had vanished in the true heart of darkness of western civilization. In a brief essay, printed in the *Partisan Review* in 1949, he outlines "a few propositions" emphasizing at the same time that "the argument can be expanded in all directions."

Evoking Nietzsche's idea about joy which wants "deep profound eternity" as his beginning he goes on to describe what he calls the main reality, because it is the model reality.

> The concentration camp is the model educational system and the model form of communality. These are abstract propositions, but

> even so they are obvious; when we fill them in with experience they are overwhelming. Unfortunately, there is nothing else into which we can fit our experience—traditions are broken and culture is unavailable. A culture is dead when the experience of men has no place in it. Our culture is an empty form, standing for a continuity of experience which is now discontinued, for the reality and inviolability of human values that are everywhere violated and denied. . . . Today the cultured man is isolated; he may still exist, but his humanity is his own. He cannot share it with anyone (apart from his own exertions) because the cultural form that conveyed humanity and asssured the interaction from one man to the next has been destroyed.[16]

As if to prove a point made earlier, Isaac Rosenfeld goes on to ask the next question.

> How is it possible? How is it possible that thousands of men, women, children and infants should be lined up in a field, to be shot before an open ditch, and that their screams should not be heard. That furnaces should be stuffed with human beings? That thousands should be marched into air-tight chambers, to be gassed or steamed to death, their naked bodies stuck together by the pressure and the heat? The death schedules are possible: efficiency; the salvaged hair, gold fillings, and wedding bands: industry. But that no one should hear the screams? We cannot understand, we are as numb as the perpetrators of the crime.[17]

In one sentence, Rosenfeld has summed up the epitome of self-loss: the identity of victim and perpetrator. A world thus described allows no choice at all. After the description of a world without choice, the only way of thinking about a different world is to imagine one which begins, once more, with immediate sense experience, hence his title for his second proposition: "The End of Alienation." The end of alienation is not announced by setting apart a post-industrial society from an industrial one, but by a deliberate and anachronistic return to the possibility of experience—a return which presents itself only in the shape of exertion.

> But joy exists only in the minds of a few poets, though all men, unaware, may yearn for it. Its real existence will require a new character of mankind, which is also to say, a new culture. . . . Our

[16] Isaac Rosenfeld, "The Meaning of Terror," in *An Age of Enormity*, ed. Theodore Solotaroff (New York, 1962), pp. 206–9.

[17] Ibid., p. 207.

> joy will be in love and restoration, in the sensing of humanity as the concrete thing, the datum of our cultural existence. It will lie in the creation of a new capacity, proof against terror, to experience our natural life to the full. What has once been transcended cannot be repeated; . . . Men will go on to seek the good life in the direction of what is joyous; they know what is terrible. May the knowledge of joy come to them, and the knowledge of terror never leave.[18]

We learn backwards indeed: Emerson, Thoreau, Adams, and William James knew how closely the demand for a new culture and a new closeness to nature would inextricably interlink terror and joy. And they knew in addition that the making of sense between these two, terror and joy, would always be an act like mending the raft rather than a guarantee for a safe voyage.

In the end any text and especially an essay in cultural history must stand alone. It will be judged as a unit of plausible or unconvincing arguments regardless of any claims to an outside theoretical authority or role model. And yet, there is no practical effort of interpretation which must not, when pressed, confess to some kind of theoretical ancestry or perhaps only inspiration. So then: if sources lying beyond our specific argument about an American allegorical tradition must be identified because they influenced the general scope of our interpretation, two should be named, if only in order to offer an explanation for the intellectual disposition which informed our approach to the American nineteenth century without, however, turning a disposition into a method. The two books in question are so different in their own right that any transformation and subsequent reproduction of what they have to say into a unified method is a practical impossibility, anyway. The first and probably most influential inspiration of our own view of cultural history has been a reading and rereading of Husserl's self-interpretation implicit in *The Crisis of European Sciences and Transcendental Phenomenology*. This late historicizing of the phenomenological fact in order to avoid the closure of presentism fulfilled the role of a constant reminder to keep history open, even when describing it in the mode of cultural history. Furthermore, the book often served as a kind of consolation when the necessities of not being able to pursue an argument further seemed overwhelmingly stringent and irritating. The exacting duty of the cultural historian to be satisfied with segments found a justification in Husserl's book, which made it all the

[18] Ibid., p. 209.

easier to discuss such masters of fragmentary thought as Emerson, Thoreau, Adams, and William James. As the citation of Isaac Rosenfeld has shown, it is very tempting to write intellectual history teleologically whether in the manner of tracing the continuity of myths and archetypes or in the mode of establishing a critical vocabulary, for example, that of antimodernism, which is then imposed on quite diverse expressions of human consciousness.[19]

What we learn from the late Husserl is that we need a teleological analysis of the middle range in order to do justice to the fact that the tradition of human consciousness whenever we try to analyze it in terms of cultural history will always be limited to having a partial beginning—and consequently a partial ending. The responsibility of cultural history therefore lies in the effort to bring to light both the sense of continuity and of disruption and replacement which constitute the other side of the partial beginning and ending. It is not enough to renarrate the history of facts and events. With Henry Adams we must pursue the question of *why*, a question which includes the acknowledgment of a debt to history by the mere fact of self-reference which it implies. Husserl's "hidden unity of intentional inwardness which alone constitutes the unity of history," when transformed into an analysis of the segment instead of aspiring to a "meaningful, final harmony" helps us to understand and makes us see the less visible, though equally important pattern in the fabric of tradition which we frequently neglect as marginal or as just a minor part of the legacy of the past.[20]

The second, somewhat unlikely companion to Husserl's role in the formation of a specific curiosity about the nineteenth century has been the influence of Theodor W. Adorno's *Negative Dialectics*, an influence of long standing, setting the overall theme of a philosophy of nonidentity. Unlike Walter Benjamin and Friedrich W. Nietzsche who are taken and occasionally used as direct witnesses to what we assume to be a teleological momentum in the nineteenth century touching directly upon pressing issues of our own times, both Husserl and Adorno stand in the background. Certainly, the art of allegorical thought lies in creating by constant configuration a recurring interplay between the visible and the invisible—but our subject matter is the

[19] See for example T. J. Jackson Lears, *No Place of Grace* (New York, 1981), whose use of the label *antimodernism* is so vague that it allows him to conclude that "superficially at odds, antimodernist, avant-gardist and advertiser have often been brothers under the skin" (p. xvii).

[20] Husserl's argument is teleological and its influence on this study is due to the nonteleological elements that his argument *implies*.

particular tradition of American allegorical thought and its specific role in the development of the Amerian cultural history in general. To what extent the American nineteenth century was to a greater or lesser degree participant in an international cultural development is a question of interpretation and obviously an implicit theme within the context of our own argument. But without preempting the interpretative bias of our choice it should be emphasized, given the background mentioned above, that our primary concern is the dialectical function of the American allegory as a cultural force *sui generis.*

CHAPTER 1

Allegory and the Work of Tradition

Thomas Eakins was a man of great character. He was a man of iron will and his will was to paint and to carry out his life as he thought it should go. This he did. It cost him heavily but in his works we have the precious result of his independence, his generous heart and his big mind. Eakins was a deep student of life and with a great love he studied humanity frankly. He was not afraid of what his study revealed to him.

—ROBERT HENRI

His art was lacking in the higher notes—poetry, the natural unthinking joy in sensuous beauty. It is a Puritanical art, austere, sombre, bitter.

—LLOYD GOODRICH

Thomas Eakins, *The Gross Clinic*, 1875. From the Jefferson Medical College of Thomas Jefferson University, Philadelphia.

In 1876 America celebrated the centenary of its own becoming. The fact that Eakins's great painting *The Gross Clinic* was not included among the works exhibited in the Art Pavilion at the Philadelphia Centennial Exhibition has been frequently commented upon. But even if the series of great exhibitions and world fairs which rapidly followed one another are interpreted as symbolic events in their own right, one should not expect too much from these high points of cultural and social self-projection; at least not in the realm of intellectual history.

That the "Centennial March," which was played at the opening of the exhibition, had been composed by Richard Wagner demonstrates more than adequately that self-celebration and adequate self-reference usually diverge. The decision to exhibit Eakins's painting in the model of a hospital ward, using it as a kind of illustration, has an ironic twist to it, which critics who see all of this as a major insult to an important work of art tend to overlook.

The decision to use *The Gross Clinic* as a piece of information is based, even if unintentionally, on an elementary grasp of the painting's allegorical nature. Displaying it as part of a documentary effort meant to make use of all the didactic and time-bound properties of true allegory. In this sense at least the painting was not dislocated but had been put in the right place.

A working tradition favors allegory. Aware of the need for abstraction, it also knows about the dangers of sterility: a tradition at work, therefore, is the self-reflective process looking for an adequate expression of its full content. Its great concern is to deal successfully with opposites and this naturally leads to a great sensitivity about time's double features of duration and arrest, of eternity and the immediate moment. Allegory, by explicitly approaching the question of the *shape* and the *meaning* of time dramatizes in art what science and philosophy fail to express. Where allegory is dominant, epistemology looks pale. Knowledge becomes clearly defined as the *necessary first step*: The second step involves the quest for synthesis. This second step is the final one—never fully accomplished.

The painting that Thomas Eakins presented to a puzzled audience in 1875 came totally without preparation. Never before, as many commentators have pointed out, had such a painting been seen in America. If it is part of tradition's work to resist the exhaustion of its sources, Eakins's contribution to the strength of American culture can hardly be overestimated. The power of his work to withstand the efforts of classification makes for an interesting episode within art criticism. Eakins has in turn been described as a realist, as a positivist, and as a naturalist. On rare occasions a critic would simply come to terms with the difficulty of his task by giving credit to the presence of a whole range of qualities in Eakins's work, if only in order to expand the meaning of the term *realism* as it might be applied to Eakins.

> The question always is: Where and in what does he discover reality? . . . For Eakins always knows far more than can be seen; he knows why what is seen takes on the appearance that it does. From the outset he bases his painting on a great deal of research into problems of anatomy and perspective and light. It is a sort of knowledge which may not be needed by other temperaments but which Eakins tracks down with an intenseness that amounts to a passion. He accepts the world in more than its visual aspect; he credits every person and every thing in it with independent existence. What he endeavors to attain is an understanding of all that exists below the surface—the solidity of things, the countering stress of bodies in action, the quiescent tensions of bodies in repose. The ways in which Eakins acquires this knowledge are all experimental and scientific, in harmony with his intellectualized conscious life. All this has by now been so often said in other words that perhaps this bare statement may be acceptable; but it is restated here to indicate the means by which his pictures go beyond a merely visual naturalism to a mental realism. And this is more than the passive understanding just mentioned; it is the active state of comprehending things and creatures and personalities from within which remakes them not only as pictures to be seen but also as pictorial organisms to be comprehended again.[1]

The act of comprehending something again is exactly the task that

[1] Virgil Barker, "Imagination in Thomas Eakins," *Parnassus* (November 1939): 8.

tradition demands and articulates in works of art that emphasize their authenticity by way of concurrent distantiation and actuality. In fact, none of Eakins's later works would achieve what *The Gross Clinic* did, in terms of dramatizing its own place and meaning in time. There is, however, a tendency in his portraits to emphasize the solitary position of the sitter that is sometimes contrasted with elements of the "outside world" that are seen in a relationship to both the viewer and the person viewed. Frequently these elements are quite obvious, like the tools of his profession in the portrait of Benjamin Howard Rand, or like the scientific formulas surrounding the portrait of Professor Henry A. Rowland on the carved frame of the painting. These are, however, only minor infractions on the genre. They are the kind of intrusions that confirm the existence of the authentic visual space that they comment upon. Such added iconographical commentaries are not yet part of the unified order of allegorical construction.

In other cases it is the obvious self-absorption of the person portrayed that we first feel as a form of withdrawal and then interpret as a resistance against pictorial fixation in time. Thus, anticipating a point to which we shall return later, the object of the painter's attention is exactly where it is—as painted—and it is somewhere else as well, at a place we only know about, because the *act* of painting has taken place. Eakins's best portraits always convey the feeling to the viewer that he is intruding into an unfinished interaction between the painter and his subject. It is as if, even in the finished portrait, the act of painting still continues: the portraits seem to defy being firmly placed, sometimes by sheer force of melancholy and sometimes by strange and unnerving elements of theatricality. Even if we want to ignore the rather dramatic composition of head and body in the portrait *Lady with a Setter Dog*, we cannot overlook the gesture of the empty right hand. The isolated gesture demands attention. This is, of course, merely another way of saying that the attention of the artist is bilocal—it concentrates on his subject and at the same time on a space in history that the subject does not occupy. The bilocality of the painter's attention is, in effect, the very mixture of narration and representation that we mentioned earlier. It is a kind of realism, one should add, that shares more with French painters like Manet and his friends among the antisalon realists than we are likely to expect from Eakins if we simply examine his educational background.

By the time of Eakins's arrival in Paris, the *bataille réaliste* was at its height. The major programmatic statements by such spokesmen for realism as Flaubert, Zola, Courbet, and Baudelaire had been made and were in circulation among intellectuals and artists. The Salon des

Refusés of 1863 had made its enormous impact, and if we allow for the possibility that Eakins was most probably exposing himself to the qualified, tempered traditionalism of Gérôme as well as to the modernism of the contemporary realist, we will understand the real nature of his education in France. We will, in addition, understand how Eakins's French education fits into his American background and enabled him to paint *The Gross Clinic*, a painting that we take to be the painterly signature of the allegorical tradition in the American nineteenth century.

However, on the surface of Eakins's development as a painter there is little advance promise of the authority of *The Gross Clinic*. There are a few details that can be isolated, but they do not really explain the explosion of stylistic will that we find in *The Gross Clinic*. Barbara Novak sums up the status of Eakins adequately when pointing out: "With Eakins, this desire for knowledge—an almost obsessive one in this case—extended to the use of the machine as tool (photography) and into mathematics. His art thus belongs, in many of its aspects, to the mensurational, machine-connected aesthetic that characterizes much American art before and after him. In his grave attempts to reconcile knowledge with art, he was perhaps the most philosophical and conscientious of American artists."[2]

Philosophy, in this sense, can only refer to his work, because we do not have any elaborated statements by Eakins on American art. There is no cogent statement on the nature of art from which we can quote; nothing, at least, in the sense of *The Art Spirit* by Robert Henri, who was a great admirer of Thomas Eakins, and who never missed an occasion to point out the significance of his work.

If we look at contemporary books on art, like those by James Jackson Jarves, *The Art-Idea*, and *Art Thoughts*, we will find that by their very orientation towards European art they make the sudden appearance of a painting like *The Gross Clinic* rather more puzzling than not. On the other hand, the tone of high idealism that one finds in such opening remarks as those of Jarves's *The Art-Idea* lends itself easily to an interpretation of American art in the nineteenth century that can draw heavily upon an equally idealistic view of transcendentalism: "Life may be likened to a sphere which includes an inexhaustible series of circles of knowledge. In the beginning we are but a simple point. But mind having the power of self-increase, each successive experience enlarges its circumference. Ultimately it may include within its grasp all love and wisdom short of Divinity."[3]

[2] Barbara Novak, *American Painting of the Nineteenth Century* (New York, 1969), p. 191.
[3] James Jackson Jarves, *The Art-Idea* (New York, 1877), p. 1

The act of looking at a painting is seen as just another indication of an open future, as an act that draws our attention away from the painting, a way of organizing actual time into a historical shape that would also identify the role of the beholder. The existence of the painting is seen as a reminder of a kind of generalized potential and growth.

> The mental processes by which we thus enlarge our circles are worthy of attentive observation, partly from the satisfaction of analyzing and appreciating the mind's growth, but chiefly indicative of the illimitable future of knowledge which they gradually open to our view, in the degree that we humbly, earnestly, and continually demand to know the secrets of Immortality.
>
> If it were not for this ever-expanding Future to tempt us on, we should speedily despair of the Present, and pronounce it only vanity and vexation.[4]

The career of Thomas Eakins has often been interpreted as a puzzling phenomenon in the making of an artist, simply because his tutelage under Jean-Léon Gérôme seemed to be exactly the expected idealistic uplift that the American artist needed, according to critics like Jarves. As we shall see there are two misconceptions at work in this assumption that will have to be corrected. One concerns the actual learning process a painter like Eakins went through when working in Paris, and the second one is related to *our* perception of a painter like Gérôme as opposed to what Eakins saw in his teacher's paintings.

Eakins, after having worked at the Pennsylvania Academy in Philadelphia, left for Paris in 1866 at the age of twenty-two to receive his formal education as an artist. If we look for the influences that shaped Eakins's artistic development before his experiences in Paris, we will have to confine ourselves to his use of Rembrandt Peale's *Graphics*, a series of drawing manuals, and the exercises that Eakins did under the instructions given in those manuals. Indeed, his *Drawing of Gears* and *Drawing of a Lathe*, both of which are in the Hirschhorn Collection, refer us to the early photographs of mechanical objects, taken by Charles Sheeler during the rise of the American avant-garde. What we see here is that the scientific bias of the American artist and his reverence of objecthood are part of an unchanging tradition. Even the influential Jackson Jarves, whose idealistic concept of art is represented in its most elaborate form in his popular volume *The Art-Idea*, finishes his book by emphasizing the role of science in the development of the arts.

[4] Ibid., pp. 1–4

If we analyze carefully the argument that Jarves presents roughly ten years before Eakins finishes his first large painting, *The Gross Clinic*, we realize that Eakins's own scientific attitude reflects his conservative ties to the craftmanship tradition of "picture-making," which in this respect locates him within the continuation of the American Enlightenment. Eakins's teaching method, as described by several of his students, seems like an answer turned into practice when compared with the questions raised by Jackson Jarves.

> In science we find no routine of individual reproduction, as in art, but a systematic unfolding of progressive truths; so that the startling or discredited discovery of one age becomes the familiar knowledge of the next. Thus a mighty whole is gradually built up. Nature gives freely, as she is pertinaciously asked.
>
> Every discovery in the laws of matter that affects the elementary substances in art-use, simply or combined, should be carefully scrutinized, to detect its practicability to enlarge or improve the means of art. Perspective, of which so little was formerly known, is now reduced by science to so simple a study that a school-girl in this respect surpasses the efforts of ancient masters.[5]

The nature of the scientific bias in American art has been interpreted in many ways, and one of the most succinct formulations has been offered by Barbara Novak, who claims that "in America there was a vested interest in the preservation of the fact, behind which we can perhaps identify deeper religious and philosophical attitudes to the substance of God's world, attitudes prescribing the analytical irreverence of Impressionism."[6]

But the question remains, what, more precisely, the "vested interest in the preservation of the fact" could have meant, if we take into account that whatever we or the contemporary beholder are supposed to see *behind* the represented fact is determined by the meaning that the representational surface is allowed to require. Emerson's view that the innermost and fundamental secrets of nature, when revealed to a man, would probably turn out to be disappointingly simple is reflected in Eakins's remark on the necessity of dissection as part of the artist's education.

> If beauty resides in fitness to any extent, what can be more beautiful than this skeleton, or the perfection with which means and ends are reciprocally adapted to each other? But no one dissects

[5] Ibid., p. 369.

[6] Novak, *American Painting*, p. 59.

> to quicken his eye for, or his delight in beauty. He dissects simply to increase his knowledge of how beautiful objects are put together to the end that he may be able to imitate them. Even to refine upon natural beauty—to idealize—one must understand what it is that he is idealizing; otherwise his idealization—I don't like the word by the way—becomes distortion, and distortion is ugliness. This whole matter of dissection is not art at all, anymore than grammar is poetry. It is work, and hard work, disagreeable work.[7]

The term and the whole idea of *beauty* stands in an ambiguous relation to the idea of the object. It is, however, the kind of ambiguity that later would produce statements like Fairfield Porter's, who in his book on Eakins in 1959 made the following emphatic use of machine-metaphor: "The French academicians painted 'machines,' that is, deliberate, elaborate paintings of great size whose purpose was the display of the artist's power. Eakins thought of painting as a deliberate construction. His paintings of scullers were executed from studies of perspective, of reflections and of anatomy put together in the studio. An Eakins 'machine' was more modest and thorough than a French academician's; it was a fixation of an idea on canvas, like the *Concert Singer*."[8]

Describing a portrait like the *Concert Singer* in terms of the machine-metaphor says something about both the process and structure of the artist's work and about the results it is supposed to achieve. Again, if we want to outline the structure of valid tradition, the most immediate analogy that comes to mind is the whole frame of reference of the camera's work that evolved around Stieglitz and his circle. The "right moment," seized after days and sometimes weeks of careful observation, was supposed to produce an image that was representative in the sense of having an autonomous status against the interruption of its historical time sphere. Whatever the image represented was seen as a concentration of historical time, its reality being based upon the condensation of external relationships achieved through artistic work.

The process, in other words, was one of inversion: the external relationships that make up a person's or an object's reality are invisible most of the time (an object being used, a person being involved in one of many activities) and become visible only by *representation*. Obviously, this analogy between the painting and the camera has a genealogy: it

[7] Cited in William C. Brownwell, "The Art Schools of Philadelphia," *Scribner's Monthly*, 18 no. 5 (September 1879): 745.

[8] Fairfield Porter, *Thomas Eakins* (New York, 1959), p. 20.

is, in short, that progression from historical painting in the traditional sense of depicting a scene to the allegorical organization of historical meaning. Eakins's apprenticeship in the studio of Gérôme, when seen in this light, has to be interpreted as the fulfillment of a circle, rather than an odd step backwards, taken against the given chronology of art history. It is a step worthy of some consideration.

In Paris Thomas Eakins began to study art seriously at the Ecole des Beaux Arts. After some delay, Eakins had obtained a letter of recommendation from John Bigelow, then the American minister to France, and although the Ecole had refused to accept any foreigners in the previous year, he was soon registered to study with Jean-Léon Gérôme, then the leading figure in the field. He was familiar with some of Gérôme's work, from the prints that he had seen at home, but it is hard to see the influence of Gérôme in Eakins's work. In fact, one is easily led to believe what John Canaday observed in 1964: "It is difficult to find anything in Eakins' art that he could have learned from Gérôme."[9] We do know, however, that he took seriously both the technical instruction and its meaning as an artistic tool that was the artist's only entrance into the realm of nature. We feel the influence of his time spent with Gérôme when we read a letter written in the tone of a student who tends to preach a bit when talking about recently acquired insights: "The big artist does not set down monkey-like and copy a coal scuttle or an ugly old woman like some Dutch painters have done, nor a dung pile, but he keeps a sharp eye on Nature and steals her tools. He learns what she does with the light, the big tool, and then color, then form and appropriates them to his own use. Then he's got a cause of his own, smaller than Nature's but big enough for every purpose. . . . With this canoe he can sail parallel to Nature's sailing."[10]

It seems that the major influence of Gérôme on Eakins was to instill a respect for his craft that, when transformed into self-respect, would allow Eakins to take himself seriously as a painter. He left the confined atmosphere of the Ecole in the fall of 1869, heading for Madrid and taking the rest of his education into his own hands. He needed the distance from his teacher.

> I have had the benefit of a good teacher with good classmates. Gérôme is too great to impose much, but aside from his overthrowing completely the ideas I had got before at home, and then

[9] John Canady, "Thomas Eakins," *Horizon* (Autumn 1964): 105.

[10] Cited in Gordon Hendricks, *The Life and Work of Thomas Eakins* (New York, 1974), p. 46.

> telling me one or two things in drawing he has never been able to assist me much, and oftener bothered me by mistaking my troubles. . . . Sometimes I took all advice, sometimes I shut my ears and listened to none. My worst troubles are over, I know perfectly what I am doing. . . . What a relief to me when I saw everything falling in its place, as I always had an instinct that it would if I could ever get my bearings all correct only once.[11]

In Madrid he studied the paintings of Velázquez, whose influence one would later notice in Eakins's portraits; but more important than one single influence is the change of language he uses when writing about the art of painting to his father.

> I have seen big painting here. When I looked at all the paintings by the masters I had known, I could not help saying to myself, "It's very pretty but it's not all yet. It ought to be better." Now I have seen what I always thought ought to have been done and what did not seem to me impossible. O, what a satisfaction it gave me to see the good Spanish work, so good, so strong, so reasonable, so free from affectation. . . .
>
> My student life is now over and my regular work is commenced. I have started the most difficult kind of picture, making studies in the sunlight. . . . Something unforeseen may occur and my picture may be a failure, these first ones. I cannot make a picture fast yet, I want experience in my calculation.[12]

One could go on to collect samples from his letters and the evidence would, by accumulation, support what he had already decided in his notebook after a visit to the Prado: "*Il faut me décider de ne jamais peindre de la façon du patron.*"[13]

As such phrases like "I want experience in my calculation" show, he was moving towards a kind of realism that, hesitantly so at first, and then with unmitigated energy, grasped at a whole domain of new, previously neglected subject matter. He was far from subscribing to any of the contemporary realist creeds and did not belong to any of the groups then discussing the issues of realism in Paris. He became, however, increasingly contemporaneous in the choice of his subject matter, and in addition to acknowledging the importance of the realists' creed that "*il faut être de son temps,*" he also managed to keep a balance between the demand for contingency and the dignity of the arrested mo-

[11] Ibid., p. 56.

[12] Ibid., pp. 58–62.

[13] Lloyd Goodrich, *Thomas Eakins: His Life and Work* (New York, 1933), p. 30.

ment in time. The efforts on his part are best exemplified in his well-known boating pictures. At this time, Eakins was still sending some of his work to Gérôme in Paris for criticism and advice, both of which he received in good measure, mostly favorable. While in the Salon of 1875, Eakins's *Pushing for Rail* had been praised for its "genuine precision" and because it had been "rendered in a way that is photographic."[14] He himself already had in mind a painting of entirely different proportions.

"I have just got a new picture blocked in & it is far more than anything I have ever done," he wrote to Earl Shinn in 1875. "I have the greatest hopes for this one,"[15] he went on to say, and he was going to be right. In a way, his *The Gross Clinic* would be his "real allegory," his very own and specific counterpart of Courbet's well-known *The Painter's Studio* of 1855. The similarities and differences between these two paintings are indicative of the relationship of allegory and realism in the mid-nineteenth century.

Eakins has provided one of the major clues for an adequate reading of his painting as allegory, by his contrapuntal use of light and color. Light and color in *The Gross Clinic* establish two separate levels of meaning, and it is their juxtaposition within a unified whole of many parts that allows us to read the painting as pictorial *allegoria permixta*. As opposed to the *tota allegoria*, the first form of allegory works with a wide range of easily accessible substitutions that help to clarify the meaning of the allegorical statement.

Thus, the color red in all its variations structures a narrative mode that incorporates the transition from a sacral tradition to a naturalistic world view, whereas, by contrast, the use of light in the painting tends to substitute the pictorial vocabulary of the secular tradition with an interlinear vision of the sacred and the profane. In the manner of allegorical intention Eakins did provide a portrait of the famous surgeon; but if Dr. Gross had several times made the demand that the great surgeons of America should be immortalized for posterity, he certainly did not expect to have his wish granted by way of allegorical dissemination. In this sense, then, he certainly was immortalized in the manner of traditional portraiture also, but only with a large number of qualifications included.

The contrapuntal functions of light and color in *The Gross Clinic* state the allegorical sense of the painting in its most extreme and openly subversive form. The de facto narrative of the pictorial alle-

[14] Hendricks, *Life and Work*, p. 87.

[15] Eakins to Earl Shinn, 1875, Friends Historical Library, Swarthmore College.

gory becomes explicit as these extremes begin to converge in the eye and mind of the beholder.

The first thing we realize when looking at the painting—before we start sorting out the various forms of confusing and irritating elements in it that we fail to grasp immediately—is our own position in relation to the painting. On the one hand, the spectator is occupying the potential place of the painter, doing a portrait of Dr. Gross at work, relying on a traditional central point of view and fall of light. On the other hand, the planimetric use of space distorts the coherence of central perspective, forcing the eye of the beholder to wander—and thus to define his own identity by way of process. The latent conflict of these two modes of looking at the painting establishes its identity. The eye of the beholder does, of course, follow a meaningful pattern. First of all there is the line of bloodied hands from those of the surgeon's assistants to his own, and both points of attention are caught in the equally red pen of the assistant writing the protocol of the operation. By simply following this single line of obvious connections the spectator has moved from color to meaning. In his final analysis he will have to account for the red pen in the hands of the note-taking assistant. The distribution of color as a narrative style forces the viewer's imagination to look for a meaningful pattern. The spatial order and proximity provoke the imposition of both an order of meaning and one of imaginative identification.

Once he has advanced so far, the attention of the spectator will be caught by the highly dramatic, mannered, and vaguely familiar gesture of the hand of the old woman at the right side of the surgeon, covering her eyes in horror. In fact she is covering her eyes with her arm, the dramatically cramped hand set free to signify the horror that she feels. Like so many elements of the overall image, the hand is set apart in order to convey meaning within the context of the whole. The familiarity of the hand stems from our knowledge of crucifixion scenes. But the beholder will not push his associations too far at a first viewing. He will return to the scene as a whole in order to understand what exactly he is seeing. Obviously an operation is being performed; but what is the position of the patient? As Sylvan Schendler has summed it up:

> Something else disturbed genteel Philadelphia. In the better known of Rembrandt's anatomy lessons, The Anatomy of Dr. Tulp, the corpse is stretched out from right to left on the canvas, its loins covered with a cloth, and although it is seen from below and foreshortened, it causes no difficulty to the spectator. By con-

trast, the position of the patient in "The Gross Clinic," seen in effect from a seat in the amphitheatre at virtually the same level as the operating table, is not at all easy to understand. The soles of Patient's feet, covered with a towel, are turned toward us and his knees are flexed to present his bare thigh to the picture viewer. Limbs, trunk and head, radically foreshortened and masked by operating clothes, the view of the patient broken up by the hands and arms of the assistants—these were elements of a human and an aesthetic mystery. If a good Philadelphian could look long enough to solve that mystery, his scrutiny brought him no comfort. The unaccustomed pose was offensive; he found himself contemplating the patient's left buttock and his anus.[16]

If the imagined viewer would care to look a little longer, he would try to focus his attention on the open incision, the obvious cause of horror for the old woman and something to be technically dealt with by the assistants. The rise and fall of their arms is confusing, even their very alignment. By slowly connecting arms, hands, and heads of the assistants, the viewer will realize that the real and the pictorial space are in even greater collision than he had at first apprehended. Someone, hidden for the most part, is cowering or crouching behind Dr. Gross: we see only one of his hands holding a clamp and his right knee protruding at the right side of Dr. Gross.

As a kind of realistic, adequately represented space the painting begins to worry the viewer who feels himself uncomfortably pushed towards problems of meaning that he has to reconstruct in terms of distorted space. So he will probably return to the head of Dr. Gross, which seems to be to such an extent a portrait in itself that he understands immediately why for a while the painting was called *Portrait of Dr. Gross*. The forehead of the eminent doctor, his graying hair are splendidly exhibited in the kind of sacral light that suits the calm surgeon: master, after all, over life and death.

Again, this part of the painting can be isolated and put into a historical context that the rest of the painting and therefore the painting as a whole refuses to represent. In many respects the historical background of *The Gross Clinic* resembles that of the Dutch tradition of the group portrait, the *shuckerstuck*. Putting it into this tradition already means a removal from its real source of origin. What Dr. Gross wanted were portraits, done with the commemorative function in mind. "There is one thing which strikes an American in viewing the great literary and scientific and charitable institutions of Europe with admi-

[16] Sylvan Schendler, *Eakins* (Boston, 1967), pp. 55–56.

ration such as he cannot feel for his own. It is the respect which is everywhere shown to the memory of their great and good men. Portraits, busts, and statues adorn alike the halls of learning and of legislation, and courts of justice, the gallery, the hospital, and the medical school."[17]

If one wants to judge Eakins's deviation from the established norms (and expectations) implicit in Dr. Gross's plea for memorial portraits, one need only compare *The Gross Clinic* with S. B. Waugh's *Portrait of Dr. Samuel D. Gross* that had been commissioned in 1874. Eakins, in contrast to Samuel Bell Waugh, moved the style of the portrait into a context of stylistic contradictions, each of which represents one aspect of reality of which the hagiographic portrait is the result, an origin that the portrait often tries to hide. As a result, we see the humanitarian pioneer of the medical profession, dictating his notes and explaining his actions to the future medical doctors in the amphitheater. He is dressed like a gentleman would be, the blood on his hand which holds the scalpel making the only contrast and disturbing the iconology of portrait and hero worship. The contemporary Philadelphian viewer had little patience with either: with the demand that both the situation painted and its realistic detail made on his good taste on the one hand, and with the intellectual provocation that the painting represented by means of its composition, and finally its meaning, on the other.

Eakins was quite aware of the shock he would provoke, and he had a number of autotypes made of the painting in order to prepare his audience for the exhibition of the painting itself. To little avail: with the exception of a long, basically favorable, but somewhat distorting review, written by his friend William J. Clark in the *Evening Telegraph*, the reviews were mainly negative. This is how a benevolent critic saw the painting:

> The picture being intended for a portrait of Dr. Gross, and not primarily as a representation of a clinic, the artist has taken a point of view sufficiently near to throw out of focus the accessories, and to necessitate this concentration of all his force on the most prominent figure, Dr. Gross. . . . To say that this figure is a most admirable portrait of the distinguished surgeon would do it scant justice: we know of nothing in the line of portraiture that has ever been attempted in this city, or indeed in this country, that in any way approaches it. . . . The work, however, is something more than a collection of fine portraits; it is intensely dramatic,

[17] Parry Ellwood, "*The Gross Clinic*," *The Toronto Quarterly* 32 (Winter 1969): 373.

> and it is such a vivid representation of such a scene as must frequently be witnessed in the amphitheatre of a medical school, as to be fairly open to the objection of being decidedly unpleasant to those who are not accustomed to such things. The only objection to the picture that can well be made on technical grounds is in the management of the patient. The idea of the artist has obviously been to obtrude this figure as little as possible, and in carrying out this idea he has foreshortened it to such an extent, and has so covered it up with the arms and hands of the assisting surgeons, that it is extremely difficult to make it out. It is a mistake to introduce a puzzle in a picture, and this figure is, at first glance, a decided puzzle.[18]

Others disliked the subject of the painting as such, and in addition disliked the presence of the old woman in the amphitheater. Negative criticism at its most explicit was published in the *Herald* of New York City, which condemned the painting as "decidedly unpleasant and sickeningly real in all its gory details, though a startlingly lifelike work." The critic of the *Tribune* did not think that such painting ("most powerful, horrible, and yet fascinating") should be in a public gallery "where men and women of weak nerves must be compelled to look at it."[19] The same paper, in a second discussion of the painting, picked out the presence of the old woman for special criticism and challenged the composition of the space as a whole.

> The patient lies extended upon the table, but all that we are allowed to see of the body is a long and shapeless lump of flesh which we conclude to be a thigh because, after eliminating from the problem all the known members, there seems nothing but a thigh to which this thing can be supposed to bear any likeness. We make out that one of the Professor's assistants is holding a cloth saturated with chloroform over the patient's face, meanwhile two students hold open with flesh-hooks a longitudinal cut in the supposed thigh; another assistant pokes in the cut with some instrument or other, and the Professor himself, holding up a bloody lancet in bloody fingers, gives the finishing touch to the sickening scene. A mile or so away, at a high raised desk, another impassive assistant records with a swift pen the Professor's remarks, and at about the same distance an aged woman, the wife or mother of

[18] Hendricks, *Life and Work*, p. 93.

[19] Reviews from the *Herald* and the *Tribune* are quoted in Hendricks, *Life and Work*, p. 97.

> the patient, holds up her arms and bends her head in a feeble effort to shut out the horror of the scene. She is out of all proportion compared with other figures, and her size is only to be accounted for on the impossible theory that she is a great distance from the dissecting table. . . . Then again, is it usual for the relatives of a patient who is undergoing a serious operation to be admitted to the room? And, whether it be or be not, is it not unnecessary to introduce a melodramatic element—wholly hostile to the right purpose—into the scene, to show us this old woman writhing her body and twisting her hands as the Professor details the doing of the scalpel in the house of life of someone dear to her?[20]

There is a pattern underlying the criticism, a pattern that is shaped by Eakins's effort and success to be faithful to a kind of realism that produces allegory. The offense to good taste aside, the contemporary criticism concentrated mainly on two issues: composition and meaning.

On the other hand, Eakins had maintained the realistic effect of the momentary instance to an extreme degree; the painting at first glance shows exactly what at this point in time could be seen from the chosen point of view. However, he turned the painting into a comment on *how* it might have come about by putting himself into the painting. (The fact that Eakins put himself back into the painting taking notes, i.e., *writing*, should not be overinterpreted. It probably is just what a painter in that position would do. It does, however, remind the viewer of the painting that he is in fact reading it, legitimizing the allegorical mixture of visual and literal components.) With the painter himself as part of the whole, the time structure of the painting changes dramatically. It becomes a statement of the general disposition of artistic interest. And seen and read in this way, it tells us about the mythical impulse guiding the realistic eye for contingency. Its unity as a real moment in time is shattered and restored as a historically unified description of the *condition humaine*, a seemingly photographic arrest of time, and archetypal elements of iconography are made to work towards the same effect. Sylvan Schendler has attempted to sum up his impressions of the painting without trying to reorder as a composition in his mind what the overlaying and overlapping levels of construction in the painting suggest to him:

> The powerful assertion of an uncompromising humanism achieves something paradoxically like religious intensity. There is something in the painting's undertone reminiscent of a Descent

[20] Ibid., p. 93.

> from the Cross, with God himself present. *The Gross Clinic* is so important in the history of American art because it raises realistic American subject matter to the level of myth with a broad and profound power and intelligence that had never been approached before. The depth of Eakins' penetration of his subject can most be felt in the head of the surgeon. His intellect did not permit him to paint a high priest of the religion of science, the embodiment of a romantic and unqualified affirmation of the will. For the great surgeon is in part the victim of his own power. In the drama being enacted in the amphitheatre Dr. Gross, poised in this moment with life flowing beneath him, caught up between contemplation and action, mediating like some god between the detachment of his students and the techniques of his assistant, dominates this community by personal force and through the intensity of his vision. And at the height of this intellectual passion he is almost lost to feeling. . . . For the Philadelphia of the time, the heroic painting might celebrate great men of great events, preferably military or political. . . . To picture any surgeon splattered with blood, the bloody scalpel in his bloody hands, was an offense to an audience which wished to be ennobled by other sorts of images. Blood could be expected in a battle scene but not in a work that spoke so strongly of the pains of mortality. Eakins' audience wished to be reminded neither of human suffering nor of the agonies of the flesh.[21]

After summing up many reasons for the hostile reaction of Eakins's audience, Schendler comes to the conclusion that in the case of Eakins, we are once more confronted with the virtually classic fate of the artist in America. "One associates the kind of introspection and deeply serious intention of which Melville and Eakins were capable with the best part of the Protestant inheritance, and the kinds of response to their work with the customary darkness of that same tradition. The reception of *The Gross Clinic*, no less than *Moby-Dick*, is a classic illustration of the shipwreck of the imagination in nineteenth century America."[22]

Shipwreck: the topos for failure! Before discussing some of the implications of Schendler's argument, we ought to point out that the original failure of the audience to understand the painting or to read it correctly as an ingenious deviation from more than one tradition can be blamed only in part on the inhibiting force of genteel taste. The

[21] Schendler, *Eakins*, p. 55.

[22] Ibid., p. 57.

so-called genteel tradition was quite capable of coping with the ordinary demands made on the canon of taste and on the abilities of the individual by artistic expression that came from the mainstream of the realistic tradition.

Seeing the genteel Victorian in America as the proverbial "frightened philistine" would only mean to subscribe more or less without discrimination to the critical imagination of the generation of Van Wyck Brooks and those after him who carried their prejudices into their own intellectual space. True enough, *The Gross Clinic* is not executed in the terms of an aesthetic that wants to poeticize "the living fact of ordinary existence," in quest for the American myth, as F. O. Matthiessen has paraphrased endeavors of that kind. Neither did Eakins stick to the rules of an acceptable kind of realism when doing *The Gross Clinic*. There is something altogether specific about the Gross Clinic, a quality of an orchestrated realistic rhetoric that transforms the historical moment into metaphysical time. It is, in fact, the very orchestration of the rhetoric of realism that causes this transformation. (Despite the scandals and rumours surrounding Eakins in later life, his portraits were realistic in the best tradition and very well received indeed.) Apart from this element of mannered realism, how else does *The Gross Clinic* differ? First of all: the reviewers quoted above were correct, even though they misunderstood the meaning of their experience when they claimed to be puzzled about the lack of a fixed point of view for themselves as viewers. Eakins plays out the order of central perspective against an order of iconological sense that puts the viewer into a position that has all the characteristics of a double bind. With the surgeon in the middle of the painting and the round shape of amphitheater in back, the viewer is in a twofold sense lured into assuming the identity provided by the anthropomorphic quality of central perspective on the one hand, and at the same time included by the enclosure of the rotund space on the other. This secure identity is shattered, however, by the dysfunctional arrangement of the figures in the plane of the image, which works against the rationality of central perspective. The viewer is thus excluded from the painting and is thrown back upon himself and his position as a spectator. As if to underline the exclusion of the viewer, the artist has put himself into the painting.

The viewer, as a result, has to resort to his powers of self-reflection in order to reestablish his identity. He is, in other words, part of what is happening only when he brings his powers of self-reflection to bear on the painting. His identity, then, is at stake, if the painting is going to be read correctly at all. There is no middle ground.

As if in confirmation of this point, most of the critics quoted showed a definite tendency to divide the image before them into elements that they liked (the head of the surgeon as a portrait) and those that they wanted out of the painting (the surgeon's bloody hands). The viewer, once he is willing to follow the path of his own reflections, will soon realize the analogy between the threat to his own identity in being simultaneously participant and observer, and the threat to the patient's identity as a victim and as someone to be restored to physical unity and health. That such a restoration is possible only at a certain price is most vividly expressed in the gesture of horror expressed by the anguished woman, whose melodramatic presence one critic deplored. In terms of iconography, her presence has been the issue of some debate, but whether we are looking at a charity case, where the law demanded the presence of a relative of the patient, or whether she is the patient's mother is of little relevance if we are talking about the painting's allegorical quality. Coming to our point indirectly, one of the contemporary critics wondered about the necessity of *choosing* to put her in at all. Again the answer goes further than iconographical veracity. She is *put* into this implausible pictorial position for what she represents: the anxiety suffered whenever transformation takes place. She herself is part of the scene of the painting *and* she represents the archetypal fear experienced in moments of violent change. Her hand, not used to cover up her face, evokes the hand of Christ nailed against the cross, but the painting does not encourage the interpreter to pursue the symbolic quality of this gesture. The blood, the body, the instruments that damage the body in order to heal: all these components are contributing to the painting's intentional ambiguity. The emotive ambiguity is worked out to its fullest, if we remember the structural relationship of the use of color and light, as mentioned before.

Narrative dislocation and fragmentary representation are the indispensable working elements of the painting. The viewer is not allowed to retreat from the painting's process of acquiring meaning by shrugging off the presence of the old woman as representing old-fashioned fear in the face of advancing science. The objects closest to him are the instruments and tools of the surgeon's work, placed there not for the easy reach of the surgeon but for the purpose of reminding the spectator that he is not only symbolically a part of what he observes. Here, too, the presence of the painter in the scene, his own reintroduction into his painting enforces the claim of the painting to represent the archetypal meaning of its subject matter. The clinical amphitheater becomes a world theater: the particular moment in time extends into history and finally the allegoric quality of the painting defines the existence of the viewer. The main axis of meaning along which the allegoric quality establishes itself is one of "being apart"; simply by being exactly where they are, all of the main participants in the scene are *also* somewhere else. The blood on the actual incision is still present at the highest level of abstraction: in the color of the objectifying, note-taking assistant, to point out one example. The surgeon is, in the quality of being portrayed, removed *from* the actual scene, whereas the actual reason why he is worthy of being portrayed in the first place is that he is *at work*. The same then is true for the viewer as we have seen; he is made to work in order to experience the whole meaning of the painting. The effort to combine the objective description of factual occurrences in their empirical appearance (the figure hidden behind the surgeon) with a meaning going beyond mere fact, produced, as the painting of Eakins shows, highly intellectual forms of expression.

Eakins's *The Gross Clinic* is, however, not merely a pictorial statement on the condition of art in its time, commenting on the involvement of the painter as a participant observer. Seen in its allegoric qualities, the image shows that at a time when art felt the danger of being tucked away safely into the realm of merely pleasing the eye and confirming good taste and a complacent view of the world, it could call on enormous resources of resistance and strength. The allegorical challenge extends far beyond the limits of art appreciation. It draws towards it the social and philosophical explanations of contemporary experience and demonstrates them to be existential experiences of humankind. The manifest disregard for rational space and its almost collagelike freedom of pictorial quotation put the viewer into the position of not only having to sort out what the image is all about, but also, in the very process of doing just that, coming to terms with the viewer's own self. This is, if we are looking for the very essence of the phrase, the literal sense of *allégorie réale*: placing the self between time and timelessness; the temporality of the self being self-reflective within the reality of history. *The Gross Clinic* achieves its highly sophisticated way of questioning the official, or perhaps merely overt, meaning of a culture in transition by unfolding in a fabric of figures and images the distance between the self and its identity in society. Against the ideology of progress it is a conservative counterstatement, utterly progressive, however, where the idea of modernity is concerned!

We have discussed Thomas Eakins's *The Gross Clinic* in some detail, not only because it was first exhibited in 1876, roughly marking the middle of the era we want to discuss, but mainly because it shows how the weakening of a dominant artistic expression forces the concentration of otherwise separated views of the world into one: the allegorical form of artistic articulation. In this role allegory becomes a functional equivalent for absent statements in literature and philosophy; it occupies, by condensation, representational narrative space.

A second, related aspect should not be overlooked, namely, the religious quality of the painting, seen in the context of secularization. To the extent that the image *The Gross Clinic* represents a world, it also has to be discussed as part of the process of self-constitution. Humanity's self, in the painting of Eakins, is one in transition. Even the single person capable of maintaining identity is part of the transitory world merely as a witness: the painter concentrating so as to see everything, but only one among many in the chain of being, visible at the far right of the actual space, a witness to both pictorial fiction and reality. The paradox, resulting from Eakins's specific way of being scientifically exact in his realism and trying to transcend reality at the same time has been described by Barbara Novak in terms of an "outside" of the painting as opposed to its actual spatial organization.

> The patient's thigh and part of the buttock seem literally disjoined from the body. Sufficient space is not allotted for the physical existence of a trunk between leg and anesthetized head. As in many of Eakins's works, however, this *seems* right, as well as curiously wrong, emphasizing the paradox implied by this method—mathematical fidelity to the realities of three-dimensional space and form *outside* the picture transferred to the two-dimensional pictorial space by multiple conceptual and perceptual means.[23]

If, as Barbara Novak points out, the picture "runs a gamut of style," such a combination of styles, which comment on each other, does indeed extend the meaning of the painting beyond the painted space in a logical manner. The logic, then, is determined to a large extent by *the world view the painter has of the world outside of the pictorial realm*, by the view he takes of the political and social reality.

Eakins had returned to Philadelphia from France via Spain in 1870. The years spent in France from 1866 to 1869, as we have pointed out before, cannot be reduced to the experience of the academic tutelage of Gérôme and his colleagues at the Ecole. The France that Eakins left behind had been politically restless and artists were very much involved in clarifying their role in a society of conflicts. Philadelphia, by comparison, was a rich, stable and—by the standards of the time—highly cultured city at its genteel best. If one of the negative charac-

[23] Novak, *American Painting*, p. 200.

teristics of genteel culture was to ignore the foundations of its own existence, to separate, in other words, knowledge and its results, material and form, Eakins was certainly the man to tell his fellow citizens not to fool themselves.

If, again, the epitome of genteel artistic expression was the quasi-symbolic fusion of form and content frequently performed in a sentimental and facile manner, then Eakins's allegoric configuration of the divergent elements of meaning into a unified whole in *The Gross Clinic* achieved the opposite result. Instead of trying to confirm the individual's desire to acquire, without work, the results of the cultural effort, thus satisfying in that way a socially enforced shallow idealism, his art demanded the involvement of active intellect. The genteel idealism knew no limits: its natural apex was the fusion of beauty and death as a kind of achieved sublimity. The soul had become the supermarket of life—with a back door, of course, as G. H. Boker's famous advice to Swinburne shows. Eakins's *The Gross Clinic* incorporated all of the essential ingredients of genteel culture—representing them, however, by means of a form of bricolage. It is an image, therefore, of the world as a unified whole of fragments: the fact of transition, of history's passing, is its crucial point, and with reference to this it alludes to the triumph of Nature.

Emerson's famous statement "Man is god in ruins" would have been an adequate title for the painting. One cannot expect, however, that the contemporary audience should have made a connection between Emerson, transcendentalism, and Eakins. Eakins, after all, represented a shockingly new and barely acceptable realism. In the same year, when *The Gross Clinic* was first exhibited at Hazeltine's Gallery in Philadelphia, Emerson published his *Letters and Social Aims*, put together by James Elliot Cabot. By that time Emerson had become the sage of Boston, if not of the New World, while Eakins was seen as the proverbial outrageous artist whose antisocial notoriety would soon assume legendary proportions. It was therefore out of the question to *read* Eakins's painting with Emerson's essay "Poetry and Imagination" in mind.

> Science was false by being unpoetical. It assumed to explain a reptile or mollusk, and isolated it,—which is hunting for life in graveyards. Reptile or mollusk or man or angel only exist in system, in relation. The meta-physician, the poet, only sees an animal form as an inevitable step in the path of the creating. . . . Science does not know its debt to imagination. Goethe did not believe that a great naturalist could exist without this faculty. He was himself

conscious of its help which made him a prophet among the doctors. From this vision he gave brave hints to the zoologist, the botanist and the optician. . . . All thinking is analyzing, and it is the use of life to learn metonomy. [24]

Eakins's painting had to be read, its allegorical qualities relying on the recognition of its rhetoric of and in history. The rhetoric of allegory transforms the realistic, empirically verified moment into an element of history and further into one of Nature. In this sense, then, Eakins's painting is the contemporary allegory of Life and Death, a quality that is only thinly disguised underneath its insistence on actuality. As if in anticipation of the jargon of the modern clinic today, the patient, humankind is reduced to "the thigh," in the sense of the painting of the wound. The hand of the assistant working on the initial incision and the hand of the woman expressing horror are geometrically aligned. The bloody scalpel of the surgeon is slightly elevated to form another straight line with the red pen of the assistant taking notes. The masses of future doctors remain largely anonymous: the allegory, being an explicit statement of the contemporary moments, points out a threshold in the professional development. A comparison between Eakins's *The Gross Clinic* and his later painting *The Agnew Clinic* confirms that real allegory, although an expression of transcendental time can only be produced out of a firm view of the actual, historical moment in an experienced present. There is no escape from this dualism.

Allegories age, as Walter Benjamin has stated, because the element of terrible insight is essential to their nature. Hence its affinity to the realm of signs, emblems, and writing. Why, then, does allegory as a major form of expression represent the vital and formative force within the cultural context of the American nineteenth century?

As a tentative beginning towards an explanation of this phenomenon we can take a hint from Emerson, who in his essay "Poetry and Imagination" praised the powers of poetry in a way that works by a strange inclusion: "Newton may be permitted to call Terence a playbook and to wonder at the frivolous taste for rhymers; he only predicts, one would say, a grander poetry: he only shows that he is not yet reached; that the poetry which satisfies more youthful souls is not such to a mind like his, accustomed to grander harmonies."[25]

[24] Ralph Waldo Emerson, *The Complete Works of Ralph Waldo Emerson,* 8 (Boston, 1885): 10.

[25] Ibid., p. 56.

From the point of view of allegory as opposed to symbol, such statements are the death sentence of the symbolic, at least as long as definition of the symbol draws its strength from its alleged closer vicinity to the idea, in other words to the romantic concept of truth. The fact that Emerson refers to Newton cannot be overlooked: the reference does more than remind us of Cotton Mather's famous statement that after Newton "Philosophy is no Enemy but a mighty and wondrous incentive to religion." Perry Miller, who in his essay "The End of the World" briefly discusses the Newtonian influence on the Puritan's theological imagination, quotes Newton's famous dictum "Hypothetes non fingo," but loses a good track through his wilderness by not paying attention to the sentence following: "Quincquid enim ex phaenomenis non deducitur, hypothesis vocanda est." This anti-Platonic implication is a kind of anticipated realism of high latency. By the time Emerson draws upon the evocative power of Newton's ear, being, as it seems, attuned to the music of spheres, he limits the potential of poetry. The world's poetry, however perfect and of a higher order than empirical science, is out of tune. As long as perfection in this world has not been achieved, poetry will always remain a potential of hope. Logically it can only reach a sort of qualified perfection at best: "Itself must be its own end, or it is nothing."[26] This leaves a large part of the world to allegory, a world that, by being known through allegory, is at the same time shown to be far from a state of perfection. It is dignified only by virtue of being the only material *capable* of perfection. The concreteness of matter, therefore, is of transcendental importance. The realistic allegory maintains a precarious balance between idealism and materialism and betrays its genesis, or rather its sudden importance since the mid-nineteenth century by calling upon tradition at a time of cultural change. Compared with the monumental effort of keeping knowledge alive in the allegorical architecture as a storehouse of memory, the pale negation of Unitarianism assumes a ghostlike pallor. When genteel culture came to dominate public life, the very same public was confronted with the sight of the work of tradition going on—and where such work achieved expression, culture most certainly was not a unified experience. Henry Adams, as part of his own resistance against the smugness of genteel culture, in his chapter on the Chicago exhibition, summed up the whole issue most adequately.

> The Exposition itself defied philosophy. One might find fault till the last gate closed, one could still explain nothing that needed explanation. As a scenic display, Paris had never approached it,

[26] Ibid., p. 54.

> but the inconceivable scenic display consisted in its being there at all—more surprising, as it was, than anything else on the continent, Niagara Falls, the Yellowstone Geysers, and the whole railway system thrown in, since these were all natural products in their place; while, since Noah's Ark, no such Babel of loose and ill-joined, such vague and ill-defined and unrelated thoughts and half-thoughts and experimental outcries as the Exposition, had ever ruffled the surface of the Lake.[27]

The irony increases to the point of furious sarcasm: Henry Adams was a good historian of culture, and throwing in the railway system *pars pro toto* must have been one of his generous, though backhanded, gestures towards his future colleagues. Anger of such quality anticipates the betrayal that is brought about by an intentional act of forgetting.

[27] Henry Adams, *Education*, pp. 339–40.

CHAPTER 2

Merlin's Laughter

The grand distinction of modern times is, the emerging of the people from brutal degradation, the gradual recognition of their rights, the gradual diffusion among them of the means of improvement and happiness, the creation of a new power in the state, the power of the people.

—WILLIAM ELLERY CHANNING

Ye were conquerors; ye were conquered! . . . I am Merlin. Then such a delirium of silly laughter overtook him that he reeled about like a drunken man, and presently fetched up against one of our wires. His mouth is spread open yet; apparently he is still laughing. I suppose the face will retain that petrified laugh until the corpse turns to dust.

—MARK TWAIN

In the year 1838, several months before William Ellery Channing delivered his lecture on the topic of "Self-Culture," H. D. Thoreau entered the following observation into his journal: "That which properly constitutes the life of every man is a profound secret. Yet this is what every one would give most to know, but is himself most backward to impart."[1] This brief entry, one among several others, was part of his preparation for his lecture at the Lyceum, his subject being the nature and characteristics of society. On the fourteenth of April, Thoreau gave his talk, and the drift of his argument can be easily reconstructed from several other notes he made while thinking over what he was going to say—but little needs to be added for our purposes, now, to the pithy remark quoted above. With one swift stroke Thoreau reduced the many-sided problems concerning society and its relation to the individual to one central issue: that of the *self*. What else, other than the self, can be meant by what he refers to as that which "properly constitutes the life of every man?" Thoreau not only makes it quite clear where any theory of society should take its beginning, he also in passing touches upon the difficulties of self-reference and the problem of an adequate language to denote "self."

From the idea of the self to a concept of social identity: this formula describes, in short, the social change in the American nineteenth century, if one wants to capture it in the realm of intellectual history. The rapid and often violent change of the American social landscape from an early industrialism within a pastoral setting into a multifunctional, highly complex society had its counterpart in the transformation of self into social identity. Far from being the result of a deterministic view of social change and its consequences, this transformation ought to be seen as a necessary functional equivalent within the collective

[1] Thoreau, *Journal*, p. 27.

and individual experience of material and social change. This should be obvious, for we are after all interested in the efforts to resist the loss of the idea of the self—and if we allow for the possibility of viable resistance, it would make little or no sense at all to argue for determinism and symmetry instead of acknowledging the existence of contingency and choice.

From self to social identity: it would be too simple to associate the first principle, namely that of selfhood, with a kind of rugged individualism saved from the early pioneering days, and to see the second as a loss of the first, due to the closing of the frontiers and to the emergence of a tightly knit social structure. The dialectics of social and intellectual change work in a different order: it was the emphatic belief in the full potential of selfhood that allowed the ideal of social identity to take shape.

In the face of a multifaceted society, which had become virtually impenetrable, both the concept of self and that of social identity worked as a means of interpretation, as defenses against the unknown.

If we realize how threatening it must have been for the individual to witness within one generation all those upsetting social changes that transformed America from an agricultural nation of small townships into a geopolitical power with a seemingly unlimited and uncontrollable economic and sociopolitical potential, we will understand that the movement from the idea of selfhood to that of social identity expressed above all a need for a social and cultural interpretation based on anxiety.

It is neither ironic nor surprising that the emphasis-shift from self to identity should in the end be seen as a process of diminishing returns. After the transformation of self into a distended social identity something was irrevocably lost. There were gains too, of course, like a sense of certainty and optimism about humankind's ability to manage its own fate. But such optimism was the result of the process we are discussing here, namely the metamorphosis of self into identity as an event of some duration. If we see this event suspended in time, we cannot be surprised that its intellectual and artistic expression mostly worked by dissemination and by the use of the abrupt voice of disoriented shock, rather than in the polished tone of the unified narrative. Allegoresis, being the conscious structuring of a specific experience in a series of tropes and rhetorical configurations introduced strange elements of mannerism and phantasmagory into the art of realism. It is not surprising that in a certain kind of fiction, as if in imitation of a society that was unsure of its own destiny, we find sense in dissemination rather than in the rhetoric of organicism. That exactly some of those texts that we have in mind, like Emerson's essays, frequently talk *about* the organic whole is a totally different matter. There are, on the other hand, examples enough that make it easy on the critic's part to point out the emblematic detail![2]

Certainly one of the most terrifying comments on the failure of practical, technological reason at the end of the American nineteenth century is the frighteningly proleptic image of Merlin's laughter in Mark Twain's *A Connecticut Yankee in King Arthur's Court*. Merlin's laughter, this powerful indictment of the present in the name of the future, is the ultimate expression of nature's victory over the attempts at her domestication. Laughter is the decisive emblem; and death—in the realm of human experience—is the final encounter between man and nature. History, once seen through the eyes of Twain as the pure accumulation of death through time, loses its chronological order. Death, removed from the individual experience within a life span, is a phenomenon of simultaneous timelessness. "We had conquered; in turn we were conquered. The Boss recognizes this; we all recognized it. If we could go to one of those new camps and patch up some kind of terms with the enemy—yes, but the Boss could not go, and neither could I, for I was among the first that were made sick by the poisonous air bred by those dead thousands. Others were taken down, and still others. Tomorrow—*Tomorrow*. It is here. And with it the end."[3]

The physicality of death, the poisonous gases, and the imagery of the holocaust evoked here may serve as a vantage point from which we may get a clear view of a landscape of despair which, in the case of Mark Twain, resisted narrative beautification. Critics of Twain's writing have often felt obliged to be apologetic about a certain uneven and sometimes almost incohesive quality of his texts, but they rarely have seen this particular fault as a result of sheer speechlessness vis-à-vis the horrors of the reality Mark Twain saw unfolding before him. If Mark Twain faced the experience of nature's triumph over man without looking for help in the camps of ideology or metaphysics, the result had to be the conscious fabrication of the allegorical structure as the most penetrating and yet provisional form of knowledge. Such provisional knowledge, which is by virtue of being *provisional* at the same time the most advanced one about life's fragile nature, does not go well with narrative unity. It is a glimpse of Mark Twain's genius, that facing an age of materialism, his allegory of Merlin's laughter

[2] The rhetoric of Emerson's essays is "emblematic" to the extent by which he makes use of visual imagery in the "hieroglyphic" tradition.

[3] Mark Twain, *A Connecticut Yankee in King Arthur's Court* (New York, n.d.), p. 318.

ends and culminates in petrification. Just as the signature of the age was one of objects, so the objectified signature qua epitaph had to be dead matter.

Our brief look into the darkness of Mark Twain's imagination, which in terms of the American allegory is much closer to Emerson's pessimism than we are likely to recognize at first sight, should also remind us how close the relationship really is between myth and allegory. Allegory exists by maintaining a precarious and barely maintained distance from myth, a distance that occasionally a simple image manages to reduce by way of construction. Hank Morgan, as we remember, lost his original identity as a practical Yankee whose "real trade," as he explains, was to "make everything; guns, revolvers, cannons, boilers, engines, all sorts of labor-saving machinery" (Twain, *A Connecticut Yankee*, p. 6), because of a literally crushing encounter with a mythical figure: "a fellow we used to call Hercules" (p. 7). Before there can be myth, however, an assembly of experience must take place.

Young Thoreau, who had given the question of the self much thought, starting typically not with a theoretical assumption about what ought to be the case, began his explorations in the realm of tangible experience. From the early awareness of sound (the experience of hearing) towards the meaning of sound in nature and from there to the individual and his relationship with society, it was a long way. In addition, Thoreau, to make matters more complicated, liked the kind of shortcuts that every traveler hates, because they take him a long way off the direct route. So the question of the self and its relationship to society were complex issues that Thoreau manages to dramatize, using Unitarian culture as a background. Nature would occupy the foreground, and thus the stage was set with Thoreau as director—even if he himself would not have liked or accepted the designation of this role.

At the time that Thoreau picked up the issue, matters had become complicated. If Channing could still claim with a certain innocence that "Nature should be studied for its own sake, because so wonderful a work of God, because impressed with this perfection, because radiant with beauty, grandeur, and wisdom, and beneficence,"[4] Thoreau had to alert his readers to the role of the individual in the pursuit of such studies. The complexity of the allegorical mode lies in the setting

[4] William Ellery Channing, *The Works* (Boston, 1890), p. 367. Hereafter cited in text as Channing, *Works*.

of the scene, in the conscious work of transformation, and it was this complexity that Thoreau had to confront.

Sometimes, as a beginning, the simple text has the advantage of highlighting the essential aspects of more complicated ideas. With this precaution in mind we should take a step backward and look at some of the crucial writings of Dr. Channing, which are certainly representative of the Unitarian culture, which so unwillingly produced transcendentalism. In all fairness, one must concede that William Ellery Channing's sermon given in 1819 at the ordination of Jared Sparks in Baltimore was never intended as a theological masterpiece. Its quality must be seen in its frank effort to put an end to the vexing and provincial squabbling between the various factions of New and Old Light Calvinists, Arminian rationalists of early Arian persuasion or worse, of Socinian leanings.

Against such scholastic, or rather more frequently, merely idiosyncratic subtleties, Channing mustered up the reasonably self-evident forces of simplified enlightenment. By bluntly asserting the basic tenets of Unitarianism in his Baltimore sermon, Channing defended Boston liberalism from the attacks launched against it in the furor of the theological pamphleteering that followed a number of provocative challenges and assaults instigated mainly by the unforgiving and power-conscious Jedidiah Morse. It is therefore the political shadow of Morse, a man already compromised by his scheming in the public arena, that looms over Channing's sermon of 1819. But apart from its political thrust the sermon managed to enlist the authority of modernism on the side of Unitarianism. In fact, it does so in an exemplary way. If one follows the accounts of the rise of Arminianism and consequently of Unitarianism in New England, more often than not it is the absence of theological substance that first strikes the observer.

Conrad Wright's *The Beginning of Unitarianism in America*, can be read like the report of a long, drawn-out battle, including the maps of strongholds, and about gains and losses of the involved parties. The debate about the respective relationship between social and theological developments may stand as it is. Two immediate conclusions can be drawn, however, from what has been described about the history of Unitarianism so far. The process of diluting the coherence of theology had started long before Channing's time. Channing himself provided the personal focus at a point in time when a central figure was badly needed. Like most personalities who rise to prominence at a time of crisis, Channing was open to projection. Even his biographers cannot escape from this particular quality of Channing's character—so at best, they try to give it shape by summary.

> Unitarians have always been prone to conceive of Channing after their own image. Sometimes he has been identified with the early Unitarianism of the nineteenth century with its Lockean background, its Arian christology, its pre-critical approach to the New Testament, its miracles, and its somewhat mechanical notion of inspiration. Again, the exponents of the idealistic monism that was the dominant force in later nineteenth and earlier twentieth century Unitarianism have pointed to features of his thought that are undeniably akin to views entertained by the Transcendentalists, have hailed him as a precursor of their movement, and have maintained that, had he lived a generation later, he would have thought as they thought. And, last of all, the so called 'humanists' have so earnestly appealed to the social aspects of his thinking, to his emphasis upon the dignity of man and upon freedom of thought, that one is sometimes inclined to believe that it would scarcely do them injustice to represent them as contending that, if he had lived today, his gospel would have been limited to a demand for education for all, a chicken in every pot, a play-ground in every school, and good sewer pipes in every street.[5]

Certainly Channing can be seen in all the ways mentioned—which is exactly the reason why, within the process of nineteenth-century secularization in America, his role was so decisive. Channing, we might say without undue exaggeration, *represents* the functionalist interpretation of secularization. The functionalist interpretation of secularization puts the whole process into the framework of the *social* structure. It tells us just as much about Channing as it does about the varieties of theory—designing if we read the functionalist theory of secularization backwards, from Niklas Luhman to Talcott Parsons. The stress is laid on primary functional, highly differentiated systems of society, where secularization serves the purpose of stabilizing an increasingly complex network of interrelated units that constitute the whole of society. Channing's multifaceted interests, his high degree of interpretability that we quoted above, is merely an example of what the theoreticians have tried to describe; an example, however, fitting one particular set of theories only.

So if one were forced to choose from any of the three attitudes of roles ascribed to Channing in the summary given above, one could safely assume that seeing him in the position described last would be quite adequate. It is revealing that Wordsworth, who could have easily

[5] Robert Lee Patterson, *The Philosophy of William Ellery Channing* (New York, 1952), pp. 63–64.

remembered him differently, when asked to recall the impression Channing had made on him answered "that there was one particular statement by Channing which he remembered clearly," namely, that Christianity "contained nothing which rendered it unadapted to a progressive state of society; that it did not put checks upon the activity of the human mind, nor compel it to tread always blindly in a beaten path."[6] To this statement his biographer Madeleine Hooke Rice added "how typically Channingesque that." Indeed, the poet, if we interpret his words adequately, remembers the perfectly modern man in the sense that the ability of Christianity to survive is guaranteed by its seemingly limitless adaptability to changing social structures.

Channing, the reluctant radical, as one of his interpreters has called him, must have realized that the adaptation of religion to social change by moving religious questions into the private realm would make a larger number of theological issues irrelevant.[7] He was reluctant indeed to concede to institutions their full sociological impact in a modern sense, preferring to shift the responsibility onto the individual. Channing, in other words, reacted to the increasing complexity of modern society by compromising in a bipolar fashion. The social institution enters into a functional relationship with the individual, a relationship that will remain stable only if the individual is subjected to implicitly institutionalized norms of behavior, attitudes, and moral standards. The balance thus achieved is rational *and* antihistorical. Social change with Channing becomes the overwhelming and, at the same time, the least overt issue. In the end the equation was quite simple: Unitarianism was rational, rationalism was modern, at least by Edinburgh standards, and no Christian could allow irrationalism to enter into his theological system.

God, who was infinitely wise, expected the use of reason, Channing explained, as a good father and teacher ought to do.

> Our leading principle in interpreting Scripture is this, that the Bible is a book written for men, in the language of men, and that its meaning is to be sought in the same manner as that of other books. We believe that God, when he speaks to the human race, conforms, if we may say so, to the established rules of speaking and writing. . . . Enough has been said to show, in what sense we make use of reason in interpreting Scripture. From a variety of possible interpretations, we select that which accords with the na-

[6] Madeleine Hooke Rice, *Federal Street Pastor: The Life of William Ellery Channing* (New York, 1961), p. 113.

[7] Jack Mendelsohn, *Channing the Reluctant Radical* (Boston, 1971).

> ture of the subject and the state of the writer, with the connection of the passage, with the general strain of Scripture, with the known character and will of God, and with the obvious and acknowledged laws of nature. In other words, we believe that God never contradicts, in one part of Scripture, what he teaches in another. (Channing, *Works*, pp. 367, 369)

Casting God into the role of the faultless father and teacher spared Channing some difficult questions about truth and time, about the relationship, also, between the conservation of selfhood and the idea of teleology.

> We are told, that God being infinitely wiser than men, his discoveries will surpass human reason. In a revelation from such a teacher we ought to expect propositions, which may seem to contradict established truths. . . . We answer again, that, if God be infinitely wise, he cannot sport with the understanding of his creatures. A wise teacher discovers his wisdom in adapting himself to the capacities of his pupils, not in perplexing them with what is unintelligible, not in distressing them with apparent contradictions, not in filling them with skeptical distrust of their own powers. (Channing, *Works*, p. 370)

Even though admitting an occasional obscurity of Scripture due to their composition over such a long period of time, Channing drives home the point that in no conceivable way could God intend to confuse or weaken his creatures. The Unitarians' horror of skepticism, resulting in a distrust of one's own power, moves into the foreground of Channing's argument. By implication at least he constructs a relationship between God and man that endows the latter with infinite resources of self-improvement, while denying God the power to call the adventure of his creation and its consequences to a sudden end. God, one might want to say, is deprived of some of his powers, so that his children can be less frightened. "To give our views of God in one word, we believe in his parental character. We ascribe to him, not only the name, but the dispositions and principles of a father. We believe that he has a father's concern for his creatures, a father's desire for their improvement, a father's equity in proportioning his commands to their powers, a father's joy in their progress, a father's readiness to receive the penitent, and a father's justice for the incorrigible" (Channing, *Works*, p. 377).

A father, we ought to add, bound by contract, which seems to throw at least a shadow of doubt on the trustworthiness of the father: "We reason about the Bible precisely as civilians do about the constitution under which we live. . . . Without these principles of interpretation, we frankly acknowledge, that we cannot defend the divine authority of the scriptures. Deny us this latitude, and we must abandon this book to its enemies" (Channing, *Works*, p. 378).

Those members of Channing's audience who were willing to indulge in the treacherous capacity of the metaphor to maintain and consequently betray some sense of its origin may have felt that they were being treated to a lesson in basic mercantile common sense. The alluring aspect was, of course, that humankind, according to Channing, could only end up in the black. In fact, Channing was merely engaging in a simple act of theological safeguarding: the power of God had to be minimized by increasing his virtues infinitely, which forced (or rather enabled) humans to become like him. The approach to modernism works by minimizing the complexities involved in the process of finding truth, in order to increase the realm of practical intellect. To the extent that the theoretical preconditions of possible selfhood diminish, the individual could expand his or her grasp of the world.

We shall have to follow Channing's development a little further in order to show how, at its prime, liberal Unitarianism produced both the culture of gentility and its rebellious counterpart. We also need to unfold the next aspect of our argument in some detail in order to demonstrate to what extent and in what way Unitarian culture managed to become so dominant within the American cultural tradition.

W. E. Channing, in his introductory address to the Franklin Lectures, which were held before a working-class audience, indicated simply by his choice of title that he was thinking about the development of the self as a practical character-building kind of exercise. The self Channing talks about resembles society at large in its economical composition. It is the microcosmic version of the social macrocosm. The idea underlying Channing's argument is that both aspects, the individual and the society, ought to strive for universal harmony, which in itself stood for rationality. Channing, like most of his Unitarian colleagues, shunned epistemology. Influenced by Scottish common-sense philosophy, he and his friends preferred a simplified dualistic ontology, designed to assert the dominance of mental activity over inert, passive matter. Nowhere in his elaborate, published version of his original lecture is Channing in doubt about the substantiality of the self he talks about. Even if one bears in mind that Channing was addressing a working-class audience, it is hard to believe how easy it was to discard essential elements of theology and philosophy without any need for explanation. It also shows how the culture of liberal Unitarianism lent itself to what Santayana, and everyone after, would refer to as the genteel tradition.

> Self-culture is something possible. It is not a dream. It has foundations in our nature. Without this conviction the speaker will but declaim and the hearer listen without profit. There are two powers of the human soul which make self-culture possible, the self-searching and the self-forming power. We have first the faculty of turning the mind on itself; of recalling its past, and watching its present operations. . . . It is worthy of observation that we are able to discern not only what we already are, but what we may become, to see in ourselves germs and promises of a growth to which no bounds can be set, to dart beyond what we have actually gained to the idea of Perfection as the end of our being. (Channing, *Works*, p. 14)

W. E. Channing saw no difficulties in the mind confronting itself; he embraced the Lockean doctrine without any reservations. "Our observation, employed either about external sensible objects, or about the internal operations of our minds, perceived and reflected by ourselves, is that which supplies our understanding with all the material of thinking. These two are the fountains of knowledge, from whence all the ideas we have, or can naturally have, do spring" (Channing, *Works*, p. 19). Like most of his contemporaries, Channing blended Locke's empiricism with Scottish moral philosophy, a mixture that made philosophers like Frances Hutcheson look more idealistic than they in fact were.

Also, like many of his contemporaries, Channing felt free, and was by the lack of a stable canon of philosophical texts forced to make up his own philosophy; and he did so with considerable results. He thus clearly represents the classical threshold phenomenon where lines of thought become seemingly entangled without yet forming a new, systematically patterned network.

Channing, too, must have felt that he was proceeding on unstable ground, just as the sensitive reader of his discourses and sermons will hardly miss the hortatory and occasionally shrill overtones in his arguments, an anxiety that seems to increase after the 1819 sermon in Baltimore. Christianity *had* to be a rational religion, Channing seems to be saying, usually preferring the fervent avowals of the desired to the proving of fact. "Christianity is a rational religion. Were it not so, I should be ashamed to profess it. . . . If I could not be a Christian without ceasing to be rational I should not hesitate as to my choice. I feel myself bound to sacrifice to Christianity property, reputation, life; but I ought not to sacrifice to any religion the reason which lifts me above the brute and constitutes me a man" (Channing, *Works*, p. 233).

Not only are the passages quoted a remarkable evidence of the Arminianism that had conquered the liberal Unitarians, they also demonstrate the extent to which the rhetoric available had to be stretched in order to reconcile the advance of science and the idea of teleologically oriented history. When reading some of the more passionate appeals of Channing to his readers and audience, one cannot help but conclude that somewhere in every Unitarian a frightened Calvinist was hidden—a Calvinist more sensitive to the threats of secularization than the liberal Unitarian could allow himself to be. The Unitarian, it seems, had a tendency to conquer by simplification, that is, by simply avoiding the intricacies of philosophical and scientific theory. As a result the Unitarian self was transformed into an individual with only a vague idea about its proper destiny in history and society. The individual, expected to make sense of a society that had become increasingly complex, was ill equipped for this task in terms of self-interpretation. Looking back at the highly intellectualized atmosphere of the enlightenment and the questions tackled then, one is slightly baffled by the intellectual complacency that seemed to govern the Unitarian mind. Certainly Henry Adams's pointed statement of 1876 that in the minds of most Unitarians of Channing's generation the conviction reigned that the limits of truth had been reached was somewhat exaggerated. But it contains an element of truth, which may help us to approach an answer to Perry Miller's question about "why Waldo and Margaret in the 1820s and the '30s should instinctively have revolted against a creed that had at least been perfected as the ideology of their own group of respectable, prosperous, middle-class Boston and Cambridge—why these youngsters, who by all the laws of economic determinism ought to have been the white-headed children of Unitarianism elected to become transcendental black sheep."[8]

The element of truth just mentioned that Henry Adams catches in passing can be brought out in detail if we look at the kind of questions that W. E. Channing did *not* raise. One wonders about the sentiments of the working-class audience that listened to Channing, ending his lecture on self-culture with a rhetorical flourish so pathetically evoking

[8] Perry Miller, *Errand into the Wilderness* (Cambridge, Mass., 1976), p. 200.

the idea of uplift and reform that it must have struck some of his listeners as downright depressing.

> Let us thank God for what has been gained. But let us not think everything gained. Let the people feel that they have only started in the race. How much remains to be done! What a vast amount of ignorance, intemperance, coarseness, sensibility may still be found in our community, what a vast amount of mind is palsied and lost. . . . And how few of us are moved by this moral desolation? How few understand, that to raise the depressed, by a wise culture, to the dignity of men, is the highest end of the social state? (Channing, *Works*, p. 36)

It took the laborious efforts of someone like the notorious Francis Bowen to provide the well-intended but vague argument of the gentle Dr. Channing with some philosophical backing, even if its solidity remains questionable.

The early Unitarian consensus on divine reason allowed one, by way of adoption, to claim that history was still on its way towards fulfillment. The Unitarian effort had gained its energy mainly by defining the world as it ought *not* to be: by its attacks on Calvinism and by its pliability within a process of social and economical development. What Francis Bowen in his *Critical Essays on Speculative Philosophy* would expound as a natural impulse (and as a natural right), namely the "principle of legitimacy," was itself the answer to an anticipated crisis of legitimacy. In that way liberal Unitarianism had occupied the fields of enlightenment, humanitarianism, and progressivism, which did not leave much room for dissenters—unless they were willing to differ radically. Such radicalism could hardly come from direct opposition. The structure of Unitarian liberalism was highly flexible, as its success would show.

If one wanted to criticize it successfully, its vulnerability had to be looked for in the place that it tried to occupy in the larger context of history. The question, in other words, was not whether its attack against Calvinism was right or wrong but whether it provided the adequate alternative to what it tried to abolish. Was Channing's "moral argument against Calvinism" an adequate argument for a different morality in terms of either a functional equivalent or simply as a demand for change? What kind of knowledge did the Unitarian attack against Calvinism indigenously possess that the Calvinists did not have? Channing gives us an implicit hint when he names the reason for the decline of Calvinism.

> Calvinism, we are persuaded, is giving place to better views. It has passed its meridian, and is sinking to rise no more. It has to contend with foes more formidable than theologians, with foes from whom it cannot shield in mystery and metaphysical subtleties, we mean with the progress of the human mind, and with the progress of the spirit of the Gospel. Society is going forward in intelligence and charity, and of course is leaving the theology of the sixteenth century behind it. We hail this revolution of opinion as a most auspicious event to the Christian cause. . . . We think the decline of Calvinism one of the most encouraging facts in our passing history; for this system, by outraging conscience and reason, tends to array these high faculties against revelation. Its errors are peculiarly mournful because they relate to the character of God. It darkens and stains his pure nature; spoils his character of its sacredness, loveliness, glory; and thus quenches the central light of the universe, makes existence a curse, and the extinction of it a consummation devoutly to be wished. (Channing, *Works*, p. 468)

If we isolate two main strains of Channing's argument, Calvinism had been brought down by the progress of society (not by theological reasoning) and because it had put God into a position that invited criticism by blaming the uncertainties of earthly life on his incomprehensibility. ("This reasoning of our opponents casts us on an ocean of awful uncertainty.") (Channing, *Works*, p. 467)

The ease with which Channing moves the weight of responsibility from theology to the progress of society indicates that the second part of his argument also serves the idea of justifying progress by absolving God from responsibility for potential calamities. Rather than accept the uncertainties of progress, Channing prefers to minimize potential disasters and disappointments with history by reducing them to human errors instead of seeing them as part of God's doing. Strictly speaking, Channing makes history a human venture, including its reduced expectations of meaning. Truth becomes knowledge and the loss of meaning is compensated for by the idea of scientific gains that can be quickly transformed into technical competence. Religious value orientation on the basis of uncertainty, providing a sense of self, based on interpretation is replaced by the ordering of experience as a function of social location.

The identity gained by social or sociologically definable position does not exclude a sense of religion, but it changes the meaning of value orientation. To the degree that such value orientation becomes a matter of the socially conscious individual the importance of mediating symbols rises. Channing's liberating call for a National Literature is part of this process. At the end of this process one should expect a canon of National Literature, just as the progress of reason does not allow for the existence of the unreasonable individual. Society, therefore, is basically right, though not perfect; but just as we cannot expect a just God to set things right, so we cannot expect ourselves to remedy social ills fundamentally either. If such social grievances exist, that is, instead of being merely an exaggeration or a misinterpretation of human nature.

> The outward condition of the poor is a hard one. I mean not to criticize it with the apathy of the stoic, to deny that pain is an evil, privation a loss of good. . . . That some of the indigent among us die of scanty food is undoubtedly true, but vastly more in this community die from eating too much, than from eating too little. . . . Our daughters are oftener brought to the grave by their rich attire, than our beggars by their nakedness. So the poor are often over-worked, but they suffer less than many among the rich who have no work to do, no interesting subject to fill up life, to satisfy the infinite cravings of man for action. According to our present modes of education, how many of our daughters are victims of ennui, a misery unknown to the poor, and more intolerable than the weariness of excessive toil. . . . Let now the condition of the poor be spoken of as necessarily wretched. Give them the Christian spirit, and they would find in their lot the chief elements of good. For example, the domestic affections may and do grow up among the poor, and these are to all of us the chief springs of earthly happiness. . . . In this country, the poor might enjoy the most important advantages of the rich, had they the moral and religious cultivation consistent with their lot. Books find their way into every house, however mean; and especially that book which contains more nutriment for their intellect, imagination and heart, than all others; I mean, of course, the Bible. . . . Even the pleasures of a refined taste are not denied to the poor, but might easily be opened to them by a wise moral culture. True, their rooms are not lined with works of art; but the living beauty of nature opens on the eyes of all her children. (Channing, *Works*, p. 73)

After dwelling at great length on the advantages that lie buried and are as of yet undiscovered in the condition of being poor, Channing spends an equal amount of time describing the material misery and deprivation of the poor and society's responsibility for various consequences of poverty, such as crime and alcoholism. Legislation, however, he contends can remedy only a few superficial symptoms of poverty. "Our chief reliance . . . must be placed on more direct and powerful means than legislation. The poor need and must receive Moral and Religious Culture, such as they have never yet enjoyed. I say Culture; and I select this term, because it expresses the development of Inward Principles; and without this, nothing effectual can be done for the rich or poor" (Channing, *Works*, p. 78).

Having thus established the similarity between the rich and the poor in the face of internalized moral culture, and while refraining at the same time from evoking the image of the masses of future educators, which would upset the balance that Channing tries to establish between the interior and the exterior side of man, he cites nature and science as the final proof of his argument.

> Such is the harmony between the religious and the philosophical spirit. It is to a higher moral and religious culture, that I look for a higher interpretation of nature. The laws of nature we must remember, had their origin in the Mind of God of this they are the product, expression and type; and I cannot but believe, that the human mind which best understands, and which partakes most largely of the divine, has a power of interpreting nature, which is accorded to no other. It has harmonies with the system which it is to unfold. It contains in itself the principles which gave birth to creation. As yet, science has hardly penetrated beneath the surface of nature. . . . Whence is light to break in on these depths of creative wisdom? I look for it to the spirit of philosophy, baptized, hallowed, exalted, made piercing by a new culture of the moral and religious principles of the human soul. (Channing, *Works*, p. 82)

Channing does not forget to mention the dark side of science, which degrades instead of serving the cause of uplift. But despite such aberrations from the course of reason, the social blueprint is clearly in place. Society will move forward, in more or less orderly ways, in the sense of an organic development guided in its evolution by the principles of a sociotheological culture. Channing in his address *Ministry for the Poor* from which the above quotations were taken, basically takes the success of society for granted, mainly because he can rely on nature as an ally. The resulting optimistic organicism, claiming over and again to have reason on its side as well, in fact diminishes the role of reason by subordinating it to the process of organic evolution.

Channing's commitments in this sense, then, were dangerous to the point that one feels tempted to see the banality of good as a predecessor of the banality of evil. If we read the diverse texts of Channing with a critical eye towards this issue, the impression becomes confirmed that he was taking a gigantic leap from the self, originally conceived as singular before God and hence thrown back upon itself in self-reflection to a conception of identity as a social role. His assessment of Napoleon Bonaparte is clearly derived from a preconceived opinion about the relationship between society and the individual. Whatever he has to say about the vice or virtue of Napoleon Bonaparte later, the beginning of his long two-part essay is significant. "We begin with observing, that it is an act of justice to Bonaparte to remember that he grew up under disastrous influences, in troubled days, when men's minds were convulsed, old institutions overthrown, old opinions shaken, old restraints snapped asunder. . . . A more dangerous school for the character cannot well be conceived" (Channing, *Works*, p. 523).

Social psychology as a beginning for reflections on Napoleon's sinister sides as well as on his merits: there is hardly a trace left of Kierkegaard's definition of the self as a relationship to itself. ("The self is a relation that relates itself to its own self, or it is that in the relation/which accounts for it/that the relation relates itself to its own self.")[9] What we get with Channing is, in fact, an acceleration of concept shaping that goes from Calvinism to a theory of the milieu, and it is not the time factor that counts, but the problem of exchanging explanatory value. (Both Emerson and Kierkegaard arrived at their most cogent formulation of concepts of the self about twenty years later in the nineteenth century.) Once again we have to account for the success of Channing's anticipation, by pointing out what it omits.

The typologies of Calvinism, whatever their relative faults and merits within the cultural context at large may have been, had, after all, one problem clearly in sight: how to reconcile the idea of a general identity with that of a singular identity. Calvinist typology seen as a result of a long historical process had reconciled the conflict between Ancient and Christian senses of identity, the first emphasizing the general and the second the singular versions of identity, by putting the burden on one's ability to identify oneself in the face of God. The change from typology in the sense of exegesis to a typologically oriented interpretation of the world changed the meaning of typological

[9] Søren Kierkegaard, *Fear and Trembling and the Sickness unto Death* (Princeton, N.J., 1954), p. 146.

thought fundamentally. Its survival could be secured only by making distinctions about the literal and the nonliteral levels of meaning, which in fact threatened the identity of the subject. The Arminian heresy had overstressed reason, as a means to maintaining the identity of man.

But Augustine's shadow, and the patristic tradition as a whole, was a legacy one could not escape from: either man was guilty or God was not perfect.

We are not interested in the theological implications themselves but in the choices they offered to those who wanted to challenge the Calvinist structure. Channing's way of escape, so to speak, was the classical one of avoiding the central issue by talking about something else. As usual such a maneuver produces a whole set of new problems, such as legitimizing one's own beginning. Channing's attack against the moral inadequacies of Calvinism is *not* really a critique of Calvinism on its own grounds, but a half-hearted discourse on what constitutes self. The second, and more interesting, aspect of Channing's attack is a kind of resigned undertone, most pronounced in the pathos of his future-oriented rhetoric. Not only does such utopian verve seem like a consolation for the present, it also works as an apology of the future, which will differ only by degrees. Such utopian elements do more than create a legendary origin for events of the past suitable to their particular pattern. Channing was wrong: Napoleon grew up under quite normal conditions, a well-loved child of a family whose status within the Corsian aristocracy was officially recognized by the French authorities, a fact that in turn won Napoleon a scholarship in the Brienne Military Academy.

More important is another lesson to be learned from Channing's example. If the decisive element in the meaningful flux of life is the pure force of social change, which he claims as his main ally against Calvinism, then there is more than just a suspicion left that such change will take place without the aid of people of reason. The minute the suspicion arises that one has to control one's ally, that ally becomes a problem and is soon seen as a future enemy. Channing's main energies would therefore be reserved for such a control—a never-ending task, had Channing identified the problem correctly.

Another way of dealing with the limits that Calvinism had come to represent was to deny radically its tenets by accepting the consequences of one's own position. If the self had to be defended it would have to be done thoroughly and not by avoiding central problems, such as original sin and the redemption of either the many or the few.

If the question was about the self, then this is where one had to start working out the problems! *This*, put simply, was Emerson's conclusion.

By altering both the romantic and Enlightenment-oriented relationship between humankind and nature, he introduced the idea of self-reference as a rational and philosophically inevitable foundation of a possible sense of self and identity. It demanded a truly metaphysical effort, and an astonishing amount of speculative energy to accomplish this kind of achievement.

Nature had to be recognized within the seemingly unnatural context of science and sociology. This, and Emerson's absolute truth, his preference, as he put it, for "the penumbra of the thing *rather* than the thing itself" are the key to the relative success and failure of what would later be known as transcendentalism. Unlike Ahab, whose proclamation "Truth has no confines" reveals the reason for his failure, Emerson realized early enough that striking through the pasteboard mask would only result in the discovery of another one. Hence his belief in the confinement of truth: "This human mind wrote history and this must read it. The sphinx must solve her own riddle." Hence also his realistic acceptance of approximation instead of absolute truth: "the axis of vision is not coincident with the axis of things and so they appear not transparent but opaque. The reason why the world lacks unity and lies broken in heaps, is, because man is disunited with himself."[10]

To these words from Nature one should add an entry in his journal from June 1835: "Man is conscious of a twofold nature which manifests itself in perpetual self-contradiction."[11]

Emerson, who would later emphasize the need for a new theory of the universe and invoke the ancient idea of a *kosmos*, first had to come to terms with the aspects of conflict and contradiction. The fact that his idea of the self included not only the possibility but the necessity of self-contradiction would eventually become the central force in the development of Emerson's concept of selfhood. Internalizing the idea of a harmonious and yet developing universe meant above all, however, that Emerson had to accept as the only appropriate way of expressing his ideas a language and a style that was highly metaphoric. What he needed and created was a rhetoric that relied on and used the logic of the metaphor. Language, or as we shall see further below, dialogue, is one of the fundamental criteria of the validity of Emer-

[10] Emerson, *Works* 1: 73–74.

[11] Ralph Waldo Emerson, *The Journals of Ralph Waldo Emerson*, ed. William H. Gilman et al. (Cambridge, Mass., 1960) 5: 51.

son's philosophy. Emerson's transcendental horizon is set by his theory and use of language. For a long time the cryptic, seemingly hermetic and paradoxical style of Emerson's writing has been used as a reason not to take him seriously as a philosopher. Especially and significantly, those who were mainly interested in Emerson as a literary figure, tended to neglect the philosophical content of his ideas. They would neutralize the impact of his thought by applying to it reductivist labels, such as pantheism, romantic imagination, orphism, and similar ill-defined generalizations. Philosophers, therefore, and this is not a real surprise, were among the first to rediscover the full meaning of Emerson's rhetoric.

In the year 1903, William James made a short oration on the occasion of the first centenary of Ralph Waldo Emerson's birth. This memorial speech deserves our attention for two reasons: William James not only betrays a profound affinity between his own thinking and that of Emerson, thus establishing a vital link between transcendentalism and pragmatism, he also sums up in a succession of luminous passages the essence of Emerson's philosophy. A brilliant example of rhetoric craftsmanship, the speech that James delivered at Concord that day demonstrates what Emerson meant in the minds of those who were willing to read him carefully, and willing also to follow the letter rather than the legend. Unlike many of his later interpreters who for the most part would remain baffled, disturbed, or enthralled by Emerson's seemingly contradictory mode of thought, James immediately identifies the central issue behind Emerson's rhetoric: "What gave a flavour so matchless to Emerson's individuality was even more than his rich mental gifts, their combination. Rarely has a man so known the limits of his genius or so unfailingly kept within them."[12]

Bestowing upon Emerson the virtue of self-imposed limitation characterizes him as the kind of thinker to whom neither the stereotyped versions of Enlightenment nor those of romanticism apply. The virtue of self-limitation immediately reminds the perceptive audience of the civic spirit that this gift carries with it: in fact the idea of self-limitation as *sophrosyne* is genealogically tied to the rise of citizenship as a force against the willfulness and power of individual tyranny. Thus the townspeople of Concord are, with one swift rhetorical stroke, placed metaphorically within the context of the genesis and the validity of civic virtues. William James does not hesitate to exploit this metaphor. In the typical rhetoric of secularization that combines the sacred with

[12] William James, *Essays in Religion and Morality* (Cambridge, Mass., 1982), p. 109.

the profane, he stresses the medium of Emerson's genius, extending his earlier image of "combination."

> This was the first half of Emerson, but only half; for his genius was insatiate for expression, and his truth had to be clad in the right verbal garment. The form of the garment was so vital with Emerson that it is impossible to separate it from the matter, they form a chemical combination—thoughts which would be trivial expressed otherwise are important through the nouns and verbs to which he married them. The style is the man, it has been said; the man Emerson's mission culminated in his style, and if we must define him in one word, we have to call him Artist. He was an artist whose medium was verbal and who wrought in spiritual material.[13]

Far from drawing upon the idealistic strain in Emerson's thought, James points out that Emerson's desire and gift for expression were, above all, inspired by an intensive awareness of concrete experience. "Other world! There is no other world," William James quotes from Emerson and goes on to make his point about the compatibility of momentary epiphany and a view of reality, which he himself would have referred to as natural realism.

> The present hour is the decisive hour, and every day is doomsday. Such a conviction that Divinity everywhere may easily make of one an optimist of the sentimental type that refuses to speak ill of anything. Emerson's drastic perception of differences kept him at the opposite pole from this weakness. . . . Never was such a fastidious lover of significance and distinction, and never an eye so keen for their discovery. His optimism had nothing in common with that indiscriminate hurrahing for the Universe with which Walt Whitman has made us familiar. . . . Emerson himself was a real seer. He could perceive the full squalor of the individual fact, but he could also see transfiguration. . . . His life was one long conversation with the invisible divine, expressing itself through individuals and particulars.[14]

The terms in which William James couches his eulogy not only display his own debt to Emerson, they also indicate a common bond both men share in the process of nineteenth-century secularization in America. Without running the risk of facile generalization, we may identify the

[13] Ibid., p. 110.

[14] Ibid., p. 114.

programmatic nature of the phrase "the invisible divine expressing itself through individuals and particulars" if we think of it as part of the process of secularization. *Expression* and *selfhood* are the key terms in the unfolding process of secularization and Emerson's life, the tenor of which, as William James put it, was determined by the "duty of spiritual seeing and reporting" (p. 116) evolved around the working out of the idea of selfhood.

The binary strain in Emerson's philosphy owes itself to a radical reliance on the experience of the self. For Emerson selfhood is the only possible point of departure on the way from the insight into humanity's essentially tragic existence to its acceptance. If abstract philosophizing was totally uncongenial to Emerson, personal experience impressed upon him, at times overwhelmingly, the tragic nature of the human condition, caught between promise and unfullfilment. Emerson knew about the precarious character of the harmonious self, he was painfully aware of both extremes, excess and self-denial, he knew intimately about the proximity of sanity and madness, he was familiar with the experience of loss and untimely death.

Emerson's subjectivism, however, had definite limits, and life's material presented itself to him within a historical matrix. If the idea of selfhood had undergone a variety of changes in the course of the nineteenth century, it was Ralph Waldo Emerson who worked out the essential alternatives that constitute the idea of the transcendentalist self, namely, the alternatives of *possibility* and *limitation*. Emerson's achievement, in short, was to tie these alternatives into an inextricable knot, thereby establishing the paradoxical condition of man as his *final* one, as his *transcendental* state of being! Time and history, self-preservation and self-improvement, or as others would simply call it, progress—these were the primary and rather disturbing issues Emerson had to confront. His idea of self-hood would remain a fragile construct for a long time: how could one conceive of an autonomous, identical self and maintain the postulate of identity within the concept of historical and social change?

The next question, coming up by way of implication, was how to account for the moral responsibility of an acting self that is based on self-contradiction. James's repetition of dualistic metaphors (marriage, combination, etc.) refers to the ancient concept of *paideia*, the condition and art of individual as well as social equilibrium. Both the individual as well as the social impact of Emerson's thinking will be discussed at some length; for now it must suffice to point out that to Ralph Waldo Emerson the idea of the self, above all, was a *self in question*.

On the tenth of April in the year 1834, Emerson entered the following remark in his journal: "Is it possible that in the solitude I seek I shall have the resolution, the force to work as I ought to work—as I project in highest, most farsighted hours? Well, and what do you project? Nothing less than to look at every object in its relation to Myself."[15]

Resolution and doubt emanate from a conceived "self" that functions as a potential center only in "relations." Emerson's seemingly innocent "myself" hides a complicated biographical process that in itself mirrors in many of its stages an equally complex but historically much more extended philosophical process.

In many ways the idea of selfhood, at the time of Emerson's entry, had become a commonplace, but under close scrutiny the accepted metaphor reveals significant traces of its origin. The "self" in question stands for an idea of humankind and the individual's place in the universe that, when freed from vague usage, becomes highly charged with subversive meaning. In order to understand Emerson's reconceptualization of the Platonic tradition and its descendants we have to remember, first of all, that in 1834 Emerson was lecturing on such topics as "The Uses of Natural History," "The Naturalist," and "Water." He was, in other words, emphasizing the meaning of the self while subscribing at the same time to the importance and function of method! The tension between a potentially unlimited self and a corrective method that reduced the self to the status of an observing instrument characterizes all of Emerson's early lectures.

It is the very same tension, though, that contains the philosophical implication tied into the process of self-constitution. The fundamental issue was that of *teleology*. It is the mark of Emerson's genius that he chose neither the idealistic nor the naturalistic way out of the dilemma he faced. Instead of making regressive choices he preferred a risky postulate that claimed the compatibility of selfhood qua subjectivity and reason qua self-limitation. The combination of the two was the key: inverted teleology could be assumed to become a rational process of self-improvement. If we want to retrace Emerson's development up to the immediate time after his return from Europe we ought to take another look at a fairly simple text by William Ellery Channing, the discourse on "Spiritual Freedom," a sermon, "Preached at the Annual Election, May 26, 1830." Emerson, in the capacity of chaplain, attended the service when Channing delivered his sermon and undoubtedly listened to it with the mixed feelings of someone who is staking

[15] Emerson, *Journals* 4: 272.

out his own territory, without title as yet, but already aware of the problem of overlapping boundaries. His brief comments on Channing's speech, if anything, betray the feelings of impatience and subdued irritation.

For us, as before, the advantage of the simpler text, Channing's sermon, lies in the possibility of extrapolating from it a clearer marking of pivotal points that in Emerson's own hyperbolic way of thinking frequently assume a proleptic quality.

Channing's argument is for "inward, spiritual liberty," which he construes as the center of all of man's activities. What must have irked Emerson, whose own development by then had reached a high degree of latency waiting to find a manifest form of expression, was the fact that Channing established his definition of spiritual liberty by reducing it to one alternative. According to Channing's argument, spiritual liberty and therefore true selfhood can only be achieved *against* a number of obstacles. Emerson's wry comment on Channing's sermon, mentioning its nobility and length ("One hour thirty-five minutes") was not merely indicative of his own preference for a rhetoric of controlled and meaningful ambiguities.[16] He must have felt the potential for his own way of seeing things—hidden underneath Channing's simple alternatives. His own inclination towards indirect expression was in itself a mirror of Emerson's view of the process of self-constitution. His main protests against Channing's argument must have been provoked by such key terms in the sermon as *power*, as in "The essence of spiritual freedom is power." In fact, some of the definitions that Channing enumerates as part of what freedom has to be achieved *against*, return in the Emersonian version of autonomy and self-reliance as the material of the process of self-constitution.

Self-construction as self-knowledge would be Emerson's beginning. With him the age indeed became introspective. Our first attention will therefore be directed towards his early journals. We will find there the seeds of later passages in his essays where he provokes the reader by replacing the metaphorically adequate "know thyself" of his lintelstone by "whim."[17] It has been argued that in passages such as these Emerson's subscription to a theory of absolute subjectivity becomes evident: we hope to show that the complex metaphorical organization of Emerson's essays as a whole do not allow such a conclusion. In fact, it virtually excludes it, because Emerson was aware of the necessarily

[16] Channing's sermon represents the exact opposite of Emerson's way of thinking. To what an extent Emerson felt both affinities and differences with regard to what Channing had to say must in the end remain a question of interpretation.

[17] Emerson, *Works* 2: 51.

proleptic character of self-knowledge. The self-reliant life of the individual in a structurally unstable society was, for Emerson, a possibility at best. Once more we can use Channing's description of the relationship between the individual and society as a background against which the Emersonian position stands out prominently. Channing's postulates were undoubtedly shared by Emerson, but he must have considered them to be innocently idealistic. "To me, the progress of society consists in nothing more, than in bringing out the individual, in giving him a consciousness of his own being, and in quickening him to strengthen and elevate his own mind."[18]

Emerson's view of the progress of society and the potential inroads made by it on the autonomous self were far more ambivalent and skeptical. And it was Emerson's mixture of hope and skepticism which would inform and leave its mark on the early body of American social thought at a point when it turned into separate fields of philosophical inquiry, social theory, and sociology.

If such assertions seem to overstate the case of Emerson's orginality, it is worthwhile to remember that Emerson's real point of departure was one of arrival. His travels in Europe had convinced him of the limitations of science, a conviction that he found confirmed in the works of Sir John F. W. Herschel, whose treatise on astronomy he read during his voyage back to America. Emerson had read Herschel's *Preliminary Discourse on the Study of Natural Philosophy* before, and despite his admiration for the size and precision of such instruments as the telescope that Giovanni Battista Amica had built for Herschel, it is clearly the latter's rather dramatic description of the human condition that had led Emerson to call Herschel's book a noble one, in a letter to his brother.

Emerson's extensive reading in the field of natural sciences was a source of inspiration at a time in his life when the process of change and transformation in his religious convictions was at its most acute stage. It is significant that despite thorough efforts, critics and biographers alike have a difficult time pinpointing a crucial moment in Emerson's life that would stand out as the singular instance of crisis.

What the absence of such a high point of dramatic reversal or simply conversion shows is the profound involvement of Emerson's thought in the crisis-ridden drift of the century as a whole. More precisely: if the century's main preoccupation was with such matters as the course of progress, manifest destiny, and the major issues of social

[18] Channing, *Works*, p. 35.

growth and the problems it entailed, Emerson's attention was still focused on the somewhat more fundamental question: what could all this possibly mean?

Turning towards writing about nature for an answer not only meant reading as widely as possible in the field of natural philosophy, it also implied a kind of stoic acceptance of Nature's way, of Nature's method to use Emerson's own way of putting it. The mere fact that Emerson should refer to Nature's method signals to the reader that little room is left for uncontrolled speculation. On the other hand, Emerson made it quite clear that it was part and parcel of nature's method to resist reductivist generalizations. Whenever Emerson became fascinated with a statement that in pithy form would express something about which he himself felt very strongly, it would invariably be entered into his journals and notebooks several times over. There is more than one entry that refers to Fontenelle's remark, that man, should he ever discover nature's innermost secret, would probably be disappointed by the simplicity of his findings.

Emerson was clearly coping with his own sense of crisis, by transforming a stoic acceptance of nature's dominance over humankind's intentions into the creation of an allegiance—and he was fully aware of the fact that such an alliance could only be had at a price.

The price was the individual's reliance on poetic powers, used as a counterbalance against gregarious instincts to dominate by means of intellect. The individual, in other words, must see the gift of imagination as a vested interest, and not as an additional attribute to be used only on specific occasions.

It is characteristic of Emerson's whole perspective on life that even his approach to such romantically charged issues as the gift of poetic imagination was basically rational and sometimes even economical in its carefully tempered ways. If we said earlier that Emerson's real point of departure was one of arrival, we should not underestimate the sense of breaking away that he must have felt when boarding the brig *Jasper*, soon to leave for Europe. In a letter to his brother William he describes his impatience with his ship's delayed departure, even though he was fully aware of the hardship that lay ahead, "that shop of horrors the sea." It also was a relief for Emerson to have managed his resignation from the ministry of the Second Church in Boston in a way that allowed him to "walk firmly toward a peace & freedom which I plainly see before me albeit afar," as he put it in another letter to his brother.[19]

[19] Ralph Waldo Emerson, *The Letters of Ralph Waldo Emerson*, ed. Ralph L. Rusk (New York, 1939) 1: 357–58.

Much was left behind in the process of departing and the future would demand a whole new ordering of experience. Once again a familiar image expresses what Emerson's position was in the course of his own life and in the mentality of the early mid-nineteenth century. In an interesting contrast Emerson enters into his diary of 1833 first an observation on Columbus and then follows it up with a description referring to his own activities.

> It takes all the thousand European voyages that have been made to establish our faith in the practicability of this our hodiurnal voyage. But to be Columbus, to steer WEST steadily day after day, week after week, for the first time, and wholly alone in his opinion, shows a mind as solitary & self-subsistent as any that ever lived.
>
> I am learning the use of the quadrant. Another voyage would make an astronomer of me. How delicately come out these stars at sea.[20]

Emerson's entry of 1833 comes in three parts that are related to each other in a way that gives us a fine chance to observe Emerson's mind at work. First there is an indirect self-reference. Emerson clearly identifies his voyage East with that which took Columbus West, the common element in both their voyages being an unknown destiny, the entering of uncharted waters. The self-subsistence Emerson credits Columbus with is his own and would later become topic and title of one of his essays that stands as a main element in Emerson's mental architecture: the idea of self-reliance. Having emphasized this quality in Columbus, he goes back to a description of his own position in reality. Metaphorical self-perception and factual account, as must be the case, mix. Once again it is the act of looking at the stars that creates identity and place in time; but it is the use of the quadrant that characterizes the image as a whole. The astronomer takes a risk by observing the stars from the ship, an image of extremes, and he reduces the element of danger by using the quadrant. Risk and uncertainty, evoked in the imagery of the voyage and the ship, coexist with the possibility of reduction by scientific control. Such precariously balanced coexistence must create anxiety: "The whole world is but a millstone to me" (p. 109). On the other hand, Emerson would not let such anxieties overwhelm him. In such moments of dramatic threat he would invariably find a formula of acceptance, rather than allowing romantic despair or aesthetic pessimism to dominate. The final sen-

[20] Emerson, *Journals* 4: 107.

tence of his statement, therefore, emphasizes the realization of the need for "separation," or for abstraction, as we would say today.

Emerson's own sense of self, as expressed in his looking at the stars through a quadrant, confirmed by his statement that another voyage would turn him into an astronomer, is profoundly related to the nineteenth century's general search for authenticity in the face of an increasing awareness of change and of a pervasive sense of crisis. If we compare Emerson's statement: "I have sometimes thought that, in order to be a good minister, it was necessary to leave the ministry. *The profession is antiquated,*"[21] with the general tendency towards professionalization in the mid-nineteenth century, we cannot miss the essential structure of the process of professionalization itself. If this process such as it shaped the American mind has to be characterized in general terms, one would have to point out that it created a state of ambivalence and ambiguity in some observers, just as it inspired optimism and hope for the future in others. It is noteworthy that Emerson calls the ministry both a profession and antiquated. Sociological studies of the New England ministry show that it had indeed developed all the characteristics of a profession, including the awareness of the existence of a marketplace and of what it stood for in terms of money, social norms, attitudes, and bargaining power.[22] In what sense, then, could Emerson, who must have recognized that the process of professionalization was gaining momentum in other fields besides theology, call the profession of the ministry *antiquated*? It seems that in the light of his new and growing fascination with the natural sciences his verdict upon the antiquated profession of the ministry has a double meaning. The first, obvious one is related to the fact that the professionalized clergy of New England seemed to be losing some of its credibility and authority in the eyes of a critical parish. Emerson's own resignation from his duties as minister of the Boston Second Church, though couched in a language of a friendly relationship between people who shared a common belief, had all the trappings and formalized attributes of business procedure. What professionalization seemed to indicate, above all, was a loss of authenticity.[23]

A second implication of Emerson's remark, who was very much aware of the efforts to organize and formalize the acquisition and distribution of knowledge, seems to be a latent distrust of the movement towards professionalization as a limitation of the self. If Channing had

[21] Ibid., p. 27.

[22] See Donald M. Scott, *From Office to Profession: The New England Ministry, 1750–1850* (Philadelphia, 1978).

[23] Ibid.

observed that in America "men have learned what wonders can be accomplished in certain cases by unions, and seem to think that union is competent to everything," Emerson (like Thoreau, Adams, and James) was definitely not one of those who believed, without reservation, in "the principle of association."[24] To the extent that the organization and professionalization of knowledge in the prewar years mirrored the rapid development of an interdependent and increasingly complex society, men like Emerson remain skeptical as to the results of social growth. It is easy to understand some of his misgivings if one takes into account the undiluted elitism that had been one of the characteristics of both the early precursors of the American Association for the Advancement of Science. The kind of elitism that seemed to accompany professionalism came to its height in some groups, like the famous Lazzaroni, which emerged as part of the AAAS. Basically all these were early groups that had tried to establish themselves as part of a scientific community in the Jacksonian age. The fundamental dilemma was how one could be an outstanding individual of virtually heroic proportions in the realm of science and research—and yet be a democratic American, in touch with the egalitarian mainstream of society at the same time? Emerson, who in 1833 lectured to the Boston Natural History Society just about a month after his return from Europe, was addressing a body of some historical significance. There is hardly a better way to demonstrate Emerson's shift from theology towards philosophy than by discussing briefly what exactly this encounter stood for. The history of scientific organizations and their internal structure enable us to understand both the general movement towards professionalization in the nineteenth century and the ambivalence it produced—and in fact reflected, when its development as a whole was concerned.

Merlin's laughter, Mark Twain's momentous statement, owes its weight to the fact that it sets the essentially allegorical themes of *anticipation* and *memory*. History interwoven with these themes, patterned upon their structure, is always a kind of history with a broken edge. Things, to put it simply, can only become worse, just as there has always been a time when they had been better. Perhaps it would be more precise to say that memory insinuates that once, at an earlier time or simply on the morning before today, the world was less tarnished and abused by human activities. His empathy and his great gift to read the transitory while it passes away enabled him to stay with the image;

[24] Emerson's sense of preserving the freedom and autonomy of self was too strongly developed to allow him to rely on institutions the way Channing did.

Mark Twain's images stand out because they are only too often buried underneath a need to explain. Critics have often complained about Mark Twain's inability to stop, in his fiction, at the right moment. They have overlooked that this is exactly the point: there is no right moment.

Allegory as a mode of thought absorbs the tension between anticipation and memory at its most tangible in the way it structures the acquisition of knowledge. Any acquisition of knowledge, and the *scientific process* of accumulating knowledge in particular is provisional, valid only within a context of frequently brief time frames and meaningful only for a particular limited purpose. Henry Adams's vision of education as a process of failures eventually led to his recognition of allegorical form as a saving device, just as Emerson's preference for the fragment over the system was the result of accepting man's being a god in ruins. The process of acquiring knowledge reflects this whole set of contradictions, and no field of particular knowledge seems to demonstrate this more aptly than man's desire to know about himself and his social reality.

One of the earliest and certainly the most revealing document to capture—in its totality—the tension active in the acquisition of knowledge in general and the emphasis shift from self to social identity in particular is Lester Ward's book *Dynamic Sociology*. The date of its publication, 1883, is misleading insofar as it had taken Lester Ward a long time not only to write the book itself, but to make the transition from being what Emerson would have called a naturalist to becoming a social scientist, whose work was used as a standard point of departure by later sociologists like E. A. Ross, R. T. Ely, and Albion Small. Before publishing *Dynamic Sociology* in 1883, Lester F. Ward had worked as a biologist, as a botanist, a geologist, and finally in the field of paleobotany. He had been an employee of the Federal Bureau of Statistics and had taken part in a number of government expeditions headed by the well-known Maj. John Wesley Powell. At the time of his return from the Wasatch Mountains expedition, Lester Ward was already working on what would later become *Dynamic Sociology*. As a result, a great deal of his interest in "reading" nature entered his pioneer work that examined society. Ward's view of sociology was holistic and universal: for him the science of society was part of a synergetically interrelated universal science of man and nature. The fact that a critic remarked that in his later books Lester Ward was "better able to restrain his temptation to preface every sociological idea by tracing its origins to starry cosmos," tells us something about the intellectual scope and format of *Dynamic Sociology*. To say that Ward's synergetic approach, when viewed from hindsight, was strikingly modern, describes little more than a certain acceleration of the process of modernization and professionalization in the social sciences of which Ward was a part. If we tried to probe a little deeper, we would have to discuss how modernism in this sense implies a certain loss of intellectual curiosity. What we think is rich and filled with explanatory quality in Ward's writing, we find so because we are willing to admit a certain amount of poverty in the same areas in more recent social theory. Lester Ward left no doubt where his basic allegiances lay and spent much time and many arguments convincing his readers about the intellectual architecture of his book. His examples are quite revealing. "It is the so-called philosophers who after all lead the scientific as they have always led the intellectual and literary world. It may not be too much to say that science will one day admit that it owes more to Immanuel Kant for publishing his 'Theorie des Himmels' than to Alexander von Humboldt for publishing his 'Cosmos'; the one a brief but profound theory of the Cosmos, the other an extended enumeration of its then known phenomena."[25]

The opposition created here between Kant and Humboldt tells us something about Ward's own ambitions as a collector, a classifier and an empirical fieldworker, namely that he wanted to transcend what he saw as the limits of all of the above. To see Lester Ward's ambition primarily as a biographical issue, as part of his personality, which it undoubtedly and necessarily was as well, would be a great mistake. What seems like biographical material, evening readings with his wife, interest in education, a constant desire to improve his standing as a scholar, all these characteristics are part of a process that tied the acquisition of knowledge to professional life. If the pages of the *Christian Examiner* contributed to the process of secularization by giving space to lengthy discussions of Coleridge and Kant, the natural scientists tried to structure *their* sense of vocation by imposing discipline upon the history that could be deciphered.

To the extent that society became complex and hard to understand, the attention of those who wondered about the fate of humankind in a disturbingly complex social environment paid attention to the larger writing of the universe. Apart from the obvious practical aspect of both geology and botany at the time of the great surveys and expeditions, which were often conducted with public funding, the theme was seldom missing in most of the resulting reports that the knowledge

[25] Lester Ward, *Dynamic Sociology* (New York, 1907) vol. 1, p. 7.

acquired in the natural sciences was important for one's ability to understand one's own fate.

In the second volume of his *Dynamic Sociology*, Lester Ward makes a statement about our place in nature—a statement that, given its general background, is clearly designed to serve a strategic purpose in the establishing of social science as a viable discipline.

> First, then, what is the attitude of nature toward man? . . .
>
> In the first place, nature stands to man in the relation of the whole to a part. Man is an integral part of the universe, and, in order to be correctly conceived and properly studied, he must be conceived as and studied as an objective phenomenon presented by nature. "Der Mensch ist selbst Erscheinung." Neither the animal and vegetable forms, nor the rock formations, nor the chemic elements, are more to be regarded as natural objects for scientific study than are individual men or human societies. The laws governing the migration of birds, or the geographical distributions of plants, or the movement of the stars, or the elective affinities of chemicals, are not more the legitimate subjects of scientific investigation than are the individual or collective actions of men or the changes that take place in human opinions and public sentiment. From the scientific point of view, all phenomena are equally legitimate objects of study.[26]

It is simply a matter of minor rephrasing to show that an interpretation of Kant in the *Christian Examiner* of 1833 came basically to the same conclusion when making the statement that you had to adopt, or rather to develop, an internalized point of view which allowed a generalized view of all things in the same light of abstraction.[27] One should not overlook the fact, however, that viewed in the long run, the complex point of departure from which Lester Ward started out led to a kind of economical reasoning that deemphasized the sense of history that the original locus standi still maintained by virtue of its metaphorical complexity.

[26] Ibid. 2: 2–3.

[27] See *Christian Examiner*, March 1833, p. 119:

> "While we are on this ground, we beg to leave to offer a few explanatory remarks respecting German metaphysics, which seems to be called for by the present state of feeling among literary men in relation to this subject. We believe it is impossible to understand fully the design of Kant and his fellows without being endowed to a certain extent with the same powers of abstraction and synthetic generalization which they possess in so eminent a degree. In order to become fully master of their meaning *one must be able to find it in himself*" (my emphasis).

There is an aspect to Lester Ward's preference of Kant's "Theorie des Himmels" over Humboldt's "Cosmos" that sheds some light on the aspect of professionalization in a cultural ambience that still regarded itself as the outcome of a predominantly religious matrix. Lester Ward's choice, if we try to see it as a deliberate one, betrays a final and probably only minute acknowledgement of the restraints that the religious heritage at this time still exercised over the efforts to professionalize the natural sciences. Sociology as a social science has, of course, always been in conflict about its own status between the humanities and the sciences, but this conflict was especially acute in an intellectual territory where self-explanation was the central issue.

If we accept that at the time when Lester Ward was himself heavily involved in geological and paleobotanical studies, Humboldt was mainly known for his work in geology, Ward's telling comparison between Kant and Humboldt has all the characteristics of a defensive reflex. Geology and fields of inquiry related to it had become an issue of considerable contention on religious grounds. Not only had Charles Lyell's work been considered atheistic for quite some time: people like Edward Hitchcock, a minister and scientist, had to make a great effort to achieve a synthesis between religion and science. His *Religion of Geology and Its Connected Sciences* appeared in 1851, but as late as 1855 men like Taylor Lewis could still attack geology on religious grounds, which he did in his notorious *The Six Days of Creation*, which was published in 1855 and would have perhaps remained less noticed, if James Dwight Dana had not drawn attention to it by his attacks. What would later be called the Dana-Lewis controversy demonstrates to what an extent geology had become a science of rather extreme metaphorical potential.[28] The idea of dramatic geological shifts as described in Lester Ward's *Dynamic Sociology* implied both humankind's unfathomable relationship to time and the consequent changes that such a relationship involved, *and* it questioned creational order.

> Geology, too, now consists of a body of established facts. The most important of them are not yet proved by actual experience, and are from their nature, incapable of such proof. Yet they are no longer questioned. Opinion, which once ran high respecting them, is now completely at rest. There remains no one to gainsay the assertion that stratified deposits found upon high mountains were once at the bottom of the sea, where they were formed. No

[28] See Sally Gregory Kohlstedt, *The Formation of the American Scientific Community* (Chicago, 1976), and Ralph S. Bates, *Scientific Societies in the United States* (New York, 1945).

one any longer disputes that the fossils found in such positions were once living creatures inhabiting the sea. And, while no one can say with any degree of definiteness how long ago these fossils lived, scarcely a cultivated man can be found who honestly doubts that it must have been, in most cases, very much more than the long-claimed six thousand years. Upon such problems, if opinion is not yet universal, it is so completely settled among all who at all comprehend the conditions of the problems that its complete unification must result from a general diffusion of an acquaintance with these conditions.

We might go in like manner through all the established sciences . . .[29]

The imagery of grand geological movements that in a literal sense turned the world upside down was used by Ward to emphasize the essential distinction that he introduced in his book: the difference between *genetic* and *telic* evolution. By the latter he meant a kind of evolutionary process that unlike natural, genetic processes, was guided by human intelligence. Telesis, in his words, was the real aim of dynamic sociology. If we want to see more in Lester Ward's contribution to the development of American sociology, we have to assess his gigantic work as an effort to break away from the hold of nature over humanity. Lester Ward's preoccupation with nature was forced upon him so that he could break away.

[29] Ward, *Dynamic*, vol. 2, p. 405.

CHAPTER 3

Ralph Waldo Emerson

We, as we read, must become Greeks, Romans, Turks, priest and king, martyr and executioner; must fasten these images to some reality in our secret experience, or we shall learn nothing rightly.

—RALPH WALDO EMERSON

Allegory and the Rhetoric of Metamorphosis

By the time Emerson wrote his essay "History," he had almost found his own voice. He had not yet achieved the certainty and the rhetorical authority that he would display in such essays as "Experience" or "Circles," but the mere fact that he dealt with the subject of history tells us that Emerson had come to terms with the art of distantiation—and that he was going to practice distantiation as an art. The first essay in the First Series, published in 1841, together with other programmatic and yet virtually established masterpieces like "Self-Reliance," "Compensation"—theologically the most audacious one—and last but not least "The Over-Soul," "History" sets a tone which gives a free reign to the allegorical voice. The fact that the elusive spoken word, *ex negativo*, represents authority over Emerson's essays is turned and transformed into a virtue. No reader will be allowed to read the essay and go away from it with firm knowledge at his or her disposal of what history is all about.

Emerson's essay "History," which, as we know from his journals, had been preceded by a long period of brooding over the issue of time, first and above all abolishes the belief that history is something that, once chronologically fixed, can be relied on as standard legacy. It would be hard to find a place anywhere in Emerson where he comes closer to Nietzsche's idea of eternal recurrence. History, as it turns out, is a sediment, a reminder of the fact that something has taken place *before*. How can this "something" be described if not in terms of selective, and hence creative, will? The result invariably is history, but what a fragile construct it turns out to be when looked upon in this light. And above all: what a torturous mixture of choice and limitation precedes history when we see it as a *result*. The affirmative voice that

Emerson seems to assume so frequently, when his friends impatiently demanded critical opinion and ad hoc statements, is a voice that has gone beyond the conflict of limitations and choice. It is the voice of someone who has faced the cruel fact that becoming is a process of being *and* of its opposite, nothingness. It is a voice, based on the insight that all historical processes are first of all imagined by humankind! So the cycle may be a figure of consolation to some, but to those who, like Emerson, saw it as a result rather than a soothing archetype, it must have been also an emblem of great cruelty.

Ontologically, Emerson, in "History," posits the self against history, which of course invites the paradox of self-constitution. Typically, therefore, Emerson's strategy of the disruptive argument begins with the title. As any close reading reveals, "History" is about the *absence* of history and about the *dominance* of time. Far from being fashionably idealistic, however, Emerson leaves no doubt that the dominance of time is anything other than a subjective and sublime product of consciousness. "Man is explicable by nothing less than all his history. Without hurry, without rest, the human spirit goes forth from the beginning to embody every faculty, every thought, every emotion which belongs to it, in appropriate events. But the thought is always prior to the fact. All the facts of history preexist in the mind as laws. Each law in turn is made by circumstances predominant, and the limits of nature give power to but one at a time."[1]

Man, then, is never really explicable—and choice, according to the limits of nature, is an eternal necessity. We have only to grasp the impact of these two statements in order to appreciate the fact that Emerson was taking a deliberate step away from what one would consider to be the dominant culture of the time.

The world that was budding in the textile industries of Lowell, Massachusetts, at the same time that Emerson's first volume of essays appeared was not the object of direct scrutiny. We must, however, understand the dialectics of resistance in order to understand Emerson's radicalism. If we do not, we are prone to mistake Emerson's lack of social engagement for elitist aloofness. Sentences like "Of the universal mind each individual man is one more incarnation. All its properties consist in him" (Emerson, *Works* 1: 10) assume a quite militant ring when seen in the context of a society in the making. That the social process of organizing a complex, strife-ridden society would inevitably have a negative influence on the individual's claim to universality was a fact that Emerson took for granted. In fact, he took the inevitable

[1] Emerson, *Works* 1: 3. Hereafter cited in text as Emerson, *Works*.

struggle between society and the individual so much for granted that part of his taking sides in this struggle was to refuse to speak the language of society. Emerson, in other words, realized that any sociological criticism shared something with its object that damaged the very intentions of the criticism. The critical thrust of his position drew its momentum from another source of energy, namely from the need to develop the *authority of the alternative position.* Configurational thought is the immediate result of such an attitude: its rhetoric is that of allegorical quotation, of bricolage and of the dark conceit. Rather than offering a straightforward criticism, Emerson developed that art of the gesture that throws the opposition off balance or at least is meant to achieve such a result. "Each new law and political movement has a meaning for you. Stand before each of its tablets and say, 'under this mask did Proteus' nature hide itself.' This remedies the defect of our too great nearness to ourselves. This throws our actions into perspective" (Emerson, *Works* 1: 5).

The particular political process is turned by the force of the image—"each of its tablets"—into a perspective of virtual timelessness and through this alliance with timelessness the self asserts itself at the specific historical moment. At the same time, the specific historical instance is important mainly to the extent that it serves an educational purpose as an open time frame that is filled in with didactically controlled *exempla.* "The world exists for the education of each man. There is no age or state of society or mode of action in history to which there is not somewhat corresponding in his life. Every thing tends in a wonderful manner to abbreviate itself and yield its own virtue to him. He should see that he can live all history in his own person" (Emerson, *Works* 1: 8).

It is the disintegrative mode of imagining that ties in with the necessity of choice that Emerson establishes as an antecedent to the historical fact. The tragic implications of this thought are obvious: if the choice is but one positive step out of time into history, much is left behind. Hence Emerson's evocation of multiplicity and metamorphosis. The individual has to become, in a manner of speaking, many different individuals, a multiplicity of personae: each fulfilled and affirmative. This is the key to the idea of a renaissance: the birth of multiplicity out of time rather than out of the linear progress of history. (The theme, incidentally, would be picked up in its most emphatic form by Melville in *The Confidence Man.*) But what we have called a beginning, so far—the birth of time—started, of course, with destruction, because history did always exist. Time, before it can become a concrete reality itself, has to destroy: time is a destructive force. "The instinct of the mind, the purpose of nature, betrays itself in the use we make of the signal narrations of history. Time dissipates to shining ether the solid angularity of facts" (Emerson, *Works* 1: 9).

The so-called "signal narrations of history" are worthy of close attention. Emerson retranslates the idea of history into the shape of a narrative, stressing the fluidity over and against the harsh, institutionalized structure of history seen as a series of factual events. "No anchor, no cable, no fences avail to keep a fact. Babylon, Troy, Tyre, Palestine, and even early Rome are forming already into fiction" (Emerson, *Works* 1: 9).

The transformation of history into time automatically brings up the issue of individual choice and it is not surprising that Emerson would observe the disappearance of history, its "passing into fiction," which his readers would understand, whereas the complementary side, the constant birth of time, would have been a concept that one would find difficult to grasp. Both "narration" and "fiction" are of course hints that one cannot overlook, but they must be seen in their full elusiveness in order to hold their weight in an argument that Emerson develops in such hyperbolic fashion. In Emerson's argument, if we try to give it a straightforward shape, all history has one vanishing point, namely *this* particular moment in the present. "All inquiry into antiquity, all curiosity respecting the Pyramids, the excavated cities, Stonehenge, the Ohio Circles, Mexico, Memphis, is the desire to do away this wild, savage, and preposterous There and Then, and introduce in its place the Here and Now" (Emerson, *Works* 1: 11).

Being now is the allegorical moment of the birth of time, and all the work that goes into the construction of *that* particular allegorical configuration that allows this birth to happen is part of man's assertion of his selfhood against the constraints of his past. Originality, in order not to be mistaken, is not the primary goal. ("Ferguson discovered many things in astronomy which had long been known. The better for him" [Emerson, *Works* 2: 15].) The point is that working *through* the past in a very literal sense must inevitably lead to the present.

> Beloni digs and measures in the mummy-pits and pyramids of Thebes until he can see the end of the difference between the monstrous work and himself. When he has satisfied himself, in general and in detail, that it was made by a person as he, so armed and so motivated, and to ends to which he himself should also have worked, the problem is solved; his thought lives along the whole line of temples and sphinxes and catacombs, passes

through them all with satisfaction, and they live again to the mind, or are *now*. (Emerson, *Works* 1: 11)

Emerson's image of the archeologist can be used as a classical example of reversal: archeology, the putting together of broken bits and pieces, serves to construe a sense of the present rather than to demonstrate how different the past had been. There is no celebration of progress at work here, but a desperate attempt to justify the existence in the present, to justify, in other words, the choice of having become an individual. History and the process of individuation are the central topic of Emerson's "History" and only when all the implications of this theme have been accounted for does the famous statement, that "all history becomes subjective," make sense. "We are always coming up with the emphatic facts of history in our private experience and verifying them here. All history becomes subjective; in other words, there is properly no history, only biography. Every mind must know the whole lesson for itself—must go over the whole ground. . . . History must be this or it is nothing" (Emerson, *Works* 1: 9–10).

Only a deliberate misunderstanding would construe the above as a plea to replace history with biography. The individual, personal biography is not what Emerson has in mind. Such a "personal history," for the Emerson who wrote "History," would be abstract and without any profound meaning. What he says, instead, is that history is measured by life—and therefore always falls short. To be more precise: history is derived from nature, and Emerson reconstructs the relationship between the two—the thrust of his argument being, of course, that the efforts of human history to disengage itself from nature must be in vain. Emerson does not deny either the fact or the plausibility of such disengagement—but rather probes, considers, and judges the effects and possible consequences of such a separation. As if drawn by some hidden logic of his argument, Emerson makes an abrupt and unprepared statement about the doctrine of similarity by difference.

> Every one must have observed faces and forms that, with-out any resembling feature, make a like impression on the beholder. A particular picture or copy of verses, if it does not awaken the same train of images, will yet superinduce the same sentiment as some wild mountain walk, although the resemblance is nowise obvious to the senses, but is occult and out of the reach of the understanding. Nature is an endless combination and repetition of a very few laws. She knows the ole well-known air through innumerable variations. (Emerson, *Works* 1: 15)

What Emerson describes as "occult" would later be called involuntary memory, or the kind of mnemosyne that works as a reminder that the layer of civilization between humankind's and nature's history is very thin indeed: "Nature is full of a sublime likeness throughout her words and delights in startling us with resemblances in the most unexpected quarters" (Emerson, *Works* 1: 15–16).

Emerson's intimations, here, of a theory of correspondence, partially analogic, is an anticipation of the philosophical style that he would later develop, both practically and in theory as well. It is with great philosophical consistency that Emerson works his way through a number of examples, drawn from the realm of the aesthetic towards his main point about the ontological difference between fact and identity. He needs to point out this difference in order to establish the idea of *truth*, and art is the best example he can find to make his point that truth can be approached only by metamorphosis. "A painter told me that nobody could draw a tree without in some sort becoming a tree. . . . It is the spirit and not the fact that is identical" (Emerson, *Works* 1: 16).

It would be a mistake if one were to understand all these efforts by Emerson to come to terms with the idea of truth while confronting the contingency of history as a flight into some kind of romantically diluted mysticism. The opposite is the case: Emerson, by insisting on the possibility of partial metamorphosis, tries to save the profane facts from pure oblivion. In many ways he anticipates William James, who would much later define humanity's agreement to attend to a particular aspect of reality as our *only* way of creating experience. Like James, Emerson creates, though on a less theoretical basis, two histories: one being the internal subjective history of the individual, and the other, its ties to the so-called "external world." Examined closely, it becomes obvious that the construction of two histories is not one of deliberate and planned parallelism. It is rather the lack of fixation in the "primeval world," as Emerson calls it, that leads to a somewhat insecure search in that realm. "The primeval world is the Fore-World as the Germans say—I can dive to it in myself as well as grope for it with researching fingers in catacombs, libraries, and the broken reliefs and torsos of ruined villas" (Emerson, *Works* 1: 23).

The search for a fixed sense of history at this stage is astonishingly fragile and has to be justified in its results by a chain of things and events that leads into antiquity and finally to a point where humankind and nature are *almost* reunified. In the end the truth remains valid, that "man is the broken giant, and in all his weakness, both his body and his mind are invigorated by habits of conversation with nature." The second kind of history, which Emerson mentions more in passing than by truly concentrating upon it, is "that of the external world, in which he is not less stricly implicated" (Emerson, *Works* 1: 28). Having admitted that much, Emerson quickly moves away from the implication of his own admission, in order to go back to his original idea of the predominance of time over factual history, by working out the affinity between "man" and his prehistorical origins: "He is the compendium of time; he is also the correlative of nature. His power consists in the multitude of his affinities, in the fact that his life is intertwined with the whole chain of organic and inorganic being" (Emerson, *Works* 1: 35–36).

Time, then, as Emerson tries to explain in his essay on history, is not a chronological phenomenon, but a correlation. Time has the shape of a correspondence, and once this relationship is clarified, history can be conceptualized. As a result, the unexpected turns out to be time's great gift to us.

> No man can antedate his experience, or guess what faculty or feeling a new object shall unlock, any more than he can draw today the face of a person whom he shall see tomorrow for the first time. I will not now go behind this general statement to explore the reason of this correspondency. Let it suffice that in the light of these two facts, namely, that the mind is One, and the nature is its correlative, history is to be read and written. (Emerson, *Works* 1: 38)

History, then, in Emerson's view is a series of relations and differs from Truth, which is characterized by identity or by displaying again and again "the same character," as Emerson states. We have to acknowledge that history is contingent. Its center may be "One," like the mind, but again, we never are able to penetrate this center: "The identity of history is equally intrinsic, the diversity equally obvious. There is, at the surface, infinite variety of things; at the center there is simplicity of course" (Emerson, *Works* 1: 14).

Emerson's distinction between time and history is far from serving the purpose of denigrating or minimizing the importance of history. What the essay suggests, by way of radical implication and overt style, is that we rethink the very essence and idea of history. Emerson wants us to see history, our history, in a metaphysical light, by which he means that somehow the series of events that constitute history according to our common-sense understanding of it must have a relationship to an unchanging truth. "Nay, what does history yet record of the metaphysical annals of man? What light does it shed on those mysteries which we hide under the names Death and Immortality? Yet every history should be written in a wisdom which divined the range of our affinities and looked at facts as symbols. I am ashamed to see what a shallow village tale our so-called History is" (Emerson, *Works* 1: 40).

Just how we can redeem history Emerson does not tell us. He gives us certain clues, though, by his own practice and by providing our imagination with certain examples that have to be interpreted.

> Broader and deeper we must write our annals—from an ethical reformation, from an influx of the ever new, ever sanative conscience—if we would trulier express our central and wide-related nature, instead of this old chronology of selfishness and pride to which we have too long lent our eyes. . . . The idiot, the Indian, the child and unschooled farmer's boy stand nearer to the light by which nature is to be read, than the director or antiquary. (Emerson, *Works* 1: 40–41)

We cannot overlook the fact that Emerson does not say that the child or the idiot are nearer to nature, but he puts them clearly nearer to the *light* by which nature is to be read. So even in these classical examples of certain individuals being nearer to nature than the analyzing or directing scientist, it is the source of light that counts. If we try to identify that light by sticking close to our text instead of evoking almost automatically the standard topics of the Platonic or New-Platonic tradition, we have to take a closer look at what Emerson calls the sanative conscience. The only conclusion to be drawn from Emerson's way of describing the problem of both cognition and individuation here is that the company of individuals he throws together at the end of his essay are closer to, and more profoundly in accordance with, their "sanative conscience." At first, one is tempted once again to see Emerson's strategy as a somewhat trite variation of playing out "nature's child" against the alienated man of learning. And as a warning against scientific hubris this is of course an Emersonian commonplace. But more important, it seems, is the fact that in all the cases quoted by Emerson, the only way that his examples can be seen as being closer to the "light by which nature is to be read" is to acknowledge the fact that we are talking of internalized nature. The idiot is the prime witness here, for there is no reason to assume that he would have any profound understanding of the external nature, as we might grant it to the Indian. So if the chain of examples is to make sense, we have to assume that in all the cases the internalization of nature and an immersion into the "sanative conscience" provide the light Emerson talks about.

The same is reflected in Emerson's own way of writing his essay on "History." It is, like all of Emerson's essays, an exercise in approximation. Since the core of history is inaccessible, Emerson's practical conclusion is to refine and cultivate the art of the correlative argument, the art of circumvention, of hyperbolic rhetoric and a pushing of his main ideas into the shape of narrowing circles.

Emerson's rhetoric, which he would later defend as a method equal in philosophical quality to the building of thoroughly conceptualized philosphical systems, is the classical allegorical device that emphasizes time by pointing out the possibility of continuation. If every fact, as Emerson points out, is a symbol, we have to choose from an infinite number of possibilities of symbolization in order to achieve some sort of coherent image of *one* world. It is, in other words, not a one-to-one relationship that binds the fact and the symbol into a kind of unified form: *the process of metamorphosis mediates and multiplies the possibilities.* There is no absolute symmetry. The emphasis on time borne out of allegory is the result of an ongoing discourse: process turns into strategy, we might say in abbreviation. Discourse as a strategic device implies on the one hand ontologically essential completeness. Epistemologically it must have a method. Significantly enough, Emerson's own imagery in his essay "History" is centered on the idea of the "fable." The fable is, of course, the essential scriptural form of conveying meaning, the New Testament being the canon of its usage and applicability.

But against such overwhelming authority one should not underestimate the equally obvious: in 1820, the young Emerson enters the following quotation and comment in his journal "Wide World," the title that he had chosen for his first set of diaries.

> Lord Bacon is indeed a wonderful writer; he condenses an unrivalled degree of matter in one paragraph; he never suffers himself to (wander), swerve, from the direct forthright or to babble or speak unguardedly on his proper topic. . . . I will add here a fine little sentence from the 30th section of the *Novum Organum.* Speaking of bodies composed of two different species of things he says: "but these instances may be reckoned of the singular (or extraordinary) heteroclite kind as being rare and extraordinary in the universe; yet for their dignity they ought to be separately placed and treated. For they excellently indicate the composition and structure of things; and suggest the causes of the number of

the ordinary species in the universe; and lead the understanding from that which is, to that which may be."[2]

There are certain figures of thought that the reader will immediately identify as anticipatory formulas with regard to Emerson's own intellectual development. Three crucial points ought to be considered, though, before an analysis of both Emerson's quotation from Bacon and his comment on it can be made. First of all, it is important to remember that the general, programmatic intention of Bacon's *Novum Organum* was to *reassert* our aspiration to knowledge. Bacon's claim was that something that had been lost must be reclaimed: our satisfaction with our own achievements have turned us into lazy fellow travelers of the world's fate. Knowledge, as Bacon points out, is a form of work in progress that can legitimately be interrupted only by moments of sudden insight. Our great, and in fact most fundamental, mistake where the progress of knowledge is concerned is in our tendency to turn such anticipatory insights into something erroneously taken for granted and presumed to be part of an established social context.

The second aspect of Bacon's overall intentions to bear in mind, because Emerson was most certainly aware of this, is that Bacon held humankind *itself* responsible for the stagnation of knowledge. His famous statement, that a way must be opened "in order that the mind may exercise over the nature of things the authority which properly belongs to it" will only be understood correctly if we bear in mind that Bacon's view of "authority" was one of distinctly differentiated *rights* ("ut mens suo *jure* in rerum naturam uti possit"). Authority, then, does not mean absolute power, but the kind of power that must obey certain legal obligation.

The third element that must have caught Emerson's attention is the strategic use Bacon makes of rhetoric in order to justify the pursuit of knowledge. The strategy of evoking the image of humankind's fall from paradise involves a warning against the ambition to obtain certainty in the realm of "moral judgement": we will have to come back to Bacon's distinction between the two essential forms of knowledge when discussing Emerson's early lectures.

With these three considerations in mind we can now take a closer look at the passage that attracted Emerson's attention. Interestingly enough, Emerson adds to his quotation one of those revealing reclaimers that usually give away something by what they leave half-finished: "There is nothing in this sentence which should cause it to be quoted more than another. It does not stand out from the rest; but it

[2] Emerson, *Journals* 1: 21.

struck me accidentally as a very different sentence from those similarly constructed in ordinary writers."[3]

Obviously, it does not suffice to let the accidental stand, leaving it supported only by the strength of its rhetorical success. ("It is common to see an author construct a fine sentence in this way with idle repetitions of the same idea, embellished a little for the sake of shrouding the deception. In this they all convey ideas determinate but widely different and all beautiful and intelligent.") The only surprise for us becomes evident when we try to determine what exactly constitutes the beauty and intelligence Emerson refers to, namely the fact how early he would feel attracted by certain modes of thought that he would later cultivate. In Chapter 30, from which Emerson quotes, Bacon draws the attention of his readers to what he calls "Bordering Instances." In Bacon's system they occupy the ninth place among "Prerogative Instances," which is not totally irrelevant because it allowed Emerson a choice between "Singular Instances" and "Instances of Power"—but he obviously preferred the less definite, the instance of *relation* deriving its value from being something "in between."

The fact that Emerson, early on in his diaries and again in his lecture of 1835 should single out Francis Bacon as a source of inspiration is remarkable—especially if one realizes that Emerson had to reach Bacon against the grain. Mainstream interpretations of the day claimed him as part, if not as the beginning, of common-sense philosophy. It took a strong and independent mind, therefore, to discover the virtures of Bacon's "dark" conceits and reconstruct his theory of rhetoric. Emerson's disposition towards the fragmentary mode of thought found early encouragement in his sensitive readings of Bacon.

Any close reading of a text, *any* adoption of an ancient, or merely distant, author as a source of authority implies that the immediate reality has become unreliable or questionable at least. Emerson's exuberant celebration of Bacon as an original authority demonstrates the link that exists between rhetoric and philosophical style. The most obvious rhetorical elements that Emerson inherited from Bacon and developed into a style of his own were those of the instructive method of demonstration and that of the selective instance that accomplishes its didactic goal by the narrowing down of possibilities. The finest example of how an Emersonian style developed out of a close reading is probably Bacon's discussion of whiteness in his *Valerius Terminus*, even though one could find many similar examples in *The Advancement of*

[3] Ibid., p. 21.

Learning. In his study of whiteness, Bacon first enumerates instances that produce whiteness, starting with very basic and tangible examples: the combination of air and water, for example. These examples, like the combination of air and glass, to name another one, are called "migratory" instances by Bacon, who ends his investigation with a generalization that sounds strangely familiar to the reader of Emerson. Working his way towards the desired generalization, Bacon writes: "It is then to be understood that absolute equality produceth transparence, inequality in simple order or proportion produceth whiteness, inequality in compound or respective order or proportion produceth all other colours, and absolute or orderless inequality produceth blackness."[4]

It would take too much space here to deal with Bacon's form of discourse extensively, even though his method of arranging an argument in terms of "direction" most certainly influenced Emerson's own rhetoric of freely assuming that one could use the whole compass of possible arguments in order to make one point. Such a rhetoric would not avoid paradox or contradiction, because the underlying idea would be that the whole drift of any argument would be to demonstrate analogies. All the facts, even those that seemed to indicate opposition, were fundamentally related. It is easy to see, therefore, how on the basis of this conviction the contradictory style of Emerson's early lectures after his return from Europe would soon turn into a philosophical style in its own right. It only took Emerson to make the step from admonition, exhortation, and persuasion to including the reader in the development and process of his argument in order to move from the pragmatic dimension of rhetoric to a philosophical mode of thought.

Philosophical Style

> The subjective thinker is a dialectician dealing with the existential, and he has the passion of thought requisite for holding fast to the qualitative disjunction.
>
> —SØREN KIERKEGAARD

> Well, & what do you project? Nothing less than to look at every project in its relation to Myself.
>
> —RALPH WALDO EMERSON

[4] *The Works of Francis Bacon* (Stuttgart, 1963) 3: 237.

With only a few exceptions, Emerson has denied his readers the privilege of metatheoretical commentaries on his own thought, adhering most of the time to the principle that philosophy is above all the process of thinking! His claim, therefore, in "The Natural History of Intellect," is by no means a modest one.

> I cannot myself use that systematic form which is reckoned essential in treating the science of the mind. But if one can say so without arrogance, I might suggest that he who contents himself with dotting a fragmentary curve, recording only what facts he has observed, without attempting to arrange them within one outline, follows a system also—a system as grand as any other, though he does not interfere with its vast curves by prematurely forcing them into a circle or ellipse, but only draws that arc which he clearly sees, or perhaps at a later observation a remote curve of the same orbit, and waits for a new opportunity, well-assured that these observed arcs will consist with each other. I confess to a little distrust of that completeness of system which metaphysicians are apt to affect. 't is the gnat grasping the world. All these exhaustive theories appear indeed a false and vain attempt to introvert and analyze the Primal Thought. That is up-stream, and what a stream! Can you swim up Niagara Falls?[5]

The answer in Emerson's case is self-evident. If we agree that the problem of redefining the relationship between theodicy, revelation, and history provided the general historical background against which Emerson tried to project his ideas, we will easily understand his insistence on the cognitive value of fragmentary thought. Indeed, Emerson's essays turn the fragmentary style into art, by combining the characteristics of the treatise with that of the Platonic dialogue. The essential latency of meaning in the treatise and the constant process of redefinition and clarification of ideas and concepts within the Platonic dialogue suited Emerson well in his preference for the unsystematic. "I please myself rather with contemplating the penumbra of the thing than the thing itself," he had written in his journal of 1833. Indeed, his style, hermetic and beyond the reach of traditional philosophical criticism, is at the same time personal and suggestively open—and part of a longstanding philosophical tradition. Truth is represented, it is expressed, which means that truth can be understood or seen even though the individual expression or representation are not necessarily identical with "the truth." Each sentence has to stand and *work* as a

[5] Emerson, *Works* 12: 11–12.

metaphor, defining its own internal limits. It is in this light that we have to interpret Emerson's early lectures which, introduced under the general heading of "science," are his first cogent exercises in defining the scope of and limits to a contemplation of the penumbral. The metaphor of the penumbral sphere justifies Emerson's emphasis on the style of thought. It shows how carefully Emerson chose his metaphors in the sense that his choice avoided any fixation on what was traditional to metaphors of light and darkness. Instead, there is a suggestion of choice and human activity and hence also an element of cognitive modesty. Emerson reduces the range of human intellectual abilities to the limits of a shadow world, evoking not only the image of the Platonic cave, but also playing upon the transition from exterior light to interior light that he had first become familiar with when reading Bacon's *Advancement of Learning*.

The penumbral style of thinking assumes that the truth is invisible, but that both object and subject, nature and mind are symbols of the invisible truth and when rightly related become emblematic, a well-constructed, telling image of the idea of the truth. Truth, then, is translated by the individual into an adequate configuration of words profoundly related to the language of things. Emerson's famous remarks that "there is no beauty in words except in their collocation. . . . In good writing, every word means something. In good writing, words become one with things," are epistemologically programmatic; they point towards his own philosophy of history as well as betraying their historical background.

If we discard the chronology of influence, Emerson's own idea of a prima philosophia, the search for which takes shape only after his return from his first visit to Europe, is designed in the pattern of the theory of the Two Books. Emerson's reading of Joseph Marie de Gérando's *Histoire comparée des systèmes de Philosophie*, his encounter with pre-Socratic materialism, a philosophy about which we find enthusiastic and fairly elaborate statements in his journal, did more than just acquaint him with the fundamental problems of approaching a prima philosophia. It also led him to questions related to the meaning of material objects (*signatura rerum*) to the analogy of natural theology (*theologia naturalis*) and biblical theology (*theologia sacrae*) and eventually to the problems of natural history and the history of man, seen as a history of secularization within an order of the divine.

The implication here is that Emerson, by dealing in his own particular style with the problems outlined above, found himself at the very core of aesthetic idealism. Being highly subjective and thus utterly objective was indeed the paradoxical aim of romantics of both schools, that of natural philosophy and that of the philosophy of identity. Emerson, of course, refused to make a decision between the two and in telltale fashion stresses the element of passivity involved, where the perception of truth is concerned. "No choice. Self abandonment to the truth (of things) makes words things."[6]

A second, larger quotation may be necessary to demonstrate that Emerson's notion of abandonment is not part of the sentimental tradition of the nineteenth century. It is, instead, a residual category of the traditional *scientia correspondentiarum,* the origin of the hermeticism of the century before, which Emerson radicalized after his own fashion.

Abandonment is used by Emerson in a dichotomous fashion, as meaning first of all an awareness of the "power of expression which belongs to external nature; or that correspondence of the outward world to the inward world of thought and emotions, by which it is suited to represent what we think."[7] This suitability, though, is not the result of a naive arrogation of the self; on the contrary, it is possible only after a totally different kind of self-abandonment, namely to the demands of reason. "All exterior life declares interior life. I could not be but that absolute life circulated in me & I could not think this without being that absolute life. The constant strife in warfare in each heart is betwixt Reason and Commodity. The victory is won as soon as any soul has leaned always to take sides with Reason against himself."[8]

The world does intrude, and the fact that the cognitive value of analogical thought had become thoroughly obsolete at the time of Emerson only shows the critical radicalism of his own intention. Emerson, as Warner Berthoff has succinctly emphasized, in a reference to *Nature,* was "solidly philosophical," and there is no reason not to see this philosophical awareness in the early Emerson as well: in his attempt to construct a dialectical relationship between the self and the world of things, with *and* against the philosophical material available to him. The result was not a dialectical method that, once developed, was only waiting to be applied to the world at large. Instead, what we get is a theory of nature that includes man's social character and is related to a dialectical concept of history that proves itself by consistently testing its own plausibility and practicality against any self-imposed restrictions of thought, regardless of their origin or purpose. Despite the obvious philosophical implications of Emerson's thought, it has been,

[6] Emerson, *Journals* 4: 428.

[7] Ralph Waldo Emerson, *The Early Lectures of Ralph Waldo Emerson,* ed. Robert E. Spiller and Wallace E. Williams (Cambridge, Mass., 1972) 1: 24.

[8] Emerson, *Journals* 5: 399.

until recently, something of an interpretative duty among Emersonians to point out over and again that Emerson was not a philosopher. The reasons for this are manifold and worthy of a critical essay all to themselves. But for our present purpose we shall have to restrict ourselves to pointing out as briefly as possible that Emerson's rank as a philosopher rests on five basic, though nonexhaustive arguments.

First: Realizing that "every philosopher feels that the simple fact of his own existence is the most astonishing of all facts,"[9] Emerson takes the idea of natural history seriously, by trying to reconstruct its narrative character. The elementary groundwork for his reconstructive effort is to be found in his early journals and more concisely, of course, in his lectures on science.

Second: Emerson's stubborn refusal to subscribe to either a system of natural philosophy or to a philosophy of identity forced him to invent his own style of philosophical investigation, which went against the grain of the great, holistic system of his time. Neither his particular mode of thought, nor his view of history was, however, without tradition.

Third: On the contrary, his conscious use of the metaphor as a medium of cognition opened for him a third way where the two main philosophical paths towards an understanding of the individual's secular existence without denying the presence of the divine seemed to be blocked by Schelling and Hegel. We therefore find him in the respectable company of Kierkegaard, Benjamin, and Nietzsche among others.

Fourth: Emerson tries to show us that the philosophical dignity of everyday events (compare "Nat. Hist. of Intell.") is not the result of a refined translation of their vulgar, undistinguished presence into one of distinct identity, but that, instead, their dignity is grammatically essential to their very existence and ability to make sense. This effort itself is philosophical in any traditional meaning of that term.

Fifth: Emerson, like some of his lesser-known contemporaries, knew that the sense of crisis that characterized the collective consciousness of the nineteenth century could find expression in a number of explanatory metaphors, ranging from the biographical via the religious to the historical. He was aware, however, that all of these individual expressions of a loss of center were part of a philosophical tradition that itself could be tracked back to the ancients, thus becoming a constitutive element in the formation of western philosophy. The historically conscious mind of man, as seen by Emerson, would never be able

[9] Emerson, *Early Lectures* 1: 23. Hereafter cited in text as Emerson, *Lectures*.

to negate the original leap from myth to logos; in fact, the very idea of tradition implied a series of repetitions of that breaking away from preidentical wholeness.

Emerson was serious about radicalizing once more, in terms of his time, the debate about the function of the absolute. In other words: Emerson's radicalism is not a result of anticipating problems that we ourselves consider modern. Emerson is our contemporary because of his sense of tradition; a moral sense, one should add. The answer to the question of whether and how the divine *Nous* could ever be identified as a subjective faculty of world-making would eventually have extremely practical—if not even political—consequences.

The political consequences, namely the establishment of individualistic liberalism, are obvious. It is equally evident that such a political persuasion could never become the basis or platform for a political movement or organization—and yet, no political movement can seriously deny the ethical dimensions of the Emersonian position. Its ethos lies in keeping open the possibility of choice, while acknowledging at the same time that the rationality of any choice could hardly ever take the form of proof. So whenever we talk about Emerson's subjectivity we have to take into account that we are dealing with the kind of personal subjectivity that legitimizes its raison d'être by limitation. The empire of the imperial self, to use a well-known topos, when all is said, is defined by the boundaries of the single, individual person.

Interestingly enough, the issue of choice became a very pressing one in Emerson's early lectures on science and would find its first results in his more elaborate and better-designed lectures on human culture. When we read Emerson's first four lectures on science, we feel a sense of urgency, a distinct desire on his part to settle something, even if at first we find it difficult to determine what exactly it is that Emerson's lectures try to come to terms with. Beyond their immediate topic, there are certain clues in all of his first four lectures that help us to understand the underlying motivation and energy of his argument. The most accessible one to a close reading is his first lecture of 1833, "The Use of Natural History." The first emphatic proposition, which Emerson makes in this introductory lecture, evokes at once the relationship of time and history in the metaphors of the complete and finished, as opposed to the ongoing, quest. It is the old and by now familiar Emersonian style of stating his view in terms of a relationship. "The earth is a museum, and the five senses a philosophical apparatus of such perfection, that the pleasure we obtain from the aids with which we arm them, is trifling, compared to their natural information" (Emerson, *Lectures* 1: 6).

The idea of the earth as a museum corresponds to the perfection of the five senses, so consequently the question of a "greater cultivation of Natural Science" establishes the possibility of history within a basically perfect correspondence by implicitly finding fault within the relationship between the two. Very much under the influence of his European experience ("I lately had an opportunity of visiting that celebrated repository of natural curiosities the Garden of Plants in Paris"), Emerson treats his audience to an extensive description of the kind of museum of natural history that *pars pro toto* stands for the museum that the earth is as a whole—only to end this lavish praise of the exhibited objects by abruptly turning away from the objective side of observable fact to their affective dimension. The process of internalization changes the tone of Emerson's whole argument. "Whilst I stand there I am impressed with a singular conviction that not a form so grotesque, so savage or so beautiful, but is an expression of something in man the observer. We feel that there is an occult relation between the very worm, the crawling scorpions, and man. I am moved by strange sympathies. I say I will listen to this invitation. I will be a naturalist" (Emerson, *Lectures* 1: 10).

Undoubtedly his audience, the members of the Natural History Society, must have been surprised by the sudden turn from the didactic tone of his lecture to an evocation of the occult. The very reason to see the earth as a museum and to treat the Jardins des Plantes in Paris as a tangible example of a "natural alphabet" was to rationalize in an enlightened fashion the act of observing the natural fact. Emerson would come back to pointing out the practical advantages of natural science, but not before giving his audience a taste of what he had meant by his intimation of an "occult relation." Sugarcoated in the form of a quotation, the point he manages to make is that we, as naturalists, are in fact not at all the natural scientists whose full capacity and abilities are exhausted in an objective study of the objective, empirically isolated fact. Listening to the invitation, as Emerson put it, and declaring oneself a naturalist meant to acknowledge a specific deficiency. "The ancient Greeks had a fable of the giant Antaeus, that when he wrestled with Hercules, he was suffocated in the grip of the hero, but every time he touched his mother earth, his strength was renewed. The fable explains itself to the body and the mind. Man is the broken giant, and in all his weakness he is invigorated by touching his mother earth, that is, by habits of conversation with nature" (Emerson, *Lectures* 1: 11).

This is indeed a far cry from a eulogy on the possible progress of organized scientific research within a professionalized science. The emphasis instead is on *habit*, and it is the personal dimension of this part of his argument that colors Emerson's lecture on the advantage of natural history. Knowledge, even in its simplest form, allows us insight into our own ways with nature—and hence, insight into our own nature. "Moreover is it not disgraceful to be served by all the arts and sciences at our tables and in our chambers and never know who feeds us, nor understand the cunning they employ? I cannot but think it becoming that every gentleman should know why he puts on a white hat in summer, and a woolen coat in winter; and why his shoes cannot be made until the leather is. Better sit still than be borne by steam, and not know how" (Emerson, *Lectures* 1: 14).

Emerson's argument is not merely directed against the limitations of specialized knowledge; in its fundamental sense it is also a plea for humankind to set guidelines for the program of science instead of becoming overwhelmed by both the speed and the specialization of scientific progress. In a low key, we hear in Emerson's lecture an anticipation of things to come: namely Henry Adams's lament in the *Education* that the best scientists were unable to explain to him the essential nature of their practical achievements, such as the Corliss engine.

In his second lecture, which had the title "On the Relation of Man to the Globe," Emerson, after mentioning the volcanic changes that so dramatically transformed the earth into the ecological unit that we now inhabit, wants his audience to understand that his real preoccupation as a naturalist is not with the larger issue of meaning. "Thus knowledge will make the face of the earth significant to us: it will make the stones speak and clothe with grace the meanest weed" (Emerson, *Lectures* 1: 30–31).

Significance is the key term, and Emerson's primary concern. The fact that it is allegorical significance that Emerson had to cope with is borne out by his insistence on the unfinished nature of the relationship between the earth as a museum and the perfect character of the perceptive senses. The act of turning away from the observed fact as an empirical datum and concentrating on the process and ways of internalization allows Emerson to claim the existence of an unfinished world without giving up the idea of perfectability and progress. He thus establishes a balance between two basically contradictory views of the universe, a balance that enables him to avoid the pitfalls of both; the idea, on the one hand, of a world without significance because everything about it is known and established knowledge allowing no further questions, and on the other hand, the danger of absolute relativism. It is therefore not simply an embellishment of his lecture, when he emphasizes the aesthetic dimension of observing nature. On the contrary: the logic of the balance that he tries to achieve necessarily produces an aesthetic, third dimension that guarantees the possibilitiy of ongoing development. The aesthetic and individualistic perception of the natural fact that is a process of constant becoming and vanishing puts man, "the broken giant," into a position to keep alive the very unknown that the natural sciences would eventually exhaust. If we realize that the basic tension in Emerson's early lectures owes its specific characteristics to the great fear of a world without meaning, we also understand to what extent he developed a modern consciousness by anticipation. Modernism here means the insistence on further discoveries in a world where such discoveries are no longer provided by the white, uncharted parts of the globe. Instead the discoveries have to be quite literally made by proposition. Emerson adequately sums up this problem by once more putting into a juxtaposition the practical advantages of the progress of science and a quite different, fundamental sort of statement that also establishes a distinctive hierarchy of relevance: "I have spoken of some of the advantages which may flow from the culture of natural science: health; useful knowledge; delight; and the improvement of mind and character. . . . The knowledge of all the facts of all the laws of nature will give man a true place in the system of being" (Emerson, *Lectures* 1: 23).

This is the side of Emerson's argument that conforms to the general view held by the proponents of scientific progress. But Emerson immediately follows up this assertion by posing a question that undermines the promise of certainty implicit in his first assertion: "The most difficult problems are those that lie nearest at hand. I suppose that every philosopher feels that the simple fact of his own existence is the most astonishing of all facts" (Emerson, *Lectures* 1: 23–24).

The wonder about this "simple fact" eludes the grasp of natural science and Emerson takes an abrupt leap from science to metaphysics by pointing out how self-reflection is the very essence of thought and the realm of the metaphor its only adequate expression.

> The strongest distinction of which we have an idea is that between thought and matter. The very existence of thought and speech supposes and is a new nature totally distinct from the material world; yet we find it impossible to speak of it and its laws in any other language than borrowed from our experience in the material world. We not only speak in continual metaphors of the morn

the noon and the evening of life, of dark and bright thoughts, of sweet and bitter moments, of the healthy mind and the fading memory; but all our most literal and direct modes of speech—as right and wrong, form and substance, honest and dishonest, etc.; are, when hunted up to their original signification, found to be metaphors also. And this, because the whole of Nature is a metaphor or image of the human Mind. The laws of moral nature answer to those of matter as face to face in a glass. (Emerson, *Lectures* 1: 24)

After having gone from the physical to the metaphysical, and especially after having driven home his point about the imperfection of human beings, Emerson could feel quite confident in closing his lecture by leaving his audience with a message that, in light of what had been said before, could hardly be considered ambiguous. Nature, he repeats, is a language the grammar and laws of which must be studied. But the end of such studies, because it would mean the end of understanding, could only be envisioned as the end of the world: "If the opportunity is afforded him, he may study the leaves of the lightest flower that opens upon the breast of summer, in the faith that there is a meaning therein before whose truth and beauty all external grace must vanish, as it may be, all this outward universe shall one day disappear, when its whole sense hath been comprehended and engraved forever in the eternal thoughts of the human mind" (Emerson, *Lectures* 1: 26).

This final sentence has an ironic twist to it. As long as nature's language and our own remain essentially metaphorical, and our capacity as a "broken giant" remains equally within the boundaries of the metaphorical dimension, or rather tension, the end that Emerson evokes could only be the product of divine restitution. This, however, was not something to be brought about by the advancement of natural science. Even though this was Emerson's first lecture after his return from Europe, there is a *distinctive style* that sets the tone and determines the quality of his argument.

Whenever the mirror image implies a static and mechanistic reproduction, Emerson introduces the elements of personal, private experience that stands for flux and variation—and for freedom. Emerson's frequent use of the counterfactual statement, usually added rather abruptly after an outline of a systematic argument, turns into a method. Knowledge, in the end, is always personal knowledge—even though it is produced and attained under the stricture of universal laws. This method, once recognized as the real quest for knowledge, its success being the achievement of knowledge, is the *work* of allegorical thought. The final success of this work lies in the establishment of the momentary balance between the universal truth and its only possible realization in the shape of fluid personal experience. Given these antecedent conditions, philosophical style must necessarily develop a format of closely linked fragments: the connection and, in that very capacity, the partial dissociation between the fragments stands for the general philosophical intention: to demonstrate and practice the possibility of choice.

Choice within limitations: that our existence is the result of a virtually minimal chance, due to a balance in nature's composition of exactly the right conditions that allow for our survival, is the dominant theme of Emerson's lecture "On The Relation of Man to the Globe." At great length Emerson describes the conditions under which we could not and did not exist. Hence his final exclamation: "Design! It is all design. It is all beauty. It is all astonishment" (Emerson, *Lectures* 1: 49).

Allegory as a mode of thought tries to recapture again and again the astonishment about the mere chance of the *right moment* for the *right insight.* "Whoever has recovered from sickness, has remarked the picturesque appearance which the most common objects wore on his first ride or walk abroad" (Emerson, *Lectures* 1: 44). It is always the imagery of danger that accompanies the idea of allegorical truth. So it is only natural that Emerson spends long passages describing the climatic and geological upheavals that eventually created the right living conditions for man, just as dangers of seafaring provided him with a natural resource of examples about the "narrow interval between perfect safety and total destruction." Emerson himself has called his lecture "On the Relation of Man to the Globe" a series of "hasty" and "miscellaneous sketches," but there is no doubt that these sketches embody the philosophical style that cannot allow itself to be formulated in the kind of idealistic system that by its very nature tries to exclude the element of chance. Humankind's existence on this globe is such a matter of dependence on a fortuitous combination of natural forces that Emerson's use of the term *creation,* where our appearance on the planet is concerned, becomes totally devoid of any theological content. Nature, on the other hand, *did indeed prepare* the globe for "man," but any praise for what seems to be the earth's readiness to allow our existence is extricated from the extended awareness of nature's potential hostility. The astonishment, in other words, that Emerson expresses so emphatically at the end of his lecture stands out from a dark background of fear: our ability to question our own existence is deeply grounded in our knowledge about our fragility. The true miracle about our existence is that it *came about* at all.

Any such thought, beyond creating its own style, had to come to terms with two major problems: namely, with the relationship between time and history; and with the question of nature as the ultimate metaphor, and hence the ultimate medium, of cognition. Nature in the latter sense would necessarily include the *natura naturans* and the *natura naturata*. It is, in fact, both the risk and the achievement of allegory as an intellectual activity to unify these two aspects of nature in the conscious mediation of immediacy and duration. If all the astonishment, wonder, and happiness about the momentary achievements of such mediation are accounted for, there is much blindness left—and a wide space for doubt and the experience of uncertainty.

Walter Benjamin, who by virtue of being a wholehearted inhabitant of his own time turned out to be the most penetrating critic of another, summed up in his "Theologico-Political Fragment" the idea and essence of what we have come to call the context of the nineteenth century.

> Only the Messiah himself consummates all history, in the sense that he alone redeems, completes, creates its relation to the messianic. For this reason, nothing historical can relate itself on its own account, to anything Messianic. Therefore the Kingdom of God is not the telos of the historical dynamic; it cannot be set as a goal. From the standpoint of history it is not the goal, but the end. Therefore the order of the profane cannot be built upon the idea of the Divine Kingdom, and therefore theocracy has no political but only a religious meaning. . . . To the spiritual restitution in integrum, which introduces immortality, corresponds a worldly restitution that leads to the eternity of downfall and the rhythm of this eternally transient worldly existence, transient in its totality, the rhythm of Messianic nature is happiness. For nature is Messianic by reason of its eternal and total passing away.[10]

Spiritual Restitution is the key issue, and the dichotomy of unity or wholeness and fragmentation or unfulfillment is the dominant theme. Benjamin's *Fragment* is both about the absence of God and about the presence of the divine. He is concerned with the primordial nature of the divine order, containing *all* the possibilities of the universe and transcending the order of secular time; it is also about the revelation of divine presence in the momentary, simultaneous conjunction of

[10] Walter Benjamin, *Reflections*, ed. Peter Demetz (New York, 1978), p. 213.

subjective volition and its concrete opposite: that singular instance when experience and truth become identical. The relationship between the finite and the infinite, which such an idea of truth continues to reconstruct, is essentially metaphoric. Truth, one might say, is by necessity a metaphor that one cannot resist: it is at the same time a concept of limitations and one of encompassing, far-reaching consequences. Truth, with Emerson, assumes a metaphorical structure, because he radicalizes the traditional idea that the Book of Scripture could be equivocal whereas the Book of Nature was open to observation.

Necessarily Emerson was therefore preoccupied with the nature of truth as well as with the truth of nature, and in order to understand each of these he had to clarify his concepts of history and language. Epistemologically speaking, we might consider Emerson's theory of knowledge mystical, but ever since the convergence of Jewish and Christian mysticism in Schelling's work at the beginning of the nineteenth century, we have been confronted with a larger design. Its fundamental ambition is to prove the possibility of history by unfolding the exegetical powers of the subjective but historically radiant insight. Truth, in other words, is what history is all about. And truth is not a timeless concept, not a given universal, but an eminently historical configuration of thoughts, an irresistible metaphor.

Benjamin's ideas about history, language, and nature point straight towards Emerson, who had his own way of approaching the issue of history, language, and nature but who was equally forceful when he had to explain the paradoxical existence of history as something based on the secularization of the eschatological. At the heart of the paradox, making it a truly devilish one, there was literally "nothing." The mere emphasis put on the powers of the idealized self had to serve as a point of departure.

> Before the revelations of the soul, Time, Space, and Nature shrink away. In common speech we refer all things to time, as we habitually refer the immensely sundered stars to one concave sphere. And so we say that the Judgment is distant or near, that the Millennium approaches, that a day of certain political, moral, social reforms is at hand, and the like, when we mean that in the nature of things one of the facts we contemplate is external and fugitive, and the other is permanent and connate with the soul. The things we now esteem fixed shall one by one detach themselves like ripe fruit from our experience and fall. The wind shall blow them none knows whither. The landscape, the figures, Bos-

> ton, London are facts as fugitive as any institution past, or any whiff of mist or smoke, and so is society, and so is the world. The soul looketh steadily forwards, creating a world before her, leaving worlds behind her. She has no dates, no rites, no persons, nor specialties, nor men. The soul knows only the soul; the web of events is the flowing robe in which she is clothed.[11]

Emerson, like Benjamin, knew perfectly well that the idea of history could only be redeemed by purifying its conceptualization from the kind of tautology characterizing its beginning. "The soul knows only the soul" had to become a kind of statement that would preclude its transformation into a progressive, cyclical, or spiral concept of history.

The critical thrust of the idea of an exorcism of Time, Space, and Nature could only be maintained if the metaphorical nature of the soul's cognitive powers was not merely accepted, but justified as the only viable form of accessible truth! Within language and without: the narrative direction inherent in the metaphor of truth was determined by two equidistant points, the reflective abolition of the subject as its own inner self or as the subject of history. The solution, of course, was in the understanding of the nature of reflection itself. As Emerson put it: "This human mind wrote history, and this must read it. The Sphinx must solve her own riddle."[12]

If the age of Emerson was one of reflection, then it was Emerson who gave that reflection a dialectical dynamic by answering an old question in a new way: how could one conceive of secular history without giving up the idea of the divine? The shape of Emerson's answer, as outlined by his work, was a gradual replacement of established and dogmatized theological substance by emphasizing its spiritual nature and looking for evidence of it in material manifestations. This rather conventional replacement of the Scripture by the Book of Nature had far-reaching consequences, because Emerson's main interest was still the possibility—empirical and ideal—of a convergence of truth and history.

Emerson, in other words, was looking for an adequate form in order to express the idea of a significant relationship between the process of history and its culmination, its ordained end. Substance, in short, changes into function and the eschatological axis is reshaped into a dialectical pattern of realization and unfulfillment. Emerson's *prima philosophia* therefore was characterized, above all, by the acceptance of the historically mediated nature of abstraction. It is not sur-

[11] Emerson, *Works* 2: 257.

[12] Ibid., p. 10.

prising, then, that at the very heart of Emerson's philosophy of history we will eventually find the germ of a theory of action, better referred to as an outline of aesthetic pragmatism, that develops through writers like Thoreau, Adams, and William James into an American tradition of political thought sui generis. The tradition in question is marked, above all, by an undertone of heretical skepticism concerning the dominance of fate over choice, by an extreme awareness of the relationship between style and cognition, by an aesthetic reconstruction of the historical and political functions of reason and experience. The tradition in question, furthermore, is pragmatic without being explicitly practical. It is characterized by the kind of soteriology that Max Weber ascribed to a certain type of intellectual, tempered, however, by a strong sense of contradiction between the justification of historical expectation and the probability of its achievement. Hence we often meet within this tradition an acquired dialectical courage, an attitude that is very much aware of its isolation from the main currents of philosophical thought.

Hyperbolically speaking, one is tempted to say that when the nineteenth century realized that its very essence was a sense of crisis, Ralph Waldo Emerson found it his task to define the name and nature of that crisis. Theodicy and history became his central themes and the invention of a language that would enable human beings to understand their place in a world where the meaning of words like *history, nature*, and *God* was dramatically changing: man, discoursing upon himself and his fate, felt obliged to redefine his sphere and Emerson's moral radicalism makes him the natural contemporary of similar intellectuals beyond his own time. Such natural companionship, indicating intellectual affinities that reach across history and social change, cannot be understood as a belated justification of a typology of intellectual modes of thought. Only by seeing the historical moment of the individual position under scrutiny in sharp focus, will we be able to evoke the outlines of a continuity that lies at the heart of diverse systems of thought trying in various ways to express the sense of a system of life. Timeless insistence does take a form, a shape to declare its identity, and it frequently achieves just that, by establishing a particular relationship between the substance of things and a specific notion of time.

Beginnings such as Emerson's, as problem-conscious as they are problem-ridden, are generally referred to and described in terms of crisis. And in fact, there is reason enough to claim that beneath the rhetorical gestures that we find in his writing, there is, as a constant presence, the expression of despair. Obviously, this kind of reading cancels out other and more familiar interpretations of Emerson, which we need not go into, and it is equally obvious that the whole idea of a dark and brooding Emerson is not an entirely original discovery. However, leaving aside Aunt Mary Moody and her famous shroud, leaving aside also the personal experience of death, the everlasting self-doubts about not measuring up to his own calling: by neglecting, in other words, all the biographical elements of hurt narcissism and life's unavoidable tragedies, we may arrive at an understanding of Emerson's despair as an essential element of his philosophy. In short: Emerson's despair is both the precondition and the result of a philosophy of history that tries to save the idea of the messianic within the unfolding of the profane. The dialectical imagination underlying Emerson's paradox demands a typological as well as an allegorical interpretation: the first dealing with the semantics of reality, the second with the semantics of words. This distinction, of course, owes its explanatory value to the tradition of theological hermeneutics, and not to its postmodernist travesty. Therefore, to quote only one example of modernist misreading, the opposite of Harold Bloom's statement is true.

> The solipsism of Emerson's transcendentalism issues finally in the supra-realism of the necessitarianism of his last great book, the magnificent *The Conduct of Life*. Dialectical thinking in Emerson does not attempt to bring us back to the world of language, and so its purpose is never to negate what is directly before us. . . . From a European perspective, probably, Emersonian thinking is not so much dialectical as it is plain crazy.[13]

From a European point of view, Emerson's dialectical mode of thought makes perfect sense for exactly the reason that Bloom fails to see, namely that it takes us back to what Hegel called the very heart of his philosophy of history: the idea of theodicy. The remarkable twist within Emerson's thought, however, is his rejection of Hegel, which forced him to find a more radical position from which to argue against Kant's antimoniamism than was possible from within the protected boundaries of systematic idealism. His breaking out of the ghetto of systematic idealism carried Emerson into that peculiar blind spot of romantic philosophy of nature and identity, where he was confronted with the task of acknowledging and coping with the weakness and irredeemable futility of the theological effort within an idealistic philosophy of history. Such an acknowledgment would demand the recog-

[13] Harold Bloom, *A Map of Misreading* (New York, 1980), p. 176.

nition of the prevailing power of mythical origin over humankind's position vis-à-vis nature. Our alliance *with* nature, for the benefit of the idea of theodicy, was thinkable only as a reminder of the power of mythical identity in its changing historical manifestations. Logically, therefore, Emerson's dialectical energy takes its beginning with the finite object. The only material evidence of the infinite that Emerson's dialectical imagination derives its momentum from is the inherent "otherness" that the finite object represents: the concreteness of nature, for Emerson, had two faces—one that talked and one that remained mute.

Both of these seemingly contradictory aspects of nature had to be integrated into a concept of time and history that would justify them as necessary contributions to history's meaningful becoming. Movement, the familiar topos of idealistic philosophy, was seen by Emerson as both a natural quality of matter (and, he would add, of God's architecture) and a process that needed interpretation. Emerson, in this way, was taking into account the changes wrought in the very idea of time by its transference from the realm of nature into the controlled environment of the laboratory.

> There is a process in the mind very analogous to crystallization in the mineral kingdom. I think of a particular fact of singular beauty and interest. In thinking of it I am led to many more thoughts which show themselves first partially and afterwards more fully. But in the multitude of them I see no order. When I could present them to others, they have no beginning. There is no method. Leave them now and return to them again. Domesticate them in your mind, do not force them into arrangement too hastily and presently you shall find they will take their own order. And the order they assume is divine. It is God's architecture.[14]

In his brief notebook of 1835, *R O Mind*, Emerson summed up the possible results of the various activities of the mind: "The best we can say of God, we mean of the mind as it is known to us" (*Journals* 5: 271). Knowledge, reflection, and ownership, understanding and reason were seminal categories within Emerson's concept of history, the resolution of their frictional placement within his thought being the idea of repetition.

Time, according to Emerson, becomes historical time, or rather history, only by its accessibility: by being available in terms of repetition. History happens again in order to happen at all. Within Emerson's

[14] Emerson, *Journals* 3: 316.

scheme of upholding the idea of potential fulfillment in history, the fundamentally religious category of repetition plays a vital part—above all where he tries to reconcile the immanent with the transcendent. Reconciliation as a residual category of the messianic, for Emerson, meant to insist on specific differences in order to point to the common origin: "Man is explicable by nothing less than all his history." Such a concept of history would provide Emerson's view of history with its necessary sphericity, thus allowing him to overcome what we might call his Augustinian moment, his realization that the dichotomy between the *civitas dei* and *civitas terrena* could not be resolved by secularizing the idea of messianic salvation and transforming it into one of worldly progress. Emerson, the philosopher of history, is a bad proponent of the idea of progress. The emphasis on "*all* his history" is of critical importance here, referring to both Emerson's philosophical program and style. That the two are basically inseparable stands as evidence of Emerson's philosophical rank: he is not defending established positions or criticizing dogmatic concepts within a given context of received terminology. His effort, on the contrary, is to provide a new sense of our everyday experience as individuals who sit in a world of their own. "Winning losers" these individuals might be, but their gain has been characterized by Emerson as well: "His own culture—the unfolding of his own nature, is the chief end of man."[15]

The very burden of cognitive relevance that has been removed from the concepts of time, space, and nature, would, once placed upon the soul, drain its traditional resources to the limit and demand a supply of additional and functionally equivalent energizing elements. The need for these is the driving force behind Emerson's eclecticism, often criticized by those who will criticize the system-oriented intellectual style of Schelling and Hegel as well, without realizing that as spies into the secrets of history, which they were, they had much in common. Emerson's constant branching out into the fields of natural sciences, anthropology, and psychology could have just as easily been the beginning of a Realenzyclopaedie, as his preoccupation with ancient philosophy and mythology might have turned into a history of consciousness.

Emerson's function in the unfolding of the allegorical tradition, however, was to create the intellectual space for a concept of truth that had to be metaphorical to the extent that it allowed for a mediation between exterior and interior nature. Such mediation, which Emerson liked to express in the imagery of sight, optics, and illusion, would

[15] Emerson, *Lectures* 2: 215.

always have a certain bias, or tendency. Never a symmetrical mediation, which would have been the cornerstone of a larger sytematical design, nature was always seen as either an ally, a neutral, or as an enemy. Each choice would imply and provoke the expression of a different self-consciousness, and Emerson tried indeed to exhaust the whole range of possible positions of self-reference. Above all, however, each individual view of nature determined the interior structure of nature as a metaphor of cognition.

Emerson's path from his early lectures to the publication of *Nature* measures the exact interior distance defining both the scope and structure of truth as metaphor. "The axis of vision is not coincident with the axis of things, and so they appear not transparent but opaque. The reason why the world lacks unity, and lies broken and in heaps, is, because man is disunited with himself. He cannot be a naturalist, until he has satisfied all the demands of spirit. . . . But in actual life, the marriage is not celebrated" (Emerson, *Works* 1: 77).

Hence the metaphorical nature of meaning: the absence of "actuality" necessitates a metaphorical equivalent, which, at the same time, allows the intellect to take stock and reaffirm its hermeneutical competence.

The fortified scepticism that we meet in the text of *Nature* owes itself to a better understanding of the theoretical side of experience. The "naturalist" in *Nature* is a construct, accepting the fact that even though prayer is "a study of truth," it is also a "sally of the soul into the unfound infinite." Whom would he address, if not himself as "man in ruins"? Narcissus had learned to interpret the image of his own making as being only a temporary one. Emerson's cosmos in *Nature* needs something beyond experience: "It is essential to a true theory of nature and of man, that it should contain something progressive" (Emerson, *Works* 1: 65). Once again Emerson's progressive sense points towards myth, backwards in other words. Nature is "faithful to the cause whence it had its origin. . . . It suggests the absolute. It is a perpetual effect. It is a great shadow pointing always to the sun behind us" (ibid.). The text of *Nature* is a careful resetting of a relationship that the "naturalist" in Emerson's lecture of 1834 still described in the shape of an ascending "ever narrowing circle, to approach the elemental law, the *causa causans*, the supernatural force."[16] But even though such images must have sounded to Emerson's audience like a standard expression of the speaker's belief in the progress of science, they could not have totally missed the tone of his final statement.

[16] Emerson, *Lectures* 1: 80.

We are born in an age which to its immense inheritance of natural knowledge has added great discoveries of its own. We should not be citizens of our own time, not faithful to our trust, if we neglected to avail ourselves to their light. The eternal beauty which led the early Greeks to call the globe Kosmos or Beauty pleads ever with us, shines from the stars, glows in the flower, moves in the animal, crystallizes in the stone. No truth can be more self evident than that the highest state of man, physical, intellectual, and moral, can only coexist with a perfect Theory of Animated Nature.[17]

Emerson's point here lies in the remark about "animated nature." It indicates a moving away from previous notions and schemes that he kept working out in his diaries, concerning humankind's role as an interpreter of nature, a moving away from the idea that nature could in any sense of the word be read in an empirical fashion. Exactly *because* Emerson understood the nature of science well enough, he was able to use its progress in order to demonstrate what there was left to do. We can trace Emerson's development from a relatively simple use of the image of nature in a vague, illustrative sense to a concise and defined sense of the metaphorical use of the term in his journals. His entries there show that before his trip to Europe he had worked out his main ideas—his encounters with professionally organized science in Europe seem to have provided, above all, the material evidence he needed to furnish and strengthen his arguments. Again, as is frequently the case in this context, Bacon has to serve as the main source of inspiration.

Bacon said man is the minister and interpreter of nature: he is so in more respects than one. He is not only to explain in the sense of each passage but the scope and argument of the whole book. He is to explain the attractiveness of all. There is more beauty in the morning cloud than the prism can render account of. There is something in it that resembles the aspects of mortal life, its epochs and its fate. There is not a passion in the human soul, perhaps not a shade of thought but has its emblem in nature. And this does not become fainter this undersong, this concurrent text, with more intimate knowledge of nature's laws, but the analogy is felt to be deeper and more universal for every law that is revealed. It almost seems as if an unknown wisdom or intelligence in us was satisfied with expressed recognition of each new disclosure.[18]

[17] Ibid., p. 83.

[18] Emerson, *Journals* 4: 95.

Written in 1833 this statement sums up a long series of entries that Emerson began in his early Wide-Wide-World-Journals, and it marks the high point of Emerson's confidence in the feasibility of a theory of animated nature. In order to understand fully the importance of Emerson's use of the emblematic, when describing the relation between man and nature, we ought to remember another statement of his about the characteristics of a perfect philosophy of man. It would have to be a true philosophy, Emerson had written, which "should give a theory of Beast and Dreams" (*Journals* 4: 289).

The text of *Nature* is Emerson's occupation of a *locus standi*, his design of such a philosophy, which takes both into account: beast and dream. He had thus moved a long way from his early use of nature as an example of God's wisdom in a quite simplistic manner, to the acceptance of Bacon's lesson, as he had drawn it from the *Advancement of Learning*, and further on to a restoration of nature within the self: the last step allowing him to develop his awareness and acknowledgment of human psychological, anthropological, and social nature.

Emerson's unequivocal statement that there was a "historical progress of man" had taken some preparation. A more than vague outline of his way towards his lectures on "Human Culture" would have to emphasize at least three stages of Emerson's development of man's moral abilities into a holistic view of history's progress. Emerson's early views of progress in general were deeply influenced by his image of the sciences, which seemed to be moving forward by means of *discoveries*, by acts of the autonomous individual, in other words. For this we have to turn to a rather lengthy entry on this subject in his journal: "It is an old remark that there are no discoveries in morals. It is the leading object of our existence, to form moral character, and the laws of morals are therefore written on the heart in luminous and ineffaceable characters. It is in our power, to extend our acquaintance into the laws of physical nature, to ponder and solve the problems of science, to measure the land and sea" (*Journals* 4: 57).

Emerson contrasts his account of the possible progress of science with the traditional view of common sense philosophy, with its moral implications, only to *reject* it in the end. The asymmetrical development of the sciences as compared to that of moral improvement of a *sensus communis* ("written on the heart in luminous and ineffaceable characters") could only be remedied by a correction of metaphorical contents. The reading of what is "written on the heart" had to become a science too, its paradigm being the admission of *discoveries*. This is the first step that Emerson takes on his way to his lecture on human culture and beyond the text of *Nature*, as it stood in 1836. How, then, could he justify the existence of *discoveries* within the realm of the moral sciences? One way towards achieving a similarity between the progress in reading the writing of nature and that of the heart would have been to allow for the necessity of a hermeneutic of morals. Not only, though, would such an idea have isolated the luminous and ineffaceable qualities of God's writing on the heart, destroying the syngraphic bond between man and nature—it would also eliminate the social context of "reading" both scriptures, that of nature and that of the heart, isolating the act of reading from the world of action. (The very idea of a *sensus communis* in the first place, was, of course, to enable everyone to act upon it—in principle.) Emerson, to avoid the dead-end argument that would separate the realities of the text from that of the world, therefore went in exactly the opposite direction. The world was too complicated to be understood in its relationship to the simple writing of the heart, and so was the heart and the "graduated forces of the passions" (*Journals* 3: 61). Emerson, continuing his deliberation on this vital subject on the fourth of January of 1827, came to the emphatic resolution: "Understand now, morals do not change but the *science* of morals does advance, we discover truth and relations of which they were before ignorant, therefore there are discoveries in morals" (*Journals* 3: 61).

Establishing an affinity between the advancement of science and the science of morals by turning the direction of the argument towards the empirical world was a first step. It was a strategic one, since we must remember that the analogy between the two sciences, exemplified in the metaphor of discovery, worked mainly on the basis of an assumed complexity, rather than on the proof of empirical procedure. The very idea of complexity, however, helped to launch the next movement of thought: away from the maze outside, towards the one represented by humankind itself. When Emerson, in 1827, had listed among the peculiarities of the age, "Transcendentalism, Metaphysics and ethics look inwards" (followed a little later by "the paper currency" and "joint stock companies") (*Journals* 3: 61), he was, in fact, already pointing out that the real sense of turning towards humankind as part of nature had to be established by *making sense* of humankind as part of nature. Natural philosophy and philosophy of history were supposed to converge in a kind of history of man who could rightly say about himself: I am.

It needed one more step, the third, to establish this kind of autonomy, which would ultimately enable Emerson to exclaim that his project was "nothing less than to look at every object in its relation to Myself" (*Journals* 4: 277). This third part of the way towards the established self is marked, above all, by a renewal and justification of skepticism. It stresses the limits of our capacity for harmony, our confinement to a shadow world of knowledge: autonomy, in other words, as the final and most advanced form of theodicy exacts a price—it would also inevitably lead towards an aesthetic compensation for the loss of syngraphic identity.

It allowed, however, the reestablishment of an enlightened skepticism: the undertow of the romantic surge towards the sublime. The driving force behind this tendency towards skepticism was—above all—the acceptance of the process of abstraction as the way to self-knowledge. Emerson had copied from Bacon's *Advancement of Learning*, which in Ralph Spedding's translation reads: "For the sensible world is inferior in dignity to the rational soul, Poesy seems to bestow upon human nature those things which history denies to it; and to satisfy the mind with the shadows of things when the substance cannot be obtained" (*Journals* 3: 11).

To insist on the autonomy of the self, even though the substance of things could not be obtained, meant two things at once which would ordinarily cancel each other out. First it implied the destruction of nature as a guiding principle, allowing its return as landscape, or as nature-as-symbol. Second it meant the construction of something as permanent as nature within the realm of the symbolic in order to hold on to the idea of humankind's history. Nature is thus reduced to its very essence, its first law and principle. Man, as Emerson quoted more than once from Fontenelle, once he perceived this simple and primary law of nature, would probably exclaim: "What! Is this all?" Knowing nature through scientific discovery to the point where its reduction bordered on the convergence of the finite and the infinite had to result in vast, unoccupied spaces inviting creativity. Man could finally become the maker of his own self, with the aid of God, who had given up hiding behind nature and instead revealed himself in man's demiurgical abilities to abstract from nature.

It was in this sense that Carlyle had made his telling remark about the apocalyptic character of Emerson's book. Emerson was serious when he repeatedly pointed out that it was not for nothing that Bacon had concluded his argument about history by deploring the absence of the highest form of historical writing: that of literary history.

Two things remain to be said: Emerson's criticism of the absence of adequate cosmogonies in his time was not merely a defiance of the received and familiar theories available to him. There is a profound skepticism involved that basically assumes that the seven days of God's work are not yet over. The incompleteness of their work not only makes God and humankind accomplices; it also forges a link between the idea of freedom and responsibility as logical components in our actions. The key term of this logic is *necessity*—or as Emerson would prefer to call it, compensation. To put it differently, the organic metaphor, in Emerson's hands, is not an idyllic term at all, but a sharply discriminating concept designed to justify human identity. As a second and final afterthought to the above, we should remember that Emerson's effort to replace the text of nature with his own text *about* nature was a topical one within the romantic tradition. There is a radical side to it, though, that one might identify as a kind of cosmic skepticism. The book about nature will be written, but who is going to read and judge it? Prayer and poiesis therefore are both marked by the same uncertainty, they are reflective and alive only as part of the quest for self-knowledge. They are, in short, answers to the semblance of a question. So, in the end, only the imaginary filled the void between the letters written on the heart and the laws of nature.

Language, Light, and Illusion

> To an instructed eye the universe is transparent. The light of higher laws than its own shines through it.
>
> —RALPH WALDO EMERSON

> In good writing, words become one with things.
>
> —RALPH WALDO EMERSON

> Through the word man is bound to the language of things.
>
> —RALPH WALDO EMERSON

Transparency is the common denominator: language and light, by establishing an intelligible reality, also demonstrate the existence of an unworldly source behind it. Or rather, not behind it, but part of it as a constitutive element. The "hermaphroditic" principle of language, which Emerson mentions, points to the extremes of our existence, characterized by the terms of *beast* and *dream*. As analogists, we must establish ourselves between the analogies: our chance as well as our fate is that of the translator: "Nature is a language and every new fact that we learn is a new word; but rightly seen, taken all together it is not merely a language (but a scripture which contains the whole truth) but the language put together into a most significant and universal book. I wish to learn the language not that I may know a new set of nouns and verbs but that I may read the great which is written in that tongue" (*Journals* 4: 95).

It must suffice for our purpose here to point out only one aspect of "the great book" that Emerson talks about. If, as Emerson points out in his *Nature*, "words are signs of natural facts," if indeed, as he goes on to say, "every word which is used to express a moral or intellectual fact, if traced to its root, is found to be borrowed from some material appearance," why then is it so difficult to "read" the great Book of Nature? Why are we, as Emerson states, always bound to mean more than we are able to express? Apparently the analogy between the language of man and the language of nature has become distorted, not because of some interference from outside, but for exactly the opposite reason. We never managed to break away totally from our natural origins, and our ability to "read" the Book of Nature is therefore severely hampered by the fact that we have no autonomous position for ourselves, no place apart that we could rightfully call our own! The common language, shared by humankind and nature and communicating itself in a series of correspondences, covers a whole range of expressions from the symbolic to the emblematic. There always remains, however, the presence of a nondistinctive meaning. The function of language, therefore, is not only to communicate, but to symbolize the silence and muteness of nature as well.

We have become very much used to the nomenclature of the regredient and progredient as applied to the imagination, due to our familiarity with psychoanalytic theory. As a result we tend to overlook the fact that the romantic tradition saw these two aspects of the imagination as dangerously intertwined. Emerson realized that there was no transcendental way out from this paradoxical nature of the imagination and accepted it as a fundamental condition of experience. The hermeticism of his essays, their dark rhetoric, when seen in this light, serves a dual purpose. They are mimetic by necessity and intentionally didactic, forcing the reader to repeat, in the process of understanding, an experience that Emerson claimed to be the point of origin of all understanding: the moment in time when language broke through the circle and identity of mythical repetition, when interpretation of the "me" became a counterfactual necessity in order to understand the "not me." The acceptance of illusion replaces the timeless circularity of myth and makes room for a concept of enlightened skepticism, namely that both meaning and truth are possible—as metaphors.

Language and light are veils with a transparency of degrees; the acceptance of illusion allows for a kind of enlightenment that would eventually realize the common origin of imagination and desire. Emerson's essays are proof of this tendency towards a growing awareness of the anthropological dimension that is our bond with nature.

Truth, therefore, had both a tangible and an intangible side, like light itself, and like language. From early on, in his journals, Emerson had been fascinated by the fact that people always express less than they mean. Language and light both contained as part of their nature indicators that pointed to negativity and unfulfillment. They were, like truth, never a complete, static self. The fact that both language and light resist transformation into an absolute state of their appearance determines their high degree of latency and thus also their usefulness as metaphors, qualities that Emerson exploited to the full. Above all they allowed him to work out his idea of truth as a hidden, but irresistible force, while working with the kind of material everybody was familiar with. At the same time, his ideas of language and light enabled him to evoke the mythical dignity of both metaphors and to dramatize in an unsentimental way his main points about humankind's existence "between" a state of loss and illusion and one of achievement and recognition. The well-known image at the beginning of "Experience" of man's awakening on a stair describes man as only half-awake, constantly confronting the phenomenon of uncertainty. Both language and light work in an indirect way: they hide and reveal at the same time, they mediate between identity and individuation. Total identity becomes a part of our mythical origin, which, when recalled, loses some of its frightening aspects and allows the individual to take a stand against an overpowering nature.

But as Emerson never fails to point out in so many variations of the best "beast and dream" theme, nature is always with us, it is "an Eternal Now." It was certainly one of Emerson's major achievements, when dealing with the problem of language to combine two aspects of it, the momentum of original power and the revealing character of its presence in the things around us. "Every form is the history of the thing," he had said in his lecture "The Uses of Natural History," and the telling of this history serves a twofold purpose. The first is a reminder of our belonging to nature—a kind of belonging that contains both a sense of mythical terror and its scientific domestication as anthropological observation and description. The acknowledgment in "Experience," that moods and resulting action are facts of life is nothing but a summing up of such scientific distancing. The second purpose of the history of language as an ongoing history is its function as a promise of future restoration. It is important to remember that Emerson treated the idea of promised or implied restoration with great care, avoiding the return of original, mythical violence in the shape of an anticipated supremacy of man over nature. He preferred a certain passivity and receptivity, and an acceptance of the nonanalogical. Language functioned as a reminder that humankind and nature were not equal, though opposite, forces; the me and the not-me were linked in an unsymmetrical way. The etymological relationship between words and things, which Emerson outlines in *Nature*, carried over into his use of the idea of things as being emblematic. Without the notion of the emblematic character of things, his demands for a marriage of natural history to "human history" would not make sense, because man the "analogist" would simply not understand his own analogies.

On the other hand, Emerson was extremely eager to avoid the fallacies and pitfalls of total understanding and identity. He allowed mythical unity to work as a corrective of total contingency, its time structure pointing into the past and the future. The analogies that we establish in order to place ourselves, are—in the end—analogies of our own choosing. Between the Book of Scripture and the Book of Nature, truth would always remain a metaphor, demanding action. The real legacy of transcendentalism, therefore, was pragmatism where it was once again assumed, as Charles S. Peirce put it in a footnote to *How to Make Our Ideas Clear*, experience is "the process whereby man with all his miserable littlenesses becomes gradually more and more embued with the spirit of god, in which Nature and History are rife."[19] But, nature had a habit of getting in the way. As Emerson put it: "Man is not order of nature, sack and sack, belly and members, link in a chain, nor any ignominious baggage; but a stupendous antagonism, a dragging together of the poles of the Universe. He betrays his relation to what is below him—thick-skulled, small-brained, fishy, quadrumanous, quadruped ill-disguised, hardly escaped into biped—and has paid for the new powers by loss of some of the old ones" (Emerson, *Works* 4: 27).

Man, the "stupendous antagonism," has always been Emerson's greatest theme: provoking his darkest thoughts on his most profound despair. All the severity and stoicism of his best thought must be seen as the result of an ongoing battle against the terrible insight expressed in such passages about the individual's basic disorientation, as in the beginning of his essay "Experience."

> Where do we find ourselves? In a series of which we do not know the extremes, and believe that it has none. We make and find our-

[19] Charles S. Peirce, *How to Make Our Ideas Clear* (Garden City, N.Y., 1958), p. 402n.

> selves on a stair; there are stairs below us, which we seem to have ascended, there are stairs above us, many a one which go upward and out of sight. But the Genius which according to the old belief stands at the door by which we enter, and gives us the lethe to drink, that we may tell no tales, mixed the cup too strongly, and we cannot shake off the lethargy now at noonday. Sleep lingers all our lifetime about our eyes, as night hovers all day in the boughs of the fir-tree. All things swim and glitter. Our life is not so much threatened as our perception. Ghostlike we glide through nature, and should not know our place again. (Emerson, *Works* 3: 45)

To accept the necessity of this ghostlike existence is the task that Emerson sets for his readers in his major essays. The long, associative paragraphs with which he confronts his audience are the *exemplum* Emerson sets: they *represent* rather than discursively unfold his argument. The reader's experience becomes part of the process that leads to the sudden aphoristic insight. Too often, however, have the brilliant formulations, by sheer quotability, overshadowed the process and the duration of their making. "The secret of the illusoriness is in the necessity of a succession of moods or objects." Emerson's practice of stretching the succession is the great art of intellectual allegory. It uses *all* possible moods in order to enhance the fruits of choice—stressing at the same time the importance of all that is left out, once the choice has been made. This is the allegorist's way of representing a world. By creating a well-lit foreground within the context of any given argument he *makes visible*, at the same time, the vast and overwhelming darkness of the background.

The reader can return, of course, and the scene of his reading will be slightly different. But the distribution of the light and the darkness will not change. This account of Emerson's allegorical construction of a cycle of possible returns is a reflection of his view of the world, which corresponds in large part to William James's idea of a pluralistic universe. It is our freedom that is at stake in both cases: the difference being one of textuality rather than one of subject matter. Emerson's mimetic desires and his reliance on the word as a sign were naturally more developed than was possible in James's case. The difference in question is also the difference between the pioneer and the inheritor. And yet, where in Emerson's essays allegoresis is frequently produced by a series of brilliant insights, so interwoven that they tend to blind and confuse, we find in the texts of William James a dark glow, which comes from the same source. Emerson's case, the need for self-actualization, frequently found its expression literally in the light of the text only—William James, the inheritor, could allow himself a greater patience, given the legacy that he had at his disposal.

American allegory, to put it in a slightly different way, survived by transformation: what seemed extravagant in 1847 had become the accepted material of philosophical discourse in 1909. As William James would put it then, in his chapter on monistic idealism in the *Pluralistic Universe*: "Things can be consistent or coherent in very diverse ways."

CHAPTER 4

Henry David Thoreau

This was that Earth of which we have heard, made out of Chaos and Old Night. Here was no man's garden, but the unhandselled globe. It was not lawn, nor pasture, nor mead, nor woodland, nor lea, arable, nor wasteland. It was the fresh and natural surface of the planet Earth, as it was made forever and ever—to be the dwelling of man, we say—so Nature made it, and man may use it if he can. Man was not to be associated with it. . . . Think of our life in nature, daily to be shown matter, to come in contact with it; rocks, trees, wind on our cheeks! The *solid* earth! The *actual* world! The common sense! *Contact! Contact! Who* are we? *Where* are we?

—HENRY DAVID THOREAU

My Journal is that of me which would else spill over and run to waste, gleaning from the field which in action I reap. I must not live for it, but in it for the gods. They are my correspondent to whom daily I send off this sheet post-paid. I am clerk in their countings-room, and at evening transfer the account from day-book to ledger.

—HENRY DAVID THOREAU

Beyond the Mask

In order to understand the essential distance that separates Thoreau from Emerson, we must take a look back, a critical one this time, at the latter's achievement. And we must bear in mind, of course, that such differences as exist between Emerson and Thoreau are the result of an almost natural proximity. Thoreau took his radical departure from practically all that was best in Emerson's essays; we can perhaps best circumscribe Thoreau's effort to go further than Emerson by asking the question how it makes sense to see the essay, or rather to see Emerson's essays, as masks. In the light of much that has been written in recent years on the relationship between the sacred and the profane—a cultural landscape that Emerson and Thoreau still inhabited—the mask is frequently described as serving a specific role in a form of ritualized violence that defines the relationship between the two.

As René Girard has pointed out in his chapter "From Mimetic Desire to the Monstrous Double," masks are "another aspect of the monstrous double": "Masks juxtapose beings and objects separated by differences. They are beyond differences; they do not merely defy differences or efface them in original fashion."[1] In this sense, Emerson's essays and their intricate and violent rhetoric are clearly masks. They juxtapose boldly in a ritual manner: the Platonizing Yankee had ample material to work with. "Masks," Girard concludes, "serve as an interpretation," and Emerson's essays by way of violent rearrangements do interpret. Defying all notions of a systematically abstract intellectual order, he persistently told his audience how to read him: "But lest I should mislead any when I have my own head and obey my whims, let me remind the reader that I am only an experimenter. Do

[1] René Girard, *Violence and the Sacred* (Baltimore, 1977), p. 167.

not set the least value on what I do, or the least discredit on what I do not, as if I pretended to settle anything as true or false. I unsettle all things. No facts are to me sacred; none are profane."[2]

The rhetorical structure of essays like "Circles," "Experience," and "Self-Reliance" is very much a structure of violence, but then this does not mean that there is an absence of order: the opposite is the case. But Henry David Thoreau would have nothing to do with the final result of rearrangements. His concern was with the fact, or to put it differently, he did not believe in the functional role of the mask. He did not share the sense of the ritual, because he did not believe in interpretation. The idea of instruction was one that he had expediently postponed: the fact would flower in a truth—one day. There are no indications that Thoreau was concerned about the when and how of that day; his preoccupation was strictly with the present. Living was his only morality, and keeping a record of life hence became the only moral duty of the individual. Given the fact that Thoreau also published essays: "Natural History of Massachusetts" (1842), "A Walk to Wachusett" (1843), "A Winter Walk," and of course produced such careful compositions as *Walden*, the fact that he lectured: all of this should not blur the fact that Thoreau, in comparison with Emerson, had dramatically changed his *locus standi* vis-à-vis nature. If we find his individual works overshadowed by his journal, we are in fact saying two things at the same time. Pushing a beautifully organized work like *Walden* back into the context of his journals seems to deprive the book of the certain status and autonomy of a work of art. But critics have always found it hard to attribute to *Walden* a safe place in the great canon of literature—so there must be, and there is, a resistance from the work's side to be safely canonized or defined by genre. The second aspect of emphasizing the journal and proclaiming it to be the heart of Thoreau's work is the implicit acknowledgment that Thoreau's amorality is in essence what sets him apart from his fellow transcendentalists. This, of course, we find in *Walden* as well.

> I went to the woods because I wished to live deliberately, to front only the essential facts of life, and see if I could not learn what it had to teach, and not, when I came to die, discover that I had not lived. I did not wish to live what was not life, living is so dear; nor did I wish to practice resignation, unless it was quite necessary. I wanted to live deep and suck out all the marrow of life, to live so sturdily and Spartanlike as to put to rout all that was not life, to cut a broad swath and shave close, to drive life into a corner, and

[2] Emerson, *Works* 2: 318.

> reduce it to its lowest terms, and, if it proved to be mean, why then to get the whole and genuine meanness of it and publish its meanness to the world; or if it were sublime, to know it by experience, and be able to give a true account of it in my next excursion. For most men, it appears to me, are in a strange uncertainty about it, whether it is of the devil or of God, and have *somewhat hastily* concluded that it is the chief end of man here "to glorify God and enjoy him forever."[3]

How close such deliberations are to animal life becomes quite apparent at the beginning of the section "Higher Laws."

> As I came home through the woods with my string of fish trailing my pole, it being now quite dark, I caught a glimpse of a woodchuck stealing across my path, and felt a strange thrill of savage delight, and was strongly tempted to seize and devour him raw; not that I was hungry then, except for that wildness which he represented. Once or twice, however, while I lived at the pond, I found myself ranging the woods, like a half-starved hound, with a strange abandonment, seeking some kind of venison which I might devour, and no morsel could have been too savage for me. The wildest senses had become unaccountably familiar. (Thoreau, *Walden*, pp. 139–40)

The difference between Emerson and Thoreau, here, is not one of the extremity of sentiments, but one of tone. Emerson could speculate about a "theory of dreams and beasts," and in occasional outbursts he would give the reader a glimpse of what he meant, but he never could adapt the matter-of-fact voice that Thoreau employed when exploring such regions of the human spirit. To be sure, even Thoreau had to add some kind of explanation to his description of nature in human beings: "I found in myself—and still find—an instinct toward a higher or, as it is named, spiritual life, as do most men, and another toward a primitive rank and savage one, and I reverence them both. I love the wild not less than the good" (*Walden*, p. 140).

But the matter-of-fact afterthought is not meant to alleviate the impact of the initial statement. Thoreau clearly dropped the mask and introduced his own physicality as the battleground of opposing forces in nature. This of course *did* include the realm of the sublime, but the body was to become part of nature, unmasked and without the ritual

[3] Henry David Thoreau, *Walden and Civil Disobedience*, ed. Owen Thomas (New York, 1966), p. 61. Hereafter cited in text as Thoreau, *Walden*. (All citations are from the Norton Critical Edition.)

of rhetoric. Hence Thoreau's style of the momentary: his descriptions and observations always rebel against their own transitory nature. Life lived, in Thoreau's view, was not something to be safely summed up at one point in time, but it was the continuation of a series of events. Each single event, unless rendered meaningless, must therefore have its own fulfillment. The journal is, of course, the adequate literary device for an artistic will that tries to capture life as a process. Where other forms of narration eventually involve some kind of ritual—the narrative time and the act of reading according to its structure, the text as a mask juxtaposed between the reader and *his* text—the diary or the journal aspires to a literary translation of physical awareness without admitting that artifice is a needed medium. As an attempt at *direct* communication, the journal tries, in vain of course, to abolish communication as a mediator. The body and the thing are supposed to merge in the word, and the identity of the writer and the reader are to become one and the same. It is not difficult to detect in Thoreau's position the concrete aesthetics of romanticism. Similarly, one can easily concede that Thoreau's long journey through idealism ended in discovering its origin in the material object and that object's impact on the senses.

"Cold and hunger seem more friendly to my nature than those methods which men have adopted and advise to ward them off." This statement from Thoreau's "Life without Principle" sums up his belief in a cathartic life without mask. But the mask we remember was the essay, and our logical conclusion therefore must be that Thoreau offered his body as a mask, the only juxtaposition between the fact and the word. Inevitably, this raises the question of replacement. What was it that Henry David Thoreau established as a ritual of his own where he went further than Emerson dared to go? In order to answer this question, it is necessary to remind ourselves that both Emerson and Thoreau wrote as members of one community, and one's attention is drawn immediately towards their different attitudes to their community. At large, of course, they both shared a disdain for the demands that society made on the individual, but whereas Emerson argued for the self from within, Thoreau was willing to set himself apart. He adopted, quite deliberately, the role of the victim who knew that his role is to establish the right distance in order to fulfill his role as the one who saves. The voice of authority that assumes the burden of setting things right cannot be a disembodied one; it needs an agent. The self in question, as a first step, has to become physical.

> At a lyceum, not long since, I felt that the lecturer had chosen a theme too foreign to himself, and so failed to interest me as much as he might have done. He described things not in or near to his heart, but towards his extremities and superficies. There was, in this sense, no truly central or centralizing thought in his lecture. I would have had him deal with his privatest experience as the poet does. The greatest compliment that was ever paid me was when someone asked me what *I thought*, and attended to my answer.[4]

Observation, comment, description, are not enough—it all has to come from the "heart," from the self that is, that needs some defining.

Above all it is the indeterminate nature of the self that favors the journal as a form of expression that keeps the future open. Interestingly enough Thoreau, in the great debate between Asa Gray on the one side and Agassiz on the other, seemed to have taken the side of Gray and Darwin, rather than subscribing to a theory of original design. In this sense, Thoreau was a teleologist, a "self-denying teleologist," as Leo Marx has called him. The quality of self-denial applies only to the question of *telos*, however, a question that seemed to have bothered Thoreau just as little as he was seriously disturbed by such questions as original sin or the fall of man. The specific position that Thoreau occupied vis-à-vis nature was that of an attentive admirer, of someone whose ability to listen would allow nature to express herself. Standing "near to nature" was his goal and he was thoroughly convinced that in his effort he went further than any of his fellow transcendentalists. Thoreau respected nature's essential otherness.

> I love Nature partly *because* she is not a man, but a retreat from him. None of his institutions control or pervade her. There a different kind of right prevails. In her midst I can be glad with an entire gladness. If this world were all man, I could not stretch myself, I should lose all hope. He is constraint, she is freedom to me. He makes me wish for another world. She makes me content with this. None of the joys she supplies is subject to his rules and definitions. What he touches he taints. In thought he moralizes.[5]

The journals Thoreau kept were, of course, the adequate medium to establish his kind of encyclopedia that would gather exactly those kinds of facts that would one day flower into truth. Amoral as Tho-

[4] Henry David Thoreau, *Reform Papers*, ed. Wendell Glick (Princeton, 1973), p. 155.
[5] Thoreau, *Journal*, p. 511.

reau's attitude towards society might seem, there is no doubt that Thoreau on his side was not beyond moralizing himself. In fact, the mere act of observing was considered to be a moral event. But again, it must be stressed that Thoreau limited this kind of "moralizing" to the extension of his corporeal self, the realm of the five senses: "Every man is the builder of a temple, called his body, to the god he worships, after a style purely his own, nor can he get off by hammering marble instead. We are all sculptors and painters, and our material is our own flesh and blood and bones" (*Walden*, p. 147).

To the extent that an essay constitutes a well-wrought piece of rhetoric that interprets, it is obvious that Thoreau's journals represent the effort to leave the juxtaposition of interpretation behind—to drop the mask and reveal the self. But the self, as Thoreau clearly saw, included the head, the mind, and being part of nature included an understanding of the past. Thoreau, in his chapter "Reading" in *Walden*, turns the written word into a universal sign, which in the end is not very different from the universality of nature: "A written word is the choicest of relics. It is something at once more intimate with us and more universal than any other work of art. It is the work of art nearest to life itself. It may be translated into every language, and not only be read but actually breathed from all human lips—not be represented on canvas or in marble, but be carved out of the breath of life itself. The symbol of an ancient man's thought becomes a modern man's speech" (*Walden*, p. 69).

The last sentence gives us an intimation of how Thoreau might have imagined the process of fact flowering into truth: they must be consciously used and brought back into a relationship with another self.

The self and the senses, however, are not identical; they constitute the possibility of identity by becoming part of a dialectical relationship of abandonment and reservation.

The Self and the Senses

The self can never be invented; it is always the result of reconstruction. Aspiring to be something here and now, it needs the past and relationships in the past. Whenever the effort of reconstruction takes place, the past becomes an allegorical present: "When first I took up my abode in the woods, that is, began to spend my nights as well as days there, which by accident was on Independence Day, or the fourth of July, 1845, my house was not finished for winter, but was merely a defense against the rain" (*Walden*, p. 57).

Thoreau knew that the sense of allegory lies in repetition and could therefore explain: " 'Renew thyself completely each day; do it again and again, and forever again.' I can understand that. Morning brings back the heroic ages" (*Walden*, p. 60). The decisive point about Thoreau's sense of selfhood is the juxtaposition of sense certainty or immediacy with versions of the past, of myth and antiquity. His *sensus sui* is profoundly related to the tension between the subjective, momentary impression and the knowledge that the immediate is implicitly part of a sequence. The self, therefore, exists as a double, its self-experience is essentially schismatic. Open-ended teleology in the sense outlined above keeps this schism alive; in fact, it turns the experience of it into a fundamental one. We have to realize that Thoreau's efforts to simplify life and get close to nature were less a flight *from* something than an endeavor to lay bare these essential paradoxes of selfhood. It is the practical intellect that tries to bring to light and must explain the nature of selfhood as an essentially paradoxical one. The fact that Thoreau considered this to be the ultimate truth is the primary structuring principle of *Walden*—and, of course, in a much less elaborate fashion, it is the guiding principle of his journals. "No face which we can give to a matter will stead us so well at last as the truth. This alone wears well. For the most part, we are not where we are, but in a false position. Through an infirmity of our natures, we suppose a case, and put ourselves into it, and hence are in two cases at the same time, and it is doubly difficult to get out. In sane moments we regard only the facts, the case that is" (*Walden*, p. 217).

But then, what is the case? Thoreau was quite aware of the fact that his view of the "sane moment" had tragic implications. He knew that it would always be a "borderline phenomenon" and there are certain stoic implications in his ideas of the self that cannot be overlooked. As he makes explicitly clear in his chapter "Solitude" in *Walden*, it is not the separation of the individual from society that is the real issue, but a fundamental solitude within the self.

> With thinking we may be beside ourselves in a sane sense. By a conscious effort of the mind we can stand aloof from actions and their consequences; and all things, good and bad, go by us like a torrent. We are not wholly involved in Nature. I may be either the driftwood in the stream, or Indra in the sky looking down on it. I *may* be affected by a theatrical exhibition; on the other hand, *may not* be affected by an actual event which appears to concern me much more. I only know myself as a human entity; and am sensible of a certain doubleness by which I can stand as remote from myself as from another. However intense my experience, I am

> conscious of the presence and criticism of a part of me, which, as it were, is not part of me but spectator, sharing no experience, but taking note of it; and that is no more I than it is you. When the play, it may be the tragedy, of life is over, the spectator goes his way. (*Walden*, pp. 90–91)

Only then, one feels free to add. Before that the self is bound to the set of the tragedy. Solitude, in this sense, is not synonymous with being alone, but it describes a human condition. The stoic element in Thoreau's view of life as a tragedy is best exemplified in his insistence that the "play" is dynamic.

We are therefore justified to read *Walden* among other things as a rite of passage, a reading that we find confirmed in his "Conclusion," and the well-known remark "Perhaps it seemed to me that I had several more lives to live, and could not spare any more time for that one" (*Walden*, p. 213).

Self-contradiction and self-preservation are the original stoic elements of Thoreau's thought that he inevitably turned into process, into a quest for selfhood. Experience, as a result, assumes a narrative quality, which means saying more than that all experience has a temporal structure. It also goes beyond the traditional concepts of a pilgrimage or a journey towards a fulfilled self. Thoreau's quest is not a slight variation from the idealistic version of *Heilsgeschichte* as *Bildungsgeschichte*—there is no tangible Hegelian side to Thoreau. The narrative quality in question is one of self-explanation in a twofold manner: the self tries to become better acquainted with its real nature by explaining the unknown sides of its own character to itself (self-explanation) and at the same time the act of self-explanation must be fixed and transformed into an act of witnessing. Both these aspects of Thoreau's work are of equal importance. The first helps to explain his preoccupation with the elementary function of the senses and the second enables us to understand how the mere fact of writing becomes a moral act in its own right. Thoreau's insistence on the realm of the senses seems like an act of putting together again what Emerson had taken apart in the famous passage in *The American Scholar*: "The state of society is one in which the members have suffered amputation from the trunk, and strut about like so many walking monsters, a good finger, a neck, a stomach, an elbow, but never a man."[6]

Thoreau's views of society were not very different from Emerson's, but by claiming the basic wholeness of the human body, he went further than merely denouncing the alienating effect that society had on

[6] Emerson, *Works* 2: 83.

the individual. He was, in fact, denying Emerson's basic assumptions about man's status as a broken giant. Using the body as an allegory, Thoreau emphasized the opposite: man—once he managed to use his senses rightly—was a giant, nothing less. God-like he descends daily as in "The Bean Field": "A long war, not with cranes, but with weeds, those Trojans who had sun and rain and dews on their side. Daily the beans saw me come to their rescue armed with a hoe, and thin the ranks of their enemies, filling up the trenches with weedy dead. Many a lusty crest-waving Hector that towered a whole foot above his crowding comrades fell before my weapon and rolled in the dust" (*Walden*, p. 108).

Thoreau turns the commonplace into a mythical scene, and as we shall see, his allegorical assembling of human faculties, starting with the physical body, served above all the purpose of aestheticizing the commonplace. If Emerson reserved the mystical experience for the rare occasion and liked to keep it in the background, a background against which he could unfold his philosophy of experience in his essays, Thoreau tried to reverse and radicalize this Emersonian position. He did not want the philosophy but the experience. Where Emerson would claim that "every natural fact is a symbol of some spiritual fact," Thoreau would have insisted that every natural fact *is* a spiritual fact. In order to find a starting point for such a view of life, Thoreau had to emphasize the self—as did Emerson—but he also had to identify the self with the body. It is quite revealing in this context to reconsider James Russell Lowell's scathing remarks about Thoreau in his essay of 1865, especially if we bear in mind the praise he had lavished upon Emerson in what has to be read as a kind of companion piece, namely "Emerson the Lecturer." Apart from accusing Thoreau of having gathered his "strawberries" from Emerson's garden, Lowell's main complaint addresses itself to an intolerable self-indulgence on Thoreau's part: "He seems to me to have been a man with so high a conceit of himself that he accepted without questioning, and insisted on our accepting, his defects and weakness of character as virtues and powers peculiar to himself. . . . He had no faculty of generalization from outside of himself, or at least no experience which would supply the material of such, and he makes his own whim the law, his own range the horizon of the universe."[7]

There is, of course, a kind of truth in the criticism that Lowell could not appreciate. The solipsism that he finds fault with is the very virtue of Thoreau's work. Thoreau himself in "Life without Principle" used

[7] James Russell Lowell, *Literary Essays* (Cambridge, Mass., 1899), 1: 369.

an argument that, for its technological aspect, complements Lowell's complaint in a succinct manner: "Commonly, if men want anything of me, it is only to know how many acres I make of their land—since I am a surveyor—or, at most, what trivial news I have burdened myself with. They never will go to law for my meat; they prefer the shell."[8]

The surveyor's complaint, in this statement of somewhat mixed metaphors, is that people take the extensions of the body and the use they can make of them more seriously than the body—as a principle—itself. They fail to see that the work of the surveyor is but a technologically extended activity of the human body itself. Thoreau, when writing in his journal about sense experience, hardly ever leaves the observation stand alone; he frequently totalizes the minute: "I hear the nighthawk squeak and a whip-poor-will sing. I hear the tremulous squealing scream of a screach owl in the Holden Woods, sounding somewhat like the neighing of a horse, not like the snipe. . . . As I go home by Haydon's I smell the burning meadow. I love the scent. It is my pipe. I smoke the earth."[9]

In the system of Thoreau's relationship to nature, sentences like the last one can usually be reversed. Whether the senses consume or whether they are being consumed, absorbed, makes no difference where absolute convergence is the goal. The senses are like open doors: the body and the world's body become one. It is the world, which Thoreau tries to preserve, that we generally ascribe to a childlike state where the distinction between the body and the outside world has not yet been established, a time we might say in order to avoid psychological terminology, when the world was still in the making: "Remember thy Creator in the days of thy youth; i.e. lay up a sort of natural influences. Sing while you may, before the evil days come. He that hath ears, let him hear. See, hear, smell, taste, etc., while these senses are fresh and pure" (Thoreau, *Journal*, p. 776).

The whole point is, of course, that the senses are always "too late," once we become aware of them they already have meaning. They have become attached; they are, to use Thoreau's own phrase, "made" for something: "To ears that are expanded what a harp this world is! The occupied ear thinks that beyond the cricket no sound can be heard, but there is an immortal melody that may be heard morning, noon, night, by ears that can attend, and from time to time this man or that hears it, having ears that were made for music" (Thoreau, *Journal*, p. 227).

[8] Thoreau, *Reform*, p. 155.

[9] Thoreau, *Journal*, p. 776. Hereafter cited in text as Thoreau, *Journal*.

If then the moment of creation can only be reenacted, the whole performance of writing becomes such a reenactment. Nature and myth are reconciled through the work of imagination, the basis of this process being the idea that they have the same origin: "I do not know where to find in any literature, whether ancient or modern, any adequate account of that Nature with which I am acquainted. Mythology comes nearest to any of it" (Thoreau, *Journal*, p. 182).

Emerson would write philosophically *about* nature, while Thoreau practiced to *read* nature again and record his readings. He was, in this sense, consciously withdrawing from "aboutness" and his quest for the concrete must strike the contemporary reader as uncannily modern—and in terms of literary theory it undoubtedly is. At the same time, however, Thoreau was not simply radicalizing the position of Emerson with a view to future development. To the extent that Emerson's own position was very much the result of a return to Puritan origins, we must acknowledge that in exactly this sense Thoreau also went further than Emerson. If we treat the brief era of transcendentalism as the kind of *epoché* where a tradition is being redefined with a view to both the past and the future, then quite clearly Thoreau's journal recaptures a large segment of the past—with a view to the future. The subtle distinction between a view of the past and the recapturing of it lies in the effort to regain, for the sake of transformation, the *material* of the past, rather than dealing with it as an *idea*. Thoreau's journals constitute the genuine effort to gather once more the protean qualities of man's relation to nature that was part of the Puritan tradition. Perhaps it means to overemphasize a viable case, but Thoreau in his journals often seems to be a kind of secularized Jonathan Edwards. Thoreau's major step towards secularization was that he did not simply "read" nature as a replacement for scripture but treated any act of such reading as an allegorizing of the self: "How plainly we are part of nature! For we live like the animals around us!" (Thoreau, *Journal*, p. 1015).

Puritan sensationalism had established a system of typological exegesis between the individual and nature; Thoreau's aesthetic individualism broke down these barriers—and paid the price of a redemption that could only be achieved through the work of allegory. The allegorized self must at once be both abstract, which means anonymous, and concrete. Thoreau observed this fact to the letter: "The ways by which men express themselves are infinite—the literary through his writings, and often they do not mind with what air they walk the streets, being sufficiently reported otherwise. But some express themselves chiefly by their gait and carriage, with swelling breasts or elephantine roll and elevated brows, making themselves moving and adequate signs of themselves, having no other outlet" (Thoreau, *Journal*, p. 477).

In an early entry in his journal, Thoreau had declared that "man is the hydrostatic paradox, the counterpoise of the system" (*Journal*, p. 72). His journals as a whole are the effort to keep the paradox in motion and practice the art of adequate self-reference. The dualism between self-denial and self-indulgence is the logical consequence of working out the structure of the paradox in question. There is no theoretical framework to systematize this kind of dualism since it is essentially pretheoretical. As Thoreau observed in the same entry just quoted: "You have studied flowers and birds cheaply enough, but you must lay yourself out to buy him."

The fact that Thoreau's vision drew nourishment from the past as well as from the future turns his journal into an encyclopedia of transformation and change in tradition. It is the chronicle of a threshold in tradition that, when seen in combination with Emerson's essays, clearly demonstrates that the transcendentalist movement took a conscious step backwards in order to move forward.

The Fact of Writing

> Write often, write upon a thousand themes, rather than long at a time, not trying to turn too many feeble somersets in the air—and so come down upon your head at last. Antaeus-like, be not too long absent from the ground.
>
> —THOREAU, JOURNAL

If we want to get a glimpse of the sacred that lies within the profane when discussing Thoreau, we have only to take a closer look at how and what he wrote about the fact of writing itself. "Be it life or death, we crave only reality," he wrote in *Walden*, and the only way to obtain reality is to become a witness. The witness is the third party if we want to use the metaphor of the court and it seems like an adequate one, for Thoreau as a writer ("facts flowering into truth") wrote for a kind of judgment day, the judgment day of man defining *his* place in the world.

> My work is writing, and I do not hesitate, though I know that no subject is too trivial for me, tried by ordinary standards; for, ye fools, the theme is nothing, the life is everything. All that interests the reader is the depth and intensity of the life excited. We touch

> our subject but by a point which has no breadth, but the pyramid of our experience or our interest in it, rests on us by a broader or narrower base. That is, man is all in all, Nature nothing, but as she draws him out and reflects him. Give me simple, cheap and homely themes. (Thoreau, *Journal*, p. 1082)

The simple and the heroic in Thoreau's vision were of course inseparable. In fact, the act of writing was a heroic achievement in its own right. The "heroism" of everyday life, to borrow the well-known phrase from Baudelaire, was Thoreau's business, and he went about it with an almost fanatical relentlessness. Emerson in *The American Scholar* had demanded that more attention should be paid to the matters of everyday life. Thoreau did just that, and in the process he developed his own theory of writing. The terms he most frequently applies when describing the act of writing are *duty, work, business,* and *obedience*. He felt that the good writer had to cultivate a kind of passivity in order not to impose his own imagination onto his subject: "It is in vain to write on chosen themes. . . . The cold resolve gives birth to, begets nothing. The theme that seeks me, not I it. . . . Obey, report" (*Journal*, p. 337). Thoreau's theory of writing implied that through the right kind of passive obedience to the given themes and impressions, the sentences themselves would preserve a kind of auratic concreteness. By writing *as part* of nature the writer would produce sentences that would be like nature. "A writer, a man writing, is the scribe of all nature; he is the corn and the grass and the atmosphere writing" (*Journal*, p. 254).

It is not at all a contradiction that Thoreau wanted his sentences to be at the same time pithy and suggestive. The concrete, by being finite, *has* to suggest. In his criticism of authors like De Quincey, Thoreau deplores a lack of restraints: "They say all they mean. Their sentences are not concentrated and nutty" (*Journal*, p. 249).

The task of the writer, according to Thoreau, was to combine restraint and suggestiveness, which, in terms of mimesis, meant to capture the infinite within the single instance.

> Sentences which suggest far more than they say, which have an atmosphere about them, which do not merely report an old, but make a new, impression; sentences which suggest as many things and are as durable as a Roman aqueduct; to frame these, that is the *art* of writing. Sentences which are expensive, toward which so many volumes, so much life went; which lie like boulders on the page up and down or across; which contain the seed of other

> sentences, not mere repetition but creation. (Thoreau, *Journal*, p. 249)

The ideas of creation and testimony remind us of religious practices like the conversion testimonial and if in many respects Thoreau's theory of writing sounds modern where the aspects of impersonality are concerned, then this only shows that one of the dominant themes of American literature has been the *morality* involved in the fact of writing. Far from being tied to a specific literary era, the quest for the *mot juste* has been a vital part of the American literary tradition. It has always involved the reconciliation of the subjective with the objective, and we have to acknowledge the Puritan legacy if we want to understand why the problems of reconciliation and redemption have, in the American tradition, always carried with them the overtones of morality and ethics. A dialectical twist is added to the problem if we realize that in order to achieve the right kind of morality that allowed the writer to write at all he had in the end assumed a position outside of the established sense of morality. Only by being extremely subjective could the act of writing approximate the desired objectivity and concreteness: "We are receiving our portion of the infinite. The art of life! Was there ever anything memorable written upon it. By what discipline to secure the most life, with what care to watch our thoughts. To observe what transpires, not in the street, but in the mind and heart of me!" (Thoreau, *Journal*, p. 261).

Such entries in Thoreau's journals have frequently provoked the criticism of absolute solipsism. The truth, however, is that Thoreau's subjectivity served as a medium to express the objectivity that lies at the core of the very *possibility* of observation. Hence Thoreau's frequent reference to the aspect of time in writing: "Improve every opportunity to express yourself in writing, as if it were your last" (*Journal*, p. 309).

The allegorist is haunted by the idea of loss, hence his preoccupation with the destructive force of time. In longer entries of the year 1852, Thoreau expounds the theme of the writer's lack of time.

> If thou art a writer, write as if thy time were short, for it is indeed short at the longest.
>
> Improve each occasion when thy soul is reached. Drain the cup of inspiration to its last dregs. Fear no intemperance in that, for the years will come when otherwise thou will regret opportunities unimproved. The spring will not last forever. These fertile and expanding seasons of thy life, when the rain reaches thy root, when thy vigor shoots, when thy flower is budding, shall be fewer

> and farther between. Again I say, Remember thy Creator in the day of thy youth!" (Thoreau, *Journal*, p. 329)

The allegorical imagination constantly rebuilds the ruin that stands as a memento of the fact that man can endure, but not prevail.

Keeping a journal in the manner of Thoreau means to occupy two positions at the same time. On the one hand, the author becomes extremely intimate with the world he describes; on the other hand he is constantly creating a distance. The second aspect of writing a journal must not be underestimated. Like an incessant talker, the keeper of the journal asserts himself and in the very act of doing so implies a unified "other," which is, of course, an imagined one. The act of keeping a journal, then, implies a certain amount of violent ordering and interference. At the same time, however, it lends a formal identity to he who interferes. The interference is the positive acting out of an imagination at work. The relentless pursuit of reality, as we find it exemplified in Thoreau's journals, is the aesthetic answer to nature's diffidence, which is experienced as a kind of threat.

It is easy to see how in this sense the keeping of a journal transforms itself into a moral duty. It becomes a virtue that the writer has taken to fulfill, like the poet who speaks for others. The keeper of the journal is exactly what the word means: he keeps a record, which others, for all the reasons Thoreau mentions in "Life without Principle," will not do. So the keeper of a journal turns himself into someone who performs the task for them. Needless to say that such self-appointed guardians of the truth are not usually met with great approval since they are constant reminders of other people's omissions. It equally goes without saying that whoever appoints himself as representing the endangered principle must be possessed by a certain sense of the grandiose. Thoreau was not known to his contemporaries for his sense of decorum. But the important fact to keep in mind is that keeping a journal in the way of Thoreau does *in fact* become a discourse on language just in the way that separate notes turn into music. In the world of Thoreau's journal the realms of politics, of nature, of society, and of the self become intimately related because they are recorded in language, the most distinctive feature of our ability to make sense. Thoreau's journals constitute, by repetition, the fundamental philosophical act of creating ideas by speaking about what I see. Keeping a record, therefore, is not a solipsistic activity, but an act of trust. It presupposes that humankind alone will remember how truth can be attained, by relying on language as the closest possible approximation to the fact.

CHAPTER 5

Henry Adams

Pessimism itself, black as it might be painted, had been content to turn the universe of contradictions into the human thought as one Will, and treat it as representation.

—HENRY ADAMS

Nothing "between" things can connect them, for "between" is just that third thing, "between," and would need itself to be connected to the first and second things by two still finer betweens, and so on *ad infinitum.*

—WILLIAM JAMES

Pioneers are normally the first to be criticized, their achievements being taken for granted while their shortcomings are held against them. Emerson had made an intellectual clearing, but the next generation wanted more: hard facts and the knowledge about the laws, which would make the space which Emerson had created inhabitable. In the end, of course, even a stubborn mind like Henry Adams's would succumb to the rule of paradox and contradiction, would in fact cultivate it and turn the essence of paradox, namely self-reference, into the ultimate form of artistic expression. Knowing this, we immediately realize that the criticism directed against the pioneer often tells us more about the critic than about the subject itself. This is certainly true if we look at the letter which Henry Adams wrote to Oliver Wendell Holmes on the occasion of the appearance of Holmes's book *Ralph Waldo Emerson* in 1885. "After studying the scope of any mind," he writes, "I want as well to study its limitations. . . . Emerson's limitations seemed to me very curious and interesting. . . . In obtaining extreme sublimation or tenuity of intelligence, I infer that sensuousness must be omitted. If Mr. Emerson was in some respects more than human, he paid for it by being in other respects proportionally less."[1]

There is, of course, an ironic and a tragic side to this comment. Written only several months before his wife's suicide, it raises the question to what extent Adams's own pose of being, in some respects an outsider and an observant bystander where ordinary life was concerned, a pose we find so carefully explained to us in *The Education*, is the direct result of an event in his life which unexpectedly destroyed his hopes for happiness. If we do not see Henry Adams's role as the distant observer in *The Education* as a reaction against the overwhelm-

[1] Henry Adams, *The Letters of Henry Adams*, ed. J. C. Levenson et al. (Cambridge, Mass., 1982) 2: 566.

ing sorrow over his wife's death, we must take his assertions seriously that he had been a born observer of the game of life rather than a player, as he points out at the beginning of *The Education*. If this is the case, and there is much evidence to support it, the irony of his criticism lies in the fact that it is exactly this role of the outsider which he shared with Emerson. In this case, the mere fact that as early as 1885 Emerson could be described in such terms as those of Adams's shows how soon Emerson had become cast in a certain image—and it tells us something about the quality of Adams's own desires which he would express and partly disguise in *The Education* and in *Mont-Saint-Michel and Chartres*.

The allegorist, though, disguises for the sake of discovery, hence his careful and often pedantic preoccupation with the process and method of his writing. The fact that the novels *Esther* and especially *Democracy* have so frequently provoked disparaging remarks from literary critics only shows that such criticism never fully realized that the legitimate mode of the nineteenth-century allegorical novel was a narrative construction of loosely linked images, each standing in a semi-autonomous relation to a series of other, equally self-contained passages centered around their own intellectual focus. The intellectual construct, in other words, does not aspire to mimesis. If we want to read a novel like *Democracy* correctly, we have to accept it as an appeal to the intellect and must avoid any kind of reading which keeps searching for epic depth. Once seen in this light, the individual image gains, as an emblem, what it cannot claim as part of a narrative context.

The final sentence in *Democracy*, preceding the postscript titled "Conclusion," therefore, shows the full extent of Adams's disenchantment with the present and his profound longing for individuation within and against the burden of history: " 'I want to go to Egypt' said Madeleine still smiling faintly. 'Democracy has shaken my nerves to pieces. Oh, what rest it would be to live in the Great Pyramid and look out for ever at the polar star.' "[2]

The Great Pyramid and the polar star: the image is one of becoming oneself again in that archetypal act of looking out at the unattainable, protected by the stones of history against the distractions and evils of the present. The cost of achieving such individuation lies in the acceptance of isolation. Also, history, as represented in the image of the Great Pyramid, is always the frozen history of the past embodied in

[2] Henry Adams, *Democracy* (New York, 1983), p. 182.

the static monument: the *ergon* of Herodotus. The full dimension of this legacy could hardly have been lost to Henry Adams the historian.

In the eye of the nineteenth-century allegorist, meaning could only be had by setting himself apart at a *significant distance*. Thus the allegorist turns narrative movement into a rite of passage, the existential overtones of which can hardly be missed. The individual has to leave his natural place in time and social space in order to obtain a sense of meaning about which he can talk only in the indirect voice. The allegorical imagination dissects, shunning away from direct participation in the ongoing historical and social process. There is a fine line which separates the realism of the nineteenth century from its allegorical counterpart. The realist narrative, to put it somewhat crudely, pretends to understand its subject matter, whereas the allegorical imagination makes claims on the past in order to show up the incomprehensible chaos of history in the making, always wondering about some real meaning hidden underneath the process of reality's constant changes. The realist, in the end, will admit that his description of the world uses as a base some kind of abstract explanatory model or logic. To the allegorist any such given model would turn into just another enigma. The energy which keeps the allegorical imagination at work is a fundamental fear of closure, or of anything ever becoming finite.

Underlying the restlessness which the allegorist's mind so frequently displays is a knowledge which cannot come to rest, the knowledge that the absolute truth cannot be had but that the search for it must continue. As a result the observer-allegorist always tells us two tales at the same time. One is about the events which he describes and the other is about his own position in relation to the act of telling the tale. The allegorical imagination, of which Henry Adams is such an outstanding example, acts out the classical double bind and turns it into a rule of life. What the psychologist would describe as the pathogenic exception becomes an accepted attitude. It is therefore not surprising that whenever we look for a major complaint about Henry Adams's private life, in his letters or in *The Education*, the great stoic who remains silent about the extreme and traumatic experiences of his existence never ceases to complain about the presence of or even about the mere danger of boredom. The quality of such boredom remains quite abstract, as it must, because it describes literally nothing. Once more we can turn to *Democracy* and use the full authority of the narrative's opening as an example of the state of mind which, attributed to Mrs. Lightfoot Lee, can be easily identified as Henry Adams's own intellectual disposition. The reason why Mrs. Lightfoot Lee goes to Washington is described in the following manner:

> It was only to her closest intimates that she honestly acknowledged herself to be tortured by *ennui.* Since her husband's death, five years before, she had lost her taste for New York society; she had felt no interest in the price of stocks, and very little in the men who dealt in them; she had become serious. What was it all worth, this wilderness of men and women as monotonous as the brown stone houses they lived in? In her despair she had resorted to desperate measures. She had read philosophy in the original German, and the more she read, the more she was disheartened that so much culture should lead to nothing—nothing. (*Democracy*, p. 3)

The reader will probably recognize early in this passage that the emphasis is on *ennui,* and that the death of the husband serves as a rationalization. Mrs. Lightfoot Lee is not fighting against the sorrow or loss or against loneliness. Grief is not her problem but that strange mixture of being, at the same time, "serious and suffering from *ennui.*" The seriousness, as we shall see, is soon revealed as an attachment to something quite different from the preoccupation with the so-called serious social or simply human problems. In fact, this particular kind of seriousness implies a distance from socially relevant issues which borders on cynicism.

> She plunged into philanthropy, visited prisons, inspected hospitals, read the literature of pauperism and crime, saturated herself with the statistics of vice until her mind had nearly lost sight of virtues. At last it rose in rebellion against her, and she came to the limit of her strength. This path too led nowhere. She declared that she had lost the sense of duty, and that, so far as concerned her, all the paupers and criminals in New York might henceforward rise in their majesty and manage every railway on the continent. Why should she care? What was the city to her? She could find nothing in it that seemed to demand salvation. What gave peculiar sanctity to numbers? Why were a million people who all resembled each other, any way more interesting than one person? What aspiration could she help to put into the mind of this great million-armed monster that would make it worth her love or respect? (*Democracy*, pp. 3–4)

The cadence of reasoning, when we follow it closely, moves in clear steps from a seemingly reasonable frustration about the single individual's helplessness vis-à-vis the insurmountable obstacles standing in the way of significant action to a kind of self-appreciation which at first glance seems lofty and self-absorbed. But the movement away from the other towards one's own self is not a process of pure indulgence nor the beginning of an intricate process of unfolding the dimensions of the individualized self. The process of self-discovery comes to a quick end in the realization that there is a given constant which propels the self-observant mind away from its center. "Was she not herself devoured by ambition, and was she not now eating her heart out because she could find no one object worth a sacrifice?"(*Democracy*, p. 4). The desire is to sacrifice—and the dominant theme of frustration is the inability to find a cause, or an object worthy of sacrifice. If we substitute the idea of sacrifice for that of self-abandonment we recognize that we are dealing with that strange ritual of self and self-reflection which can only find an artificial equilibrium in the guise of proud loneliness.

The sense of unfulfillment comes to its logical conclusion in the previously quoted image of the Great Pyramid. We cannot omit the fact, of course, that Henry Adams gave his novel the subtitle "An American Novel," and rather than seeing this as an encouragement to read the novel as a thinly disguised account of the actual Washington which Henry Adams observed and wrote about, we shall claim this subtitle as an indication that the epic quality of the narrative lies in the epic American quest for fulfillment—bound to the unhappy consciousness that a genuine synthesis of self and self-sacrifice will never happen. Self-sacrifice, then, is an integral part of self-realization; it is the essential part of the bipolar disposition of the historically conscious mind in search of an unmediated sense of historical unity.

The reader of *The Education* finds himself confronted with this kind of bipolarity at the very beginning of the book. Before we turn to a close reading of that particular beginning, we should acknowledge the fact that even if we make the concession that *The Education* was written at the end of Henry Adams's career, the similarity of the figural schemes between the two narratives, *Democracy* and *The Education*, lends a timelessness to Henry Adams's writing which stands above the individual occurrence in his life. Henry Adams's pose of the aloof observer or, rather, as the observant consciousness, had its origin in the larger scheme of American history which transcended the limitations of his career as an individual. It is with this profound insight into the subjective/objective mode of being that Henry Adams sets out to present, in *The Education*, his life as allegory. Architecture serves as the key metaphor of sedimented history and Adams exploits this metaphor to its full extent in order to juxtapose it with the beginning of a young life which can only become itself under such a burden of history through a series of losses. The dominant theme at the beginning of *The Education* is the fated interplay between the limitless history which has passed and the fragility of a new beginning. The structure of this interplay is set: history comes first: "Under the shadow of Boston State House, turning its back on the house of John Hancock, the little passage called Hancock Avenue runs, or ran from Beacon Street, skirting the State House grounds, to Mount Vernon Street, on the summit of Beacon Hill; and there, in the third house below Mount Vernon Place, February 16, 1838, a child was born, and christened later by his uncle, the minister of the First Church after the tenets of Boston Unitarianism, as Henry Brooks Adams."[3]

This is as impersonal a beginning as one could possibly imagine, and exactly of this tone it becomes archetypal and even carries certain Biblical associations with it, which are raised directly to the surface: "Had he been born in Jerusalem under the shadow of the Temple and circumcised in the Synagogue by his uncle the high priest, under the name of Israel Cohen, he would scarcely have been more distinctly branded, and not much more heavily handicapped in the races of the coming century, in running for such stakes as the century was to offer" (Adams, *Education*, p. 3).

The typological connection made here between the world of Boston and the whole tradition of American millenialism and its ideas of manifest destiny is obviously intended, though not without a certain irony, given the fact of Henry Adams's well-known anti-Semitism. Still, history had to be stretched beyond even the far-reaching extension of the Adams family such as they were. A prodigal child was born, there is no doubt, and in all seriousness the challenge of such prodigality had to be met. And in the fashion which becomes the essential structure of *The Education,* Henry Adams goes on to construe how such a challenge could be met at all in the shape of a paradox. On the one hand he acknowledges the burden of history and its appeal to a serious awareness of it: "Probably no child born in the year held better cards than he. Whether life was an honest game of chances, or whether the cards were marked and forced, he could not refuse to play his excellent hand. He could never make the usual plea of irresponsibility" (Adams, *Education*, p. 4).

Not only do the metaphors of game and cards irritate the reader who expects a moral treatment of life's great task under the shadow of such a portentious beginning. He will also be taken by surprise when he contemplates the conclusion drawn from the negation of ir-

[3] Adams, *Education*, p. 3. Hereafter cited in text as Adams, *Education.*

responsibility: "As it happened, he never got to the point of playing the game at all; he lost himself in the study of it, watching the errors of the players; but this is the only interest in the story, which otherwise has no moral and little incident" (Adams, *Education*, p. 4).

Thus a stance is established which stands out against all contradiction, hyperbolic figures of speech and love for paradox: the sense of the education in question lies not in participation and action but in observation. At the same time, though, we are promised the kind of observation which knows the rules of the game, because how otherwise could the observer watch "the errors" of those who are actively involved in playing the game of life? Only he who knows the rules can identify the mistakes. Once again the reader is prepared for a particular kind of narrative, namely one which will teach him about a given time span seen through the eyes of an omniscient observer. But once again his immediate hopes are disappointed because Adams changes the tone, which is set out at the beginning, for a third time by returning to the child in the most concrete terms of sensual perception. This time we are not dealing with the archetype but with a tangible array of first impressions, those of color and taste, of physical discomfort and sound. But what would have been a commonplace about education for the average child is quickly turned into an event rich in consequences.

> He was not good in a fight, and his nerves were more delicate than boys' nerves ought to be. He exaggerated these weaknesses as he grew older. The habit of doubt, of distrusting his own judgement and of totally rejecting the judgement of the world; the tendency to regard every question as open; the hesitation to act except as a choice of evils; the shirking of responsibility; the love of line, form, quality; the horror of *ennui*; the passion for companionship and the antipathy to society—all these are well-known qualities of New England character, in no way peculiar to individuals but in this instance they seemed to be stimulated by the fever, and Henry Adams could never make up his mind whether on the whole, the change of character was morbid or healthy, good or bad for his purpose. His brothers were the type; he was the variation. (Adams, *Education*, p. 6)

Setting himself apart is only the first step taken at the beginning of *The Education*. Henry Adams's real goal in the opening chapter of the book is to establish a narrative persona which not only describes the contradiction and contingencies of life but a narrative consciousness which *represents* a double consciousness. Adams, in his preface, gives us a glimpse at the problem which he intends to tackle by reminding his readers of the example of Jean Jacques Rousseau, whose "Confessions" next to Augustine's were most on his mind whenever he thought about his own project. He draws a significant distinction between himself and Rousseau concerning the purpose and above all the strategy of the confessional mode. Also, of course, by referring to Rousseau in the preface, symbolically dated 16 February 1907, the date of his sixty-ninth birthday, he at least in part aligns himself with the great tradition of the confessional narrative, breaking out of the formal limitations of the New England tradition: "As educator, Jean Jacques was, in one respect, easily first; he erected a monument of warning against the Ego. Since his time, and largely thanks to him, the Ego has steadily tended to efface itself, and, for the purposes of model, to become a manikin on which the toilet of education is draped in order to show the fit or misfit of the clothes. The object of study is the garment not the figure" (Adams, *Education*, p. xxx).

In his own case, Henry Adams warns his readers, things are somewhat more complex. The distinction between the manikin and the clothes as objects of demonstration will have to go. The didactic task of *The Education* can only be achieved by including the manikin: "The manikin therefore has the same value as any other geometrical figure of three or more dimensions, which is used for the study of relation. For that purpose it cannot be spared; it is the only measure of motion, of proportion, of human condition; it must have the air of reality; must be taken for real; must be treated as though it had life. Who knows? Possibly it had" (Adams, *Education*, p. xxx).

The life of the manikin, which we first encounter as the early life of the young boy in the narrative, is defined in terms of a conflict of the self due to a large variety of contradictions in the world which surrounded it. But Henry Adams in his effort to establish a representative double consciousness focuses his attention on the most general of all possible dichotomies, one provided by nature: winter standing for death and the fight against it; summer representing the forces of life. Nonidentity as a characteristic of life between extremes soon becomes a habit, creating among other things a kind of perverse inclination towards self-hatred: "The chief charm of New England was harshness of contrasts and extremes of sensibility—a cold that froze the blood, and a heat that boiled it—so that the pleasure of hating—oneself if no better victim offered itself—was not its rarest amusement. . . . The violence of contrast was real and made the strongest motive of education. The double exterior nature gave life its relative values" (Adams, *Education*, p. 7).

The results of the exposure to such dichotomous contrasts on the child were the acquisition of a double consciousness—"from earliest childhood the boy was accustomed to feel that, for him, life was double" (Adams, *Education,* p. 9)—at the same time, however, a narrative technique is established which represents a view of the world. Henry Adams, using the traditional structure of narrative time in autobiography, emphasizes the pervading quality of the double consciousness: "The bearing of the two seasons on the education of Henry Adams was no fancy; it was the most decisive force he ever knew; it ran through life, and made the division between its perplexing, warring, irreconcilable problems, irreducible opposites, with growing emphasis to the last year of study" (Adams, *Education,* p. 9).

Anticipating the end of the beginning means to introduce a constant, something stable amid the general display of examples, episodes, and sketched segments of life. *The Education,* as the reader must realize, will be a study in opposites, not conducted in the realm of abstract cultural analysis alone, but using as its material the specific experience of a life which has been lived. At no point, therefore, can we improve on the final "Possibility it had" of the introduction. Instead we must and do learn our first lesson of *The Education* in the course of its opening pages, namely that the distinction between the real and the artificial must be abandoned as we follow the course of the narrative, and that narrative technique and historical reality are reflections of each other. The dialectic relationship of the two cannot be overlooked: Henry Adams does not simply employ a narrative strategy to make a point, but instead of moving from the concrete to the abstract in the final chapters of the book, he leaves no doubt that the narrative strategy is the result of *his* insights into the nature of experience. In essence, Henry Adams's view of experience was that it could only be had at the cost of its ordering. He thought that not only were these costs enormous but that they were a necessity—and humankind's only protection against the utter and cruel playfulness of nature. The conscious ordering of life's contingency was in addition a moral task; civilized life depended on it, limited as it might turn out to be. The ultimate and unattainable goal was the "instinctive mastery of form" which Henry Adams had admired in his father—but the first lesson of *The Education* would be that what was appropriate and possible for the father had become impossible for the son. Social and historical change did not allow the instinctive ordering of life: unity could be experienced only through self-consciousness and through the alienation from untamed nature, which it necessarily implied.

In both chapters on Boston and on Harvard College, Henry Adams manages to combine the feelings of strong and unshakable belonging with sudden insights of isolation and unreality. The world inhabited by the boy as he grows older assumed structure and coherence and at the same time it became increasingly questionable. On the one hand there was certainty and a belief in the established social structure which was dominated, as Henry Adams points out, "by the professions." The sum of all this stability was as obvious as it would turn out to be deceptive: "Viewed from Mount Vernon Street, the problem of life was as simple as it was classic. Politics offered no difficulties, for there the moral law was a sure guide . . . ; doubts were waste of thought; nothing exacted solution. Boston had solved the universe; or had offered and realized the best solution yet tried. The problem was worked out" (Adams, *Education*, p. 33).

What exactly was the nature of the problem, though? With hindsight Henry Adams gives the reader an advance warning, a contrast to the above self-certainty, but too general in its scope yet to be of specific explanatory value: "All experience since the creation of man, all divine revelation or human science, conspired to deceive and betray a twelve-year-old boy who took for granted that his ideas, which were alone respectable, would be alone respected" (Adams, *Education*, p. 48).

Any education, we can surmise at this point, is less an education for a special purpose than a process of undoing and dissolving previously held beliefs. The shock of loss and of control over reality struck the harder where beliefs had been held for certain and in high esteem. Doubt could overcome the boy as dramatically as his will to believe in the reality of values was strong: "in spite of the long-continued effort of a lifetime, he perpetually fell back into the heresy that if anything universal was unreal, it was himself and not the appearance" (Adams, *Education*, p. 63).

This is, of course, just another way of saying that the whole experience as represented in *The Education* claims to be universal—and the protagonist of the narrative becomes the Everyman of his time. By the time that Henry Adams has taken us from Berlin to Rome he has also shed the pretext of suffering simply from the shortcomings of a piecemeal education and he is ready to take on the general forces of history. If previously the question had been what a young man ought to learn in a practical sense, Rome sets Henry Adams free to occupy the role of the observer. Disposition becomes a habit: the young boy who felt himself to be an outsider has grown up to be a tourist. The image of the tourist is, of course, just a playful version of the serious observer, as we are soon to learn. The practical intention of the educational experience is finally resolved in an attitude of pure aestheticism. But even the extreme aestheticism was accompanied by a lesson. Rome, being "the worst spot on earth to teach a nineteenth-century youth what to do with a twentieth-century world" (Adams, *Education*, p. 90), taught a lesson about history which the practical Boston would necessarily miss. With his eyes on Boston, Henry Adams carefully formulated the essence of the lesson in the manner of an understatement: "In theory one might say, with some show of proof, that a pure scientific education was alone correct; yet many of his friends who took it, found reason to complain that it was anything but a pure scientific world in which they lived" (Adams, *Education*, p. 88).

The same idea dramatically structures the heart of the chapter devoted to Rome, where the image of Rome as "a gospel of anarchy" is used to exploit thoroughly the idea of the chaos of history.

> To a young Bostonian, fresh from Germany, Rome seemed a pure emotion, quite free from economic or actual values, and he could not in reason or common sense foresee that it was mechanically piling up conundrum after conundrum in his educational path, which seemed unconnected but that he had got to connect; that seemed insoluble but had got to be somehow solved. Rome was not a beetle to be dissected and dropped; not a bad French novel to be read in a railway train and thrown out of the window after other bad French novels, the morals of which could never approach the immorality of Roman history. Rome was actual; it was England; it was going to be America. Rome could not be fitted into an orderly, middle class, Bostonian, systematic scheme of evolution. No law of progress applied to it. Not even time-sequences—the last refuge of helpless historians—had value for it. (Adams, *Education*, pp. 90–91)

In Rome history reveals itself as nature, mysterious and, in the end, defying analysis. The transformation of history into nature characterizes the essential paradox of aesthetic individualism and practical intellect. It provokes both the artistic and the scientific dimension of Adams's thought, which we find interwoven in his speculative essays on history. In its many variations the theme would always be the same, namely that only by will and imagination could humankind impose some kind of order onto an anarchic universe. The sense-making effort of *The Education* is to lay bare the structure of the imagination at work. If Rome stands for the transformation of history into nature, it is in the chapter titled "Chaos" that nature and death are shown as the epitome of this transformation. History as nature in Rome represented—still—the possibility of certain lessons to be learned as either a tourist or as a historian. Hearing about his sister's accident in Lucca, with tetanus having already set in, Henry Adams realized that "the last lesson—the sum and term of education—began then" (*Education*, p. 287). Under the impression of his sister's death and nature's oblivious cruelty, society becomes entirely unreal.

> Society became fantastic, a vision of pantomime with a mechanical motion; and its so-called thought merged in the mere sense of life, and pleasure in the same. The usual anodynes of social medicine became evident artifice. Stoicism was perhaps the best; religion was the most human; but the idea that any personal deity could find pleasure or profit in torturing a poor woman, by accident, with a fiendish cruelty known to man only in perverted and insane temperaments, could not be held for a moment. For pure blasphemy, it made pure atheism a comfort. God might be, as the church said, a substance, but He could not be a Person. (Adams, *Education*, pp. 288–89)

Nature—"a chaos of anarchic and purposeless forces" (p. 289)—could only be redeemed in the realm of artifice. Man, confronting these forces, could find some kind of refuge only by creating his own artificial sense of order.

The writing of *The Education* in itself was such an act of creating an artificial universe—as any writing of an autobiography is. We know from *The Letters of Henry Adams* that the life of the person was rather different from the one which we find represented in the persona of *The Education*. The early letters which the young Henry Adams sent home from Berlin and Dresden show us an astute, ironical observer of the world in which he lived. There is hardly a trace of the preoccupation with failure and ignorance which becomes the dominant theme of *The Education*. In Rome Henry Adams went sightseeing, rode a horse into the Campagna and indulged in romantic descriptions of landscape and scenery in long letters to his brother Charles Francis Adams, Jr.: "Of all glorious things here I think a ride on the Campagna in the morning or the evening sun is the most beautiful. There one has Rome and Italy, the past and the present, all to oneself. There the old poetic mountains breathe inspiration around."[4]

The *Letters* are vivid comments on a typical *Bildungsreise*—the chapter "Rome" in the *Education* is part of a complex design meant to serve

[4] Adams, *Letters* 1: 144.

as an interpretation of a pessimism which addressed itself to the course and development of the world. Nothing less would do.

Three main sources fed Adams's aesthetic pessimism: the ambition to write, to recreate a world, was the primary source. The second was a will to understand an increasingly complex world, and the third was a counterpart to the second, namely an extreme tendency towards self-contemplation. It is of course the right mixture of all three components which makes the man of letters. Both the ambition to express his experience and an early, but not yet fully developed, inclination to become self-absorbed are clearly visible even in his early letters. Adams wrote letters home the way other people kept diaries. His diary, however, was open to immediate inspection. Within the sheer bulk of letters which the young Henry Adams sent home from Europe the reader will always detect an attempt to place himself, Henry Adams, to find for himself the defined point of observation. He obviously enjoyed being on the fringe of events, a participatory observer, whose stance would not change over the years. His will to understand was necessarily influenced by the gigantic leaps which science took in the nineteenth century and as early as his essay on Lyell's *Geology*, which was published in the *North American Review*, he had dealt with the problems posed by scientific generalizations. In *The Education* we encounter the classical polarity with which the man of letters constantly tries to come to terms: the desire, on the one hand, to fully understand, and the fear that the process of learning might come to an end. Fear and desire in this sense, of course, work towards the same goal in the end, that of rediscovery and reaccentuation. The symbolic place of the man of letters is always on the steps of Ara Coeli, brooding over the why and how of things. So, on the occasion of the Chicago Exhibition, Henry Adams repeated the experience:

> One sat down to ponder on the steps beneath Richard Hunt's dome almost as deeply as on the steps of Ara Coeli, and much to the same purpose. Here was a breach of continuity—a rupture in historical sequence! Was it real, or only apparent? One's personal universe hung on the answer, for, if the rupture was real and the new American world could take this sharp and conscious twist towards ideals, one's personal friends would come in, at last, as winners in the great American chariot-race for fame. (Adams, *Education*, pp. 340–41)

But the brooding did also include the opposite possibility, the end of idealism and the triumph of materialism, the end of a whole clan which had taken a complete set of values by which the world was run for granted and the rise of industrial capitalism setting free "energies" which demanded some kind of control. The polarities which Henry Adams is setting up are quite extreme, and they must be, because in the end it is the self-absorbed historian again, who moves into the foreground of the stage: "The historical mind can think only in historical processes, and probably this was the first time since historians existed, that any of them had set down helpless before mechanical sequence. Before a metaphysical or a theological or a political sequence, most historians had felt helpless, but the single clue to which they had hitherto trusted was the unity of natural force. Did he himself quite know what he meant? Certainly not!" (Adams, *Education*, pp. 342–43).

It is the "Certainly not" which keeps the quest for education going, and furthermore it is only within the limits of acquired ignorance that the conscious historian is allowed to set up symbols which try to help him to understand what he cannot comprehend otherwise. In this sense, Adams's statement about the way historians work is quite revealing with regard to his own narrative technique in *The Education*: "Historians undertake to arrange sequences—called stories, or histories—assuming in silence a relation of cause and effect" (Adams, *Education*, p. 382).

We can almost take this statement as a clue as to how we are supposed to read *The Education*, for the more the mind which organizes the narrative lapses into a silence where the problems of cause and effect are concerned, the more we are led into a narrative texture which combines story and history, the very abstract force—and the concrete examples of abstract forces: the dynamo and the virgin. Apart from this classical polarity which Adams sets up, there is also the much more impenetrable world of those new discoveries in microphysics which even the scientists could not adequately explain:

> Langley could not help him. Indeed, Langley seemed to be worried by the same trouble, for he constantly repeated that the new forces were anarchical, and especially that he was not responsible for the new rays, that were little short of parricidal in their wicked spirit towards science. His own rays, with which he had doubled the solar spectrum, were altogether harmless and beneficent; but Radium denied its God—or what was to Langley the same thing, denied the truths of his science. The force was wholly new. (Adams, *Education*, p. 381)

Facing in reality what had once "figured only as a fiction of thought," Adams, the self-proclaimed "conservative Christian anarchist," felt free to order reality according to his own laws of fiction *and* thought:

"Adams proclaimed that in the last synthesis, order and anarchy were one, but that the unity was chaos" (Adams, *Education*, p. 406).

The only way to establish a sense of understanding within a unity which was chaos was to create a context of symbols and work with them—to create, in other words, an autonomous world held together by the logic of its own structure. Again the scientist is used as an example to show what the literary intellectual in the role of the man of letters should do in order to achieve some sense of ordered experience: "After once admitting that a straight line was the shortest distance between two points, no serious mathematician cared to deny anything that suited his convenience, *and rejected no symbol*, unproved or unprovable, that helped him to accomplish work" (Adams, *Education*, p. 388; my emphasis).

It is in this context that Henry Adams reminds the reader that the task of the man of letters amidst all the confusion which he observes as either historian or as intellectual observer (the tourist) is to write. In a fascinating aside Adams explains in a microscopic version a theory of writing which sheds some significant light on his understanding of writing as an act of provisional ordering. Writing becomes a necessity, an almost existential act, where intentions seem to count little and the instinctive doing almost takes over.

> In such labyrinths, the staff is a force almost more necessary than the legs; the pen becomes a sort of blind-man's dog, to keep him from falling into the gutters. The pen works for itself, and acts like a hand, modelling the plastic material over and over again to the form that suits it best. The form is never arbitrary, but is a sort of growth like crystallization, as any artist knows too well; for often the pencil or pen runs into side-paths and shapelessness, loses its relations, stops or is bogged. Then it has to return to its trail, and recover, if it can, its line of force. (Adams, *Education*, p. 389)

The ordering of experience through the act of writing as described in this brief passage is not very different from the way the child's mind ordered the mysterious world by which it found itself surrounded at the beginning of *The Education*. The man of letters orders experience in a piecemeal fashion, always knowing that what the pen achieves at one point in time will last for only so long. Henry Adams not only acknowledged this fact of constant limitation but turned it into practice in the whole composition of *The Education*. The more he generalizes the more he breaks down his own theories and generalizations into sets of counterstatements. It is in the process of outlining theories of history that Henry Adams most emphatically stresses the importance of the image: "Images are not arguments, they rarely even lead to proof, but the mind craves them, and, of late more than ever, the keenest experimenters find twenty images better than one, especially if contradictory; since the human mind has already learned to deal in contradictions" (Adams, *Education*, p. 489).

Henry Adams, in a world of chaos, puts all his hopes on the mind's ability to work in contradictions, which also meant, of course, that for the mind nothing was really irreversible. The image which he chooses in order to demonstrate the mind's ability to work by and through self-reflection is that of a comet: "but the simplest figure, at first, is that of a perfect comet—say that of 1893—which drops from space, in a straight line, at the regular acceleration of speed, directly into the sun, and after wheeling sharply about it, in heat that ought to dissipate any known substance, turns back unharmed, in defiance of law by the path on which it came. The mind, by analogy, may figure as such a comet, the better because it also defies law" (Adams, *Education*, p. 489).

Self-reflection, or, as Adams would put it, self-contradiction, is the true path to self-knowledge, the rhetorical expression of self-contradiction being the metaphor—and, of course, the configuration of metaphors in the shape of allegory.

Mont-Saint-Michel and Chartres

> To feel the art of Mont-Saint-Michel and Chartres we have got to become pilgrims again. . . .
>
> —HENRY ADAMS

> There cannot be a true complementarity between architectural and historical critical discourses: they can converse with each other, but they cannot complete each other, because the two find themselves, inevitably, in competition.
>
> —MANFREDO TAFURI

Henry Adams did not believe in facts; he was concerned with meaning—and, of course, with the obvious paradox that he could not have the one without the other. He was an analogist, in the Emersonian sense; but the price he had to pay for a sensible analogy had risen since the midcentury. In a world of commodities, where everything seemed to cheapen, sense, as Henry Adams saw it, had become scarce.

By his way of solving it, he showed that he understood the inherent problem, buried at the heart of the paradox: the problem of self-reference. This fact alone bestows upon *Mont-Saint-Michel and Chartres* a literary rank which few works achieved in the era of American literary realism.

And in anticipation of issues which will be discussed a little later, one should add that Henry Adams also preferred truth to the limitations of proof. He therefore played, or rather *worked* with the idea of probability in order to create unifying images. Like Nietzsche he had come to realize that the only justification for the world's existence had to be an aesthetic one. Like Nietzsche he was profoundly troubled by his own findings, recognizing only too well the consequences of his solutions to the world's dilemma.

Much ink and hard labor have been spent to show how and where Henry Adams abused available facts. *Of course* he only knew about Lord Kelvin's work from hearsay, and he never really considered himself a medievalist proper. So when he referred to himself as "a mixture of Lord Kelvin and St. Thomas Aquinas," he was merely once again turning the horns of the old dilemma towards himself: one horn being the idea of a universal, law-abiding order, the other being the idea of free will. Looking at the advances of science and reducing it *metaphorically* to mathematical formulas, his ideas gravitated almost naturally towards the world of Thierry of Chartres. In the School of Chartres, architecture was treated as a cosmological metaphor, significant in its geometrical and arithmetic parts. But Adams also knew that the old analogies and metaphors could only be of limited value for his own time and that the sentimental evocation of earlier periods of history was of no use whatsoever. In fact, Adams radicalized the late nineteenth-century commonplace of aestheticism by emphasizing its opposite, the world of social processes. Ecclesiology was one thing, Maxwell's demon quite another, and the world of J. P. Morgan even yet another. Within such multiple universes even failure had to be relative and however hard Henry Adams tried to represent failure, playing out his fantasies of order and unified experience in the medium of self-reference, which he did in *Mont-Saint-Michel and Chartres*, the book became a success as a piece of tough imagination, sometimes almost impenetrable and always preferring the quirky association or the odd, unexpected line to the facile solution. Adams's niece, one should remember, traveled with a Kodak: odd and proleptically fanciful images were Adams's specialty. But then he was also part of a tradition. As Richard Poirier has pointed out: "That the New World offered architectural opportunities on a scale never equaled before or since scarcely needs repeating, any more than does the explanation that American writers have therefore been addicted to metaphors of 'building' and to theories about the proper housing for expanded states of consciousness."[5]

A reminder may be necessary, though, about the tradition and the logic of the architectural metaphor. Walter Benjamin made the following observation, which may help us to get our argument on the right track:

> Architecture has never been idle. Its history is more ancient than that of any other art, and its claim to being a living force has significance in every attempt to comprehend the relationship of the masses to art. Buildings are appropriated in a twofold manner: by use and by perception—or rather by touch and sight. Such appropriation cannot be understood in terms of the attentive concentration of a tourist before a famous building. On the tactile side there is no counterpart to contemplation on the optical side.[6]

Adams, of course, would not have the one without the other and we are therefore invited on what he refers to as a "pilgrimage" and what, for at least our next three arguments, we will simply call a narrative text. In a very fundamental way Henry Adams "sets the scene"—and understanding the scene is our greatest problem. The first obstacle we find ourselves confronted with is Henry Adams's love for posturing, his need for role playing. There is no need to go into the well-known biographical details which probably determined his particular fondness for the role of the virtually omnipotent observer; there is no necessity here for psychohistory. The individual desire for absolute control, which only the observer can hope to acquire through the negation of influence, is an interesting relic of a general dilemma which the historiographer has to face.

Thus we may say that the ambiguities of Herodotus, to whom we turn when we are looking for the origins for historiography, became the virtue of Henry Adams. The architectural metaphor (*ergon*) was transformed by Henry Adams into an image in the modern sense, a necessary, unifying concept: fiction becomes a must where historiography reaches its limits.[7] With a certain amount of playfulness, always reminding us of Thoreau's famous sentence in *Walden*, "I made the

[5] Richard Poirier, *A World Elsewhere* (London, 1978), p. vii.

[6] Walter Benjamin, "The Works of Art in the Age of Mechanical Reproduction," in Hannah Arendt, ed., *Illuminations* (New York, 1973), p. S.242.

[7] Compare G. Steinkopf, *Untersuchungen zur Geschichte des Ruhmes bei den Griechen* (Würzburg, 1957), pp. 73–76.

sun go up," Henry Adams was willing to push the issue of scientific laws to an extreme, where the understanding of history was concerned. Hence the scientific bias of *The Letter* which made even F. J. Turner wince when he gave his presidential address to the American Historical Association in 1910. Hence also his insistence on the role of imagination and feeling as legitimate parts of historical description. If the "rule of phase applied to history," the title of Adams's final essay on a scientific theory of history, results in a quasi-mathematical formula, imagination becomes a complementary force in its own right, the equivalent in the end to that "hyperspace of Thought" Henry Adams talks about when pointing out that "the true mathematician drew breath only in the hyperspace of Thought; he could exist only by assuming that all phases of material motion merged in the last conceivable phase of immaterial motion—pure mathematical thought."[8]

Between these two extremes—the law, applied to history, and the realm of pure thought, both extremes being vanishing points of *history as reality*—Adams put as a kind of constant the mind that remains a reflection of the human self from, as he put it, "the unknown depths of nature."

> The reflection or projection of the mind in nature was the earliest and will no doubt be the last motive of man's mind, whether as religion or as science, and only the attraction will vary according to the value which the mind assigns to the image of the thing that moves it; but the mere concentration of the image need not change the direction of movement any more than the concentration of converging paths into one single road need change the direction of travel or traffic.[9]

Two rather distinct figures of speech are constructed around what Henry Adams tries to tell us about the relationship of image and reality: one being that of the circle, describing the inherent continuity of the mind, caught in its own cage by being at once an organ of reflection and projection—the other being that of the straight line, the single road as a concentration of converging paths. Both figures are familiar topoi of the philosophy of history, cosmological self-sufficiency

[8] Henry Adams, *The Degradation of the Democratic Dogma*, ed. Brooks Adams (New York, 1949), p. 267. The affinity here to ideas of the School of Chartres are obvious as their differences in philosophical meaning are intriguing. Compare Thierry on the principle of creation: "Sed creatio numerorum rerum est creatio"; N. Harding, "The creation and creator of the world according to Thierry of Chartres and Clarembaldus of Arras," *Archives d'Histoire doctrinale et litteraire du moyen-age* 30 (1955).

[9] Adams, *The Degradation*, p. 289.

represented by a circular movement, to which nothing can or need be added as opposed to linear development translated into theories of evolution progressing in a variety of forms, harmoniously or in disruptive leaps, leading either to utopian bliss or ending in chaos and apocalyptic disorder.

Given the background of this rather crudely abbreviated topological tradition we are, perhaps, able to understand the bias which motivated Henry Adams's acceptance of the paradox—a bias, of course, which would eventually lead from acceptance to solution. Mythical man, living a life of circular repetition, had no need for history because the question of origin and telos did not exist, hence no need for historiography either: where nothing is in danger of being forgotten there is no reason to remember. Once the circle was broken, historiography moved into its legitimate place, indicating a sense of history, awkwardly at first, because things and events were undoubtedly there, but how did they make sense? Historical consciousness needed the normative-transcendental ideas and had to turn them into images in order to maintain the objectivity of the fact. Fiction and fact, or rather historiography and fiction are part and parcel of history, and the logic and narrative shape of both are determined by what we assume the latter to be. There is no way to avoid the assumption—a philosophical scandal of course, but the result also of intricate debates about theories of history and their philosophical standing—all of which we need not talk about because we are dealing here only with Henry Adams, whose scientific theory of history was, as he knew well enough, a bit more than just an assumption. It was primarily an allegorical figure of thought asking for its own destruction so that the idea of history might be saved.

This process of salvation, which is the essence of both books *Mont-Saint-Michel and Chartres* and *The Education of Henry Adams*, is structured by the effort of collecting empirical facts in order to prove the existence of the imagination. This way they *make* sense—and they do not if we assume that Henry Adams took the scientific theory of history seriously in a literal fashion instead of using it as a provocative metaphor. There is nothing puzzling then about his statement in *Mont-Saint-Michel and Chartres*: "For us poetry is history, and the facts are false" on the one hand and his intense concentration on facts, especially in the shape of architectural detail, in the same book on the other hand.[10] Both books—*Mont-Saint-Michel and Chartres* and *The Ed-*

[10] Henry Adams, *Mont-Saint-Michel and Chartres* (London, 1950), p. 89. Hereafter cited in text as Adams, *Mont-Saint-Michel.*

ucation of Henry Adams—try to reunify the phenomenon in itself with the idea which permeates its very structure as meaning.

The unification of event and meaning in terms of historiographical truth, a problem which Herodotus tried to solve by putting the burden on neither the facts nor on humankind, creating instead a tentative web of interconnected actions and events, thus in a way inventing tradition against his own preference for factual objectivity, became a working principle with Henry Adams. Having made the decision that there was no real difference in the end whether one subscribed to the epistemological position of Locke, Berkeley, or Hume, when he stated: "There are but two schools: one turns the world onto me; the other turns me onto the world and the result is the same," there was nothing left but the *process* of reunifying event and meaning.[11] The emphasis, here, is on the notion of *process*, because it generates the idea of artifice. The imperative of the artificial does more than cover the last two of the four levels of tension which R. P. Blackmur ascribes to *Mont-Saint-Michel*.[12] In addition to accounting for "the tension of Adams' plea for unity as vision in human terms," and "the tension of Adams' own spiritual autobiography," the imperative of the artificial was also Henry Adams's countermove against the inroads made by history as he witnessed it in its scientific and philosophical justification of his idea of individuality.

Tension as latent energy looking for an adequate form in order to avoid dissolution—this is, in brief, the formula on which Henry Adams put his hope for the individual—and the answer was art. Once more we ought to remember to what an extraordinary degree his imagination was inspired by sculpture.[13] Adams saw both architecture and sculpture as the arrested processes of an active imagination. The art of interpretation lies in releasing these energies: the interpretation works as discovery, as the kind of remaking for which only a chosen few are gifted. And in *Mont-Saint-Michel* Henry Adams tried nothing less than to recreate—in the form of an image—a universe.

It is easy to forget, once immersed in the book *Mont-Saint-Michel and Chartres*, that like many of Adams's brief flights from contemporary social and political life, this time, as on other occasions before, an overwhelming disgust with the general corruption around him had overcome him previous to his leave-taking. His geopolitical interests, his

[11] Henry Adams, in Brooks Adams, ed., *The Degradation of the Democratic Dogma* (New York, 1949), p. 251.

[12] R. P. Blackmur, *Henry Adams* (New York, 1980), p. 179.

[13] Compare Ernst Scheyer, *The Circle of Henry Adams: Art and Artists* (Detroit, 1970), pp. 212–49.

love for political intrigue, and his constant ruminations about the state of international financial affairs had always had a quixotic element about them. The observer of the political world could not disguise his feelings of helplessness. The more Henry Adams, in the years before he seriously began with the writing of *Mont-Saint-Michel*, pretended to be a kind of cynical, geopolitical chess player, the more he was, at the same time, looking for a historical period of relative unity in its social, cultural, and political aspects.[14] The fourth century of the Byzantine empire struck his imagination—it was obvious that he was looking for a model in the past to hold up against the present. The present he had come to regard with a marked mixture of revulsion and fear, the general theme of his swan song being that the end of civilization was imminent: "Then, at least we shall have the Passion, the Agony, the Bloody Sweat, and the Resurrection."[15]

Like many of his contemporaries, Adams was a worried man, but he added a personal flavor of wishful thinking to the general anxiety about the future. In *Mont-Saint-Michel*, Cassandra's voice changes from the doomsday tune to a more conciliatory one about the past. If the rationality of the present, which Adams identified with Wall Street, was hurrying towards its own destruction with the logic of capitalism in economics and finance, the realm of feeling and imagination had to serve as an alternative vision of how a civilization might work. If we look at the structure of *Mont-Saint-Michel*, we realize immediately that it answers his brother's letter about the meaning of unity in an unexpected way, unexpected at least to someone as economically oriented as Brooks Adams: "I admit I do not quite grasp what you mean by our civilization being a unity. I can't see it that way. If you mean there have always been trade centers and at trade centers one form of mind has been developed, I agree. If you mean there has been a regular sequence of growth in any one place, in any one direction, I fail to catch on."[16]

Henry Adams had been misleading his brother unintentionally, how unconsciously we do not know. His brother did not pick up the clues when Henry Adams began to talk with increasing insistence about "psychic energies." In fact, Brooks Adams must have missed much of

[14] Adams knew that history could not be reversed. The unity he had in mind had to be extrapolated from the most avant-garde elements of *present* history. These historical forces were general ones, hence his avoidance of the first personal pronoun in both *Education* and in *Mont-Saint-Michel.*

[15] Compare Ernest Samuels, *Henry Adams: The Major Phase* (Cambridge, Mass., 1964), p. 168.

[16] Compare Ernest Samuels, *Adams*, p. 181.

the meaning and personal history behind his brother's barely controlled hysteria. Henry Adams's ravings about corruption, decay, and universal death do indeed betray a profound personal need. The bipolarity between male and female principle which structures *Mont-Saint-Michel* and his belief in the more humane female principle, which surfaces in a succession of highly charged metaphors, are both indicative of a wounded psyche looking for some kind of relief, if not consolation, in conjuring up a world where transition and unity were not necessarily irreconcilable. So, where his brother Brooks was seriously looking for a law in history, Henry Adams's ambition was the recreation of a period, the representation of a historical process as a narrative text. He wanted to leave a legacy, an *ergon* all his own, a monumental image, which could serve as a mirror to a contemporary world which, as Henry Adams saw it, had lost out on the possibilities of capitalism and was already on its way towards an equally uninspiring domination by the trade unions. So both from a personal point of view and from his assessment of the contemporary political and social situation, Adams set out to create a text. The relevance, or pragmatic consequences of science, of knowledge, and of governing laws and rules were all subsumed under the impact and meaning of the narrative. As far as the difference between narrative and non-narrative knowledge were concerned, Adams immediately drew the conclusion from his movement towards the realm of narrative knowledge.

Insisting on the validity of process instead of searching for first principles does not only create a specific form of thought but changes the status of both, that of fiction and that of historical fact. It also, of course, produces a specific sense of history, one which critics like to call tragic, sometimes pessimistic. How true this is remains to be seen. The direct result of giving up any idea of first principles is a conception of truth which one might call interactional; it presupposes reality to be elusive in principle and fixed only by agreement. General theory and epistemology being both blind alleys, with sensible agreement now excluded, the only way out is the creation of shared images.

So there they are: the narrator-uncle in *Mont-Saint-Michel and Chartres*, and his companion, the niece with the Kodak, serving in many roles, most importantly the role of audience and that of emblematic youth, closer to mythical immediacy than the narrator, who represents old age and wisdom, as well as symbolizing the twentieth century with its atrophy and the loss of organic experience.[17] A time

[17] The image of the Kodak represents the dialectical interrelationship of both distance and vicinity qua contemplation.

span is defined, biographically at first, and then geographically and historically. The stress is on limitation, not on totality, historical time becomes a function of discourse, history itself is a potential sequel to be extrapolated from established symbols: "Some future summer, when they are older, and when I have left, like Omar, only the empty glass of my scholasticism for you to turn down, you can amuse yourself by going on with the story after the death of Saint Louis, Saint Thomas and William of Lorris, and after the failure of Beauvais" (Adams, *Mont-Saint-Michel*, p. 375).

These are the parting words of the uncle to his niece at the end of *Mont-Saint-Michel*: she will have to write a book of her own, as every coming generation must: "The pathetic interest of the drama deepens with every new expression, but at least you can learn from it that your parents in the nineteenth century were not to blame for losing the sense of unity in art."[18]

So stories must and will be told lest history should cease to exist: there is a shared causality behind the relationship of history and fiction. The relationship has always been a strained one, and in our case the truth is obvious, as Hayden White points out in "The Burden of History": "For we should recognize that *what constitutes the facts themselves* is the problem that the historian, like the artist, has tried to solve in the choice of the metaphor by which he orders his world, past, present, and future. We should ask only that the historian show some tact in the use of his governing metaphors that he neither overburden them with data nor fail to use them to their limit; that he respect the logic implicit in the mode of discourse he has decided upon."[19]

Henry Adams's root metaphor, as Stephen C. Pepper would have called it, was "unity." In exasperation with his brother, Brooks Adams had found himself forced to admit in a letter quoted previously that Henry was carrying the meaning of "unity" too far for his understanding. Henry Adams, of course, would not have written his *Mont-Saint-Michel* had he subscribed to either of the two reductivist ideas his brother had mentioned. His problem was to demonstrate the necessity of unity within diversity for the sake of meaning. He could not accept the solution of ideology or of fetishism: just as much as he accepted the possibility of choice (Byzantium had been his first option before he decided to concentrate on the Middle Ages), so he accepted the need for historical accuracy.

Unity, then, had to be deduced from the realm of cognitive method.

[18] Ibid.

[19] Hayden White, *Tropics of Discourse* (Baltimore, 1978), p. 47.

If we take a step backward from the actual point in time when Henry Adams began writing his *Mont-Saint-Michel* and take a look at the craft of historical writing in the nineteenth century, the qualitative leap which Henry Adams represents becomes obvious. The question of style with regards to a rendition of facts had become a commonplace within the historiographical debate with such highly literary figures like G. Bancroft, W. H. Prescott, and Henry Adams's "brother-in-history" Francis Parkman, who had spelled out the rules of the game.[20] The question of design had troubled each of these historians who were fully aware of their role as men of letters. It was Henry Adams who, just before he started his *Mont-Saint-Michel,* gave the old problem a new and unnerving twist. He justified the need for design and arrangement of historical material by pointing out what these means of expression could *not* do, namely to remain an ornamental and at the same time function as a cognitive device which worked as a cooperative force of cognition, together with self-evident facts, data, and the modes of historical interpretation.

If one wants to understand the profound gap between Henry Adams's view of the problem in question and the ideas of Bancroft, Parkman, and John Lothrop Motley, all one has to do is take a brief look at Henry Adams's text "The Tendency of History," which he sent to the American Historical Association in 1894 where it was read in place of the expected presidential address which Adams did not want to deliver. The letter, in modern parlance, announced a paradigm change by pointing out the inevitability of scientific norms to which the historian had to succumb and by hinting at the limits of scientific explanations. At his deceptive best, Henry Adams points at the pressures which the scientifically oriented historian would have to face when turning from the discovery of historical laws to their application and prognostic use. The end of his text baffled the audience then, but it seems rather revealing when studied from hindsight.

> Beyond a doubt, silence is best. In these remarks, which are only casual and offered in the paradoxical spirit of private conversation, I have not ventured to express any opinion of my own; or, if I have expressed it, pray consider it as withdrawn. The situation seems to call for no opinion, unless we have some scientific theory to offer; but to me it seems so interesting that, in taking leave of the association, I feel inclined to invite them, as individuals, to consider the matter in a spirit that will enable us, should the crisis

[20] Compare Samuels, *Adams*, and David Levin, *History as Romantic Art* (Stanford, 1959).

arise, to deal with it in a kindly temper and a full understanding of its serious dangers and responsibilities.[21]

Senses of Chartres

> Materialia immaterialibus, corporalia spiritualibus, humana divinis uniformiter concopulas, sacramentaliter reformas ad suum puriores principuum; his et huiusmodi benedictionibus visibiliter restauras, etiam praesentem in regnum coeleste mirabiliter transformas, ut . . . coelum et terram, unam republicam potenter et misericorditer efficias . . .
>
> —ABBOT SUGAR

> Nothing is sadder than the catastrophe of gothic art, religion and hope. One looks back on it all as a picture; a symbol of unity; an assertion of God and Man in a bolder, stronger, closer union than ever was expressed by other art; and when the idea is absorbed, accepted, and perhaps partially understood, one may move on.
>
> —HENRY ADAMS

Abbot Sugar's book *De Consecratione Ecclesiae Sancti Dionysii* serves as an adequate background against which the *literary* struggle in *Mont-Saint-Michel and Chartres,* which is after all the essence of the metaphorical pilgrimage of uncle and niece, stands out in a clear shape. Sugar's book is about the building of a church as a metaphysical process, a kind of description of real work intended to enlighten the reader about its supernatural meaning. The architectural metaphor serves as a cosmic one, expressing a universal order and reconciling the *vita activa* with the *vita contemplativa.* The universe and its order are composed: and it is our *work* to understand the composition. Adams, of course, was not a mystic in the traditional sense, but the School of Chartres, its Christianity and Platonism provided the material Henry Adams needed in order to create his own image of possible unity. His intense pessimism and despair forced upon him the belief in the function of the image: he believed in the necessity of fiction as a redemptive force against destructive nihilism. History would always

[21] Levin, *History*, p. 423.

"happen," of course, but it would be meaningless without fiction. In this respect, too, Adams was closer to Nietzsche than he probably would have cared to admit, since he was asking implicitly for a new breed of men. He would eventually do so in his chapter "Nunc Age" of the *Education*.

His *Mont-Saint-Michel*, however, was intended to play out the full drama of space and time which the constitution of an image demands. There is a kind of given material in *Mont-Saint-Michel and Chartres*. Time, of course, and space, the natural and social surrounding of humankind as the matrix of historical units, the great historical moments, and of course the appearance of the great individual at the right moment, usually put there by Adams himself: "Poetry was not usually written to prove facts" (*Mont-Saint-Michel*, p. 19). And so they speak to us: the poets, the theologian, the politicians, the monks and mystics as well as kings and queens and of course the Virgin herself, all of whom are eventually cast in the same role; they produce images which structure our historical attention. Images it seems are necessary: they undoubtedly have a cognitive function, not just as a *biblia pauperum* for the theoretically unenlightened, but in the process of theory construction itself. In this sense, and in this sense only, *Mont-Saint-Michel* is a theoretical text about the meaning of history, valid for our own time. "Images are not arguments, they rarely even lead to proof, but the mind craves them, and, of late more than ever, the keenest experimenters find twenty images better than one, especially if contradictory; since the human mind has already learned to deal in contradictions" (*Education*, p. 489).

The image is the first step away from nature, not an abstraction yet but already sending the beholder on his way. The image, in other words, is the beginning of our education and a reminder of its own potential futility. In the realm of theoretical discourse Henry Adams liked to admit the shortcomings of his way of presenting the problem: "In any case the theory will have to assume that the mind has always figured its motives as reflections of itself, and that this is as true in its conception of electricity as in its instinctive imitation of a God. Always and everywhere the mind creates its own universe, and pursues its own phantoms: but the force behind the image is always a reality—the attraction of occult power" (*Education*, p. 481).

When seen as a process, however, the unfolding of the image begins to resemble the *ergon* of Herodotus, as a monument, as an achievement, as an act worthy to be remembered. In a literal sense, we read *Mont-Saint-Michel* because, as the last sentence of the introduction states so bluntly: "The uncle talks." And he talks despite the fact that a sense of history, according to Adams, is a highly artificial construct—at best reminding the individual of the various possibilities of his or her existence as a historical being, but hardly telling much about the nature of history. In the end, nature will prevail, and as a consequence art is as necessary as it is doomed. Obviously this kind of concept implies both a nonmimetic idea of art and a theory of reality, which concedes that history is a borderline phenomenon, a process of ongoing acts of world-making, where little can be said about their success or failure. History, in other words, is the great "as if" experience on the one hand, and on the other hand, the raw material. Reality, therefore, has two sides to it: docile and domesticated, serving one's desire for self-expression, and at the same time volatile, elusive, and highly explosive, suddenly assuming tyrannical power as *factum brutum* instead of conforming to efforts of vision—or of control. In a moving chapter in the *Education*, entitled "Chaos," Henry Adams gives us a condensed version of this sense of reality which divides the individual by separating one's assumption of power as guaranteed by reason from one's helplessness vis-à-vis the *factum brutum*. The passage concerning the death of his sister is worth quoting at some length.

> He found his sister, a woman of forty, as gay and brilliant in the terrors of lockjaw as she had been in the careless fun of 1859 lying in bed in consequence of a miserable cab-accident that had bruised her foot. Hour by hour the muscles grew rigid, while the mind remained bright, until after ten days of fiendish torture she died in convulsions. . . . One had heard and read a great deal about death, and even seen a little of it, and knew by heart the thousand commonplaces of religion and poetry which seemed to deaden one's senses and veil the horror. Society being immortal, could put on immortality at will. Adams being mortal, felt only the mortality. Death took features altogether new to him, in these rich and sensuous surroundings. Nature enjoyed it, played with it, the horror added to her charm, she liked the torture, and smothered her victim with caresses. Never had one seen her so winning. The hot Italian summer brooded outside, over the market-place and the picturesque peasants, and, in the singular color of the Tuscan atmosphere, the hills and vineyards of the Apennines seemed bursting with mid-summer blood. The sick-room itself glowed with the Italian joy of life; friends filled it; no harsh northern lights pierced the soft shadows; even the dying woman shared the sense of the Italian summer, the soft, velvet air, the humor, the courage, the sensual fulness of Nature and man. She

faced death, as women mostly do, bravely and even gaily, racked slowly to unconsciousness, but yielding only to violence, as a soldier sabred in battle. For many thousands of years, on these hills and plains, Nature had gone on sabring men and women with the same air of sensual power. (Adams, *Education*, p. 287)

The beauty of nature, incorporating poetry and terror, its playful cruelty, as it is seen by Henry Adams, is not Kant's any longer, it is not the kind of beauty which attracts reason (*sittliche Vernunft*); it is instead the very opposite, a reminding force, displaying its mythical origin and thus destroying the self-certainty of enlightenment and its belief in the natural progress of rationality. Beauty of nature is the menacing, categorically different opposite and as such it changes the character of art, and its relationship to the idea of history. In essence, I think, the sense of reality as experienced and accepted by Henry Adams in the passage just quoted destroys two vital assumptions underlying the traditional theory of art as mimesis: (a) reality does not contain realms of self-evident substance, serving as a lasting, ontologically safe exemplum mundi; (b) reality is not a holistic entity, neither as idea nor as a projection of the subjective self.

Instead of being mimetic, art assumes the function of an allegorical counterfactual statement; its truth is not based on verisimilitude, but on the *fact* of its creation by the individual knowing and understanding one's faculty of producing consistent elements of reality, which are one's very own—worlds apart, worlds of potential possibilities, aesthetic worlds constructed as pattern of self-reference. It is this normative concept of art which Adams projects with force—and, as sober-minded critics have pointed out, with a reckless disregard of historical accuracy onto the thirteenth century. But then we know by now that Adams was not interested in historical accuracy for its own sake. He used facts to make a plea for art.

The art-idea corresponding to Adams's theory of reality eventually carries the book as a whole, becoming its sole raison d'être, subsuming what on a different level of discourse seems to be "factual account of historical events." Not only does the uncle-narrator, from the very beginning, insist on the importance of feeling as a medium of cognition. In the course of their tour he eventually goes so far as to present the Virgin herself as being true only as art. Theology is discussed as art, and so in the end is society when held together by a shared ideal.

If chaos, as Henry Adams has pointed out, is the law of nature, and order the dream of humankind, and if history is both incoherent and immoral as well as a catalog of the forgotten, the tour turned into pilgrimage from Mont-Saint-Michel to Chartres is the affirmation of an illusion, the insistence at the same time on the reality of illusion expressed as art. The monuments are there, and we are told that their presence is "an exceedingly liberal education of anybody, tourist or engineer or architect, and would make the fortune of an intelligent historian, if such should happen to exist, but the last thing we ask from them is education or instruction" (Adams, *Mont-Saint-Michel*, p. 40).

Instead, Henry Adams tells us time and again: "We want only their poetry." The emphasis is on instinct, feeling, and expression, and the pilgrimage, accordingly, turns into an exercise of recreating a lost illusion; its real place is that of imagination: "We are not now seeking religion; indeed, true religion generally comes unsought. We are only trying to feel Gothic art. For us, the world is not a schoolroom or a pulpit, but a stage, and the stage is the highest yet seen on earth" (Adams, *Mont-Saint-Michel*, p. 106).

Niece and uncle move upon this stage acting out a command of space and time, of dialogue among themselves and self-reflection, which as artifice and form tries to achieve what is said about Chartres:

> Like all great churches, that are not mere storehouses of theology, Chartres expressed, besides whatever else it meant, an emotion, the deepest man ever felt—the struggle of his own littleness to grasp the infinite. You may, if you like, figure in it a mathematic formula of infinity—the broken arch, our finite idea of space; the spire, pointing, with its converging lines, to unity beyond space; the sleepless, restless thrust of the vaults, telling the unsatisfied, incomplete, overstrained effort of man to rival the energy, intelligence and purpose of God. Thomas Aquinas and the schoolmen tried to put it in words, but their Church is another chapter. In act, all man's work ends there;—mathematics, physics, chemistry, dynamics, optics, every sort of machinery science may invent—to this favour come at last, as religion and philosophy did before science was born. All that the centuries can do is to express the idea differently: a miracle or dynamo; a dome or a coalpit; a cathedral or a world's fair; and sometimes to confuse the two expressions altogether. (Adams, *Mont-Saint-Michel*, p. 109)

As actors on the stage, as companions of an imagined tour, as participants involved in a fictional dialogue, niece and uncle not only acquire the autonomy usually granted to fiction, they also assume a power of interpretation which overwhelms and in effect goes beyond their given subject matter. Next to the two monuments Mont-Saint-Michel and Chartres, a *third* one is created: *Mont-Saint-Michel and Char-*

tres—the book. Calling this assumption of cognitive equality a "literary experiment" may be modest where the critic is concerned. When Henry Adams describes his own literary career as a failure he "makes" sure that we do not miss the point, that he is talking about failure on a grand scale. In fact, if we look at the failure of the ideal of unity as it is described in *Mont-Saint-Michel and Chartres*, failure when Henry Adams talks about it means the nearest possible approximation to success. A letter, referring to the autobiography, could have been written with reference to *Mont-Saint-Michel*, without losing any of its ambition disguised as self-deprecation:

> When I read St. Augustine's Confessions, or Rousseau's, I feel certain that their faults, as literary artists, are worse than mine. We have all three undertaken to do what cannot be successfully done—mix narrative and didactic purpose and style. The charm of the effort is not in winning the game but in playing it. We all enjoy the failure. St. Augustine's narrative subsides at last into the dry sands of metaphyiscal theology. Rousseau's narrative fails wholly in didactic result; it subsides into still less artistic egotism. And I found that a narrative style was so incompatible with a didactic or scientific style, that I had to write a long supplementary chapter (really three) to explain in scientific terms what I could not put into narration without ruining the narrative. . . . My experiment of trying to find the exact point of equilibrium where the two motives would be held in contact was bound to be a failure. (Adams, *Mont-Saint-Michel*, p. 645)

The narrative cannot stand unsupported—but then, on the other hand, it has to try again and again—failure being a measure of success, in the sense that it defines a relationship which is one of distance: our memory of unity and our existence in multiplicity. To put it differently: monuments will be erected, serving the illusion, but by realizing that the illusion, seen as the scar of emancipation, is the condition of our existence as historical being, the edge of failure becomes not a medium of hope—but a necessary part of our freedom: "While man moved about his relatively spacious prison with a certain degree of ease, God being everywhere, could not move. In one respect, at least man's freedom seemed to be not relative but absolute, for his thought was an energy paying no regard to space or time or order or object or sense; but God's thought was His act and will at once, speaking correctly, God could not think. He is" (Adams, *Mont-Saint-Michel*, p. 375).

We are and think and act, imperfectly so; but expressing in our best art exactly this imperfection, is, as Henry Adams would have put it, our only hope: "true ignorance." This, his final and philosophically highly charged paradox defines the essential threshold: modern "man," in order to become a pilgrim again, has to rely on his most refined powers of reflection.

CHAPTER 6

William James

Whatever things have intimate and continuous connection with life are things of whose reality I cannot doubt.

—WILLIAM JAMES

The lunatic's visions of horror are all drawn from the material of daily fact. Our civilization is founded on the shambles, and every individual existence goes out in a lonely spasm of helpless agony. If you protest, my friend, wait till you arrive there yourself.

—WILLIAM JAMES

In the Introduction to his father's Literary Remains, William James quotes approvingly from a work written on his father's philosophy. The question that he cites would in a variety of forms haunt him throughout his life: "Mr. James looks at creation instinctively from the creative side, and this has a tendency to put him at a remove from his readers. The usual problem is: Given the creation, to find the Creator; to Mr. James it is: Given the Creator, to find the creation. God is; of His being there is no doubt, but who and what are *we*?"[1]

William James's doubts were of a different sort than those of his father's, but the final question he undoubtedly shared. And if we see William James in the tradition that we have outlined so far, it is mainly for his effort to create the vision of a universe that would allow a reasonable answer to the question, "Who and what are *we*?"

James stood on a threshold, being a man of science and trying at the same time to keep science in its proper place, keeping the universe open for a variety of answers. It is typical that he always regretted having called one of his books *The Will to Believe*, instead of making his intentions clearer by calling it "The *Right* to Believe." His preoccupation with the individual's *right* to find an answer to the question about one's own self without being tied to one single, dogmatic philosophical system is probably his most Emersonian streak. William James, like Emerson, tried desperately to keep the idea of individuality alive, an idea that he found deeply threatened by a growingly complex and interdependent society. Like his father, Henry James, Sr., William James saw more in the body of society than a conglomerate of institutions and individuals. Again, William James's explanation of his father's work throws a considerable light on his own thought.

> 'Nature' and 'Society,' if I understand our author correctly, do not differ from each other at all in substance or material. Their sub-

[1] James, *Essays*, p. 6.

> stance is the Creator himself, for he is the sole positive substance in the universe, all else being nothingness. But they differ in form; for while Nature is the Creator immersed and lost in a nothingness self-affirming and obstructive, Society is the same Creator, with the nothingness saved, determined to transparency and self-confession, and traversed from pole to pole by his life giving rays. The *matter* covered by both these words is Humanity.[2]

William James, even though his own thought took a different turn where the issue concerned the question of "Humanity," was nevertheless profoundly influenced by his father's concerns. Henry James, Sr., under the influence of Swedenborg, had tried throughout his life to work out a scheme of redemption for man, a scheme that vaguely approached a configuration of ideals that we today would associate with a sort of Christian socialism. Even though Henry James, Sr., never developed a systematic scheme of his ideas, many of his individual convictions would return in the thought of his son. First of all, Henry James the father respected science, but only within a limited realm. He made it quite clear that science could make no ontological claims. In fact, Henry James established a hierarchy of knowledge that put science between immediate sense perception and philosophy.

> There are three realms of life in a man, one exterior or physical, one interior or psychical, one inmost or spiritual; or one realm of the body, one of mind and soul, and one of spirit; and each of these realms claims its proper unity or organization, the first being *sensibly* organized, the second being *scientifically* organized, the third being *philosophically* organized. Now each of these organizations or unities demands of course its own appropriate light. The sun is the light of sense. Reason is the light of science. Revelation is the light of philosophy. Each of these lights is absolute in its own sphere, and good for nothing out of it.[3]

The content of this passage is equally important as the style, if we view it with an eye to the writings of William James. The abstract concepts that could easily lead to a rigid system of thought are firmly couched in a metaphorical language. Even if we grant that Henry James, Sr., was still in many ways trying to think in analogies, we cannot overlook the fact that in such works as *The Principles of Psychology*, William James would make use of the same technique. It is certainly an exaggeration to compare *The Principles* to *Moby-Dick*, as Jacques Bar-

[2] Ibid., pp. 9–10.

[3] Frederic Harold Young, *The Philosophy of Henry James, Sr.* (New York, 1951), p. 93.

zun does in calling our attention to the mixture of the concrete and the abstract, but the philosophical tradition of mediating between the two for the sake of selfhood does exist. The man of letters takes the act of writing far too seriously in order to stay as close as possible to the realm of abstraction. As in the case of Henry James, Sr., the act of writing is too much a question of morality to leave it to just one aspect of the spirit. In a brief passage on morality, Henry James, Sr., has outlined what in other terms might equally well be regarded as a theory of writing, as it would be practiced by his son William: "The best and briefest definition of moral existence is, the alliance of an inward subject and an outward object; and of spiritual existence, the alliance of an outward subject and an inward object. Thus in moral existence what is public or universal dominates what is private or individual; whereas in spiritual existence the case is reversed, and the outward serves the inward."[4]

Not only is it hard to resist the temptation to compare such statements with modern theories of poetry and cite Ezra Pound and T. S. Eliot as the suitable examples of a longstanding tradition, it is equally hard to resist doing the opposite. It does not make much sense to see tradition as an uninterrupted flow of predecessors and successors. Replacements take place, and our business here is simply to pay respect to the influence of the father. If James did not follow in his father's philosophical footsteps, it is for exactly the reason that the most important influence the father had was to encourage the son to *think* for himself. In this Henry James, Sr., had set a living example. At the core of William James's philosophy we therefore find the insistence that individual freedom relies on the ability to think for one's self—and again, in the case of William James, this self needed some defining.

In a typical manner William James defined the self *against* something rather than attempting a technical definition. "Whatever universe a professor believes in," he wrote in the opening pages of *Pragmatism*, "must at any rate be a universe that lends itself to lengthy discourse."[5] And we are not far from the truth if we assume that James would end up defining the self as a form of lengthy discourse. The self for James was intricately a part of what he called "experience," and hence it makes sense to see the self as part of an ongoing—and risky—process rather than to establish it as a firm entity confronting the world. The matter that for James was of primary importance was

[4] Ibid., p. 227.

[5] William James, *Pragmatism and the Meaning of Truth* (Cambridge, Mass., 1981), p. 10. Hereafter cited in text as James, *Pragmatism*.

the fact that this concept of the self implied establishing at the same time the inevitability of choice. The freedom, to put it in a paradox, to not make a choice did not exist. So James defined the self as one that was constantly involved in its own creation. The risk-taking factor was one of which James was very much aware—but besides being a philosopher, he was also enough of a psychologist to realize that without these risks life would be incomplete. The universe, like the self, was *One* and *Many* at the same time. The self, then, is made up of opposites—or of "disjunctions," as James would have called them.

We are therefore constantly dealing with fragments: both where the notion of selfhood is concerned and where we deal with external reality: "Every examiner of the sensible life *in concreto* must see that relations of every sort, or time, space, difference, likeness, change, rate, cause or what not, are just as integral members of the sensational flux as terms are, and that conjunctive relations are just as true members of the flux as disjunctive relations are. This is what in some recent writings of mine I have called the 'radically empiricist' doctrine."[6]

The examiner of the sensible life *in concreto* is, classically, the man of letters and what William James has to say in *A Pluralistic Universe* is not only applicable to the professional philosopher but applies equally to any examiner of life. James had some fairly negative things to say about the specialized philosopher that need not be repeated here; it is sufficient to point out the fact that throughout his work, William James thought of his ideas of man thinking as being applicable in general. But even at his most radical moments, James was caught in the same dilemma that had made all the difference between Emerson and Thoreau. He saw the dilemma himself and described it.

> I am tiring myself and you, I know, by vainly seeking to describe by concepts and words what I say at the same time exceeds either conceptualization or verbalization. As long as one continues *talking*, intellectualism remains in undisturbed possession of the field. The return to life can not come about by talking it is an *act*; to make you return to life, I must set an example for your imitation, I must deafen you to talk, or to the importance of talk, by showing you, as Bergson does, that the concepts we talk with are made for purposes of *practice* and not for purposes of insight. (James, *Pluralistic*, p. 131)

In a nutshell, William James, by evoking the problem of practice, has put the problem of the man of letters back where it belongs, namely

[6] William James, *A Pluralistic Universe* (Cambridge, Mass., 1977), p. 126. Hereafter cited in text as James, *Pluralistic*.

in the realm of ethics. This is, of course, exactly the realm where it had been located all along.

In a veritable tour de force and as a kind of climax, William James in *Principles* explains that there is "a mental structure which expresses itself in aesthetic and moral principles. Many of the so-called metaphysical principles are at bottom only expressions of aesthetic feeling," he points out. One might be tempted to read this as a kind of letdown, but we have to bear in mind that for James the phenomenon of "aesthetic feeling" was not of an inferior order. What he tries to point out is the equality of one state of mind with the other—and he does it by correlating both to Nature: "Nature is simple and invariable; makes no leaps, or makes nothing but leaps; is rationally intelligible; neither increases nor diminishes in quantity; flows from one principle, etc., etc."[7]

That James would place both the aesthetic principle and the moral principle into the realm of experience demonstrates his basic affinity to Emerson and Thoreau: "Life is one long struggle between conclusions based on abstract ways of conceiving cases, and opposite conclusions prompted by our instinctive perception of them as individual facts."[8]

Reading such statements by James in *Principles*, one cannot help but see retrospectively how Thoreau's journals seem to be a veritable case study for James's work in psychology. But then we have to remember that even though James was familiar with the scientific psychology of his day, his great work *The Principles of Psychology* is by no means limited to the explanation of scientific data and experiments. It is a book with a mission, namely to assert the self against any possible reduction of it to a simple stimulus-response robot. Even when James must become highly technical, his mission finds a way of expressing itself. Consider the following passage from "The Perception of Reality." Having dealt at great length with the working of the mind and its reaction to outward stimuli, James suddenly introduces the following passage.

> To many persons among us, photographs of lost ones seem to be fetishes. They, it is true, resemble; but the fact that the mere materiality of the reminder is almost as important as its resemblance is shown by the popularity a hundred years ago of the black taffeta "silhouettes" which are still found among family relics, and of one of which Fichte could write to his affianced: "Die Farbe

[7] William James, *The Principles of Psychology* (Cambridge, Mass., 1981), p. 1265.
[8] Ibid., p. 935.

> fehlt, das Auge fehlt, es fehlt der himmlische Ausdruck deiner lieblichen Zuege"—and yet go on worshipping it all the same. The opinion so stoutly professed by many, that language is essential to thought, seems to have this much of truth in it, that all our inward images tend invincibly to attach themselves to something sensible, so as to gain in corporality. Words serve this purpose, gestures serve it, stones, straws, chalk-marks, anything will do.[9]

The self, in other words, is the idea of something having become alive and the whole world is its material. James, in his distinction between the brain and the mind, a distinction that is, after all, the underlying concept in his theory of the reflex arc, made mind stand for a resource of potential selves. The stream of consciousness literally "works" and it is of no small significance that James insisted over and over again on the importance of "relations." Abstractions were always incomplete. So the mind, or the self, with James, always functioned within a realm of concrete experiences that were constantly changing. The self changes accordingly and again we are reminded of Emerson and Thoreau and *their* ideas about the changes that a living self had to go through. It is not surprising, as was pointed out earlier, that James in his speech about Emerson would betray such an affinity for his subject. If, as James had pointed out, "The true is only the expedient of our thinking," the center, of course, had to be the individual thinking as Emerson put it. The result of James's effort to demystify the idea of truth was to keep alive the ability to adapt the new, to incorporate the unexpected, and in this sense too James's opinions about life are very close to the repeated assertion of Thoreau that life only made sense being alive. The emphasis is on the activity, on the work involved, on the idea in other words, that in order to live our lives consciously we have to *make* sense!

Throughout his *Pluralistic Universe* James is concerned with the necessity of vision. Even in his criticism of Hegel he grants the German philosopher a kind of vision that is marred only by Hegel's belief in an absolute system. If we were to read *A Pluralistic Universe* against the grain, and read it side by side with *The Varieties of Religious Experience*, we might quickly come to the conclusion that the greatest horror that James could conceive of was the absence of vision. The absence of vision can be equated with a view of life that had come to a standstill. It is the task of the man of letters to prevent this from happening: "our visions are usually not only our most interesting but our most respect-

[9] Ibid.

able contributions to the world in which we play our part" (James, *Pluralistic*, p. 10).

To keep the vision alive is the work of a conscious mind, and James did not confine himself to the professional philosopher when he emphasized the need for vision: "Let me repeat once more that a man's vision is the great fact about him" (James, *Pluralistic*, p. 14).

Vision turned into consciousness is the individual's emancipation from a "multifarious" nature that James described in a fascinating passage about the life that meets nature unprotected.

> The thought of very primitive men has hardly any tincture of philosophy. Nature can have little unity for savages. It is a walpurgisnacht procession, a checkered play of light and shadow, a medley of impish and elfish friendly and inimical powers. "Close to nature" though they live, they are anything but Wordsworthians. If a bit of cosmic emotion ever thrills them, it is likely to be at midnight, when the camp smoke rises straight to the wicked full moon in the zenith, and the forest is all whispering with witchery and danger. (James, *Pluralistic*, p. 15)

James's great gift as a stylist comes out again and again in such imaginative scenes that he produced for his audience, and it is in such passages where he practices what he preaches. The criticism, therefore, that he is popularizing too much, is quite unfounded. James tried to be a practical philospher and part of this effort meant not to treat his audience to what he himself always attacked as "vicious intellectualism." It is his quality as a man of letters that makes his work so accessible—even where he deals with fairly technical aspects of philosophical systems. In this sense *The Pluralistic Universe* is a fine example of what the man of letters can achieve by making ideas clear that would otherwise be hard to comprehend for a general audience. At the same time, something is always lost. The man of letters, as the example of William James shows clearly, wants his audience to understand *and* go beyond the fact of understanding alone. In this sense the man of letters is, to a certain degree, a fictionalist manqué, he invents bits and pieces, but only in the fragmentary mode. It is easy to understand why in *The Varieties* William James speaks with such great sympathy and understanding about mysticism. There is a mystic in every man of letters: he wants to convince by creating and yet cannot allow himself the freedom of being freely creative. If we want a brief definition, the example of William James shows us that the man of letters is a rational mystic, well aware of his limitations. This, as in the case of James, creates a constant feeling of slight futility: the man of letters makes the best of his limitations, which does not mean that he is happy about them. Regret is always around the corner—and William James frequently wanted to change something that he had written or said. But James knew about the danger of aspiring to perfection: "Beautiful is the flight of conceptual reason through the upper air of truth. No wonder philosophers are dazzled by it still, and no wonder they look with some disdain at the low earth of feeling from which the goddess launched herself aloft. But woe to her if she returns not home to its acquaintance; Nirgends haften dann die unsicheren Sohlen—every crazy wind will take her, and like a fire-balloon at night, she will go among the stars" (James, *Pragmatism*, p. 197).

As James demonstrated, you could use poetical language even when warning your audience not to be carried away by flights of fancy. William James's style frequently enabled his audience to understand the meaning of pragmatism much better than philosophical explanations would. James, the writer, was using a language the audience was familiar with. If, on the one hand, James wrote and spoke very much in an Emersonian tradition, he avoided the dark conceit and the paradox. Both are replaced in the writing of William James by the invention, the fabricating of the *adequate scene*. These scenes stand out from the rest of the text and the reader is constantly challenged to use both imagination and reason: " 'I yielded myself to the perfect whole,' writes Emerson; and where can you find a more mind-dilating object? A certain loyalty is called forth by the idea; even if not proved actual, it must be believed in somehow. Only an enemy of philosphy can speak lightly of it" (James, *Pluralistic*, p. 28).

The reader is invited to doubt by being enticed. He is supposed to see and feel the persuasive side of what he must criticize. There is a Socratic side to James's way of presenting an argument that lends a democratic style to his thought. Even where he condemns and criticizes he is willing to see some element in his opponent's thought that is worthwhile considering. Again, James is practicing what his philosophy is all about by granting his adversaries the right to their mistakes. James does not concern himself with showing that the object of his criticism was wrong; instead he tries to show his readers *why* someone like Hegel went the wrong way. The democratic style of James's thought is part of a tradition that tries to include the reader in the process of understanding: it is a practical intellect at work. It is in his essay "The Will to Believe" that we get the best demonstration of how the practical intellect of William James worked. The essay is an argument for a holistic view of man. As he succinctly put it, the will to believe is an act of freedom, not limited by the proofs of science, but is, rather, a question of the heart: "A moral question is a question not of what sensibly exists, but of what is good, or would be good if it did exist. Science can tell us what exists; but to compare the *worths*, both of what exists and what does not exist, we must consult not science but what Pascal calls our heart."[10]

It is not difficult to equate the appeal to the heart, as James put it, with the reference to the self as we know it from Emerson and Thoreau. There are passages in James's *Pluralistic Universe* where the reasons of the heart assume such an important role in establishing systems of knowledge that the reader is immediately reminded of Emerson's view of the self as a guiding principle for a reality that is constantly in the process of becoming.

> What really *exists* is not things made but things in the making. Once made they are dead, and an infinite number of alternative conceptual decompositions can be used in defining them. But put yourself *in the making* by a stroke of intuitive sympathy with the thing, and the whole range of possible decompositions coming at once into your possession, you are no longer troubled with the question which of them is the more absolutely true. Reality *falls* in passing into conceptual analysis; it *mounts* in living its own undivided life—it buds and burgeons, changes and creates. (James, *Pluralistic*, p. 117)

Emerson's or Thoreau's plea for a living reality would have sounded very similar and it is quite significant that William James could make his plea for an open reality at a time when science was much more advanced than it had been in the days of transcendentalism. Once again there is the strong sense that William James is holding on to something (vision) that in the course of tradition seemed most threatened. This does not mean that James, whose ideas about the future were quite articulate, was a conservative traditionalist. Nothing could be further from the truth. Like his predecessors, however, he felt the need to go backwards in order to keep unanswered questions alive, instead of simply having them replaced by new questions. It would be equally wrong to label this position antimodernist. The truth is that Emerson, Thoreau, Adams, and James all regarded the future as part of an ongoing tradition and their main worry was that established distinctions in the course of time might become blurred. They all tried to preserve the complex. William James explained the nature of his crit-

[10] William James, "The Will to Believe," in *The Writings of William James* ed. John J. McDermott (New York, 1967), pp. 729–30.

icism in *A Pluralistic Universe*, and we see immediately that his great concern was to maintain a view of the whole.

> Place yourself similarly at the centre of a man's philosophic vision and you understand at once all the different things it makes him write or say. But keep outside, use your postmortem method, try to build the philosophy up out of the single phrases, taking first one and then another and seeking to make them fit 'logically,' and of course you fail. You crawl over the thing like a myopic ant over a building, tumbling into every microscopic crack or fissure, finding nothing but inconsistencies, and never suspecting that a centre exists. (James, *Pluralistic*, p. 117)

The man of letters must always be concerned with the preservation of the center. At the same time he knows that the work of such preservation is an act of imaginative making. His sense of tragedy is the result of the insight that against the broad strokes of history, his task is the constructive work of assembling the parts which allow the recreation of the *image* of the center which once existed. It is the work of approximation, or, as James called it, "retrospective patchwork" where the individual handling of the problem is concerned. The quest, of course, is to "Place yourself at the point of view of the thing's interior *doing*, and all these back-looking and conflicting conceptions lie harmoniously in your hand," but James knew about the difference between quest and fulfillment.[11] Hence his frequent descriptions of a sense of the void, of a dread and anxiety provoked by the leveling force of history when seen as nature.

Against the transformation of history into a careless force of nature the man of letters posits the making of sense through artifice. The *making* of sense necessitates choice, and the whole drift of James's later work goes towards defending the necessity and the right of choice. James's emphatic plea for pluralism underlines this right. In his view only a pluralistic universe could be considered compatible with human nature. Essentially it is this compatibility which James tries to establish. His language shows that the philosopher was indeed above all concerned with the problem of establishing the place of humankind in a universe which would confront humankind as a "monstrosity" as he called it: "Perhaps the words 'foreignness' and 'intimacy' which I put forward in my first lecture express the contrast I insist on better than the words 'rationality' and 'irrationality'—let us stick to them, then. I

[11] As he had made it quite clear in his major writings, fulfillment was unattainable. One might even go so far as to say that he was obsessed with making this point.

now say that the notion of the 'one' breeds foreigness and that of the 'many' intimacy, for reasons which I have urged at only too great length, and with which, whether they convince you or not you are now well acquainted" (James, *Pluralistic*, p. 145).

James's desire to abolish foreignness, even though he goes through the motion of criticizing on quite technical points a large variety of philosophical systems, is clearly related to the Emersonian efforts to reconcile humankind and nature, despite their fundamental disparity. They both, in the end, work out a system of inclusions and relations. Nowhere does James sound more like Emerson than in the conclusion to *The Pluralistic Universe*: "Thus does foreignness get banished from our world, and far more so when we take the system of it pluralistically than when we take it monistically. We are indeed parts of God and not external creations, on any possible reading of the panpsychic system" (p. 143).

James's God and Emerson's Oversoul are closely related. In both cases the individual can see itself as part of a larger design. The whole idea of James's version of pluralism is to keep the principle of this design alive. In this sense he is indeed a true Emersonian.

> For pluralism, all that we are required to admit as the constitution of reality is what we ourselves find empirically realized in every minimum of finite life. Briefly it is this, that nothing real is absolutely simple, that every smallest bit of experience is a *multum in parvo* plurally related, that each relation is one aspect, character, or function, by way of its being taken, or by way of its taking something else; and that a bit of reality when actively engaged in one of these relations is not *by that very fact* engaged in all the other relations simultaneously. (James, *Pluralistic*, p. 145)

James's lectures are not only first-rate examples of how the legacy of transcendentalism survived through change, they also demonstrate in their style how *urgent* a part of tradition becomes once it is threatened with replacement. James, whose later works have been criticized for an excessive romanticism (so by A. O. Lovejoy), does indeed at times seem to be more romantic than someone like Emerson. The style of his lectures often seems to convey a message, which must be brought across before it is too late. No wonder then that James did not feel it necessary to be cautious in his way of expression of what he thought to be a fact, namely the threat to pluralism. His insistence that pragmatism was not an idealistic philosophy only troubled those critics who tried to be more radically empirical than James allowed himself to be.

It is quite ironic that at a time when philosophy became seriously professionalized, James made the effort to put the interest in the individual back into the center of a profession which was quickly branching out into different schools and factions. Obviously his father's speculative energies were kept alive in the son, together with the courage to speak out and to admit that any specific issue was not yet settled. James was not troubled at all when he had to confess that he had not solved a problem yet—indeed, he liked to let his audience participate in the effort of finding the way out of a dilemma. Hence we frequently encounter in his printed lectures appeals to the audience to make up their own minds. The suggestive mode of presenting an argument had been a genuine Emersonian stylistic device which we find in James's work as well, even though he shied away from getting more deeply involved in the rhetoric of allegory. James's original participation in the allegorical tradition was one of *content*, not one of rhetoric. His vision of the universe and his technical conceptualization of it forced the individual to accept reality as an allegorist, to deal with reality in a "piecemeal" fashion, as James would have put it. This pluralistic universe compels a person to accept the fact that whatever part of that person's reality is held to be true at any given moment is only a segment and due to change: "Meanwhile the incompleteness of the pluralistic universe thus assumed and held to as the most probable hypothesis, is also represented by the pluralistic philosophy as being self-reparative through us, as getting its disconnections remedied in part by our behavior" (James, *Pluralistic*, p. 148).

Self-reparation is, of course, the key phrase here, enforced by the "through us." Sentences like these can hardly ever become a bone of contention in a technical philosophical debate. They are statements which make a point about a view of existence—and as William James has pointed out so often, one can accept them or do the opposite; either choice may turn out to be reasonable. It is at this point, that it seems appropriate to point out that Richard Rorty sees a great similarity between James and Nietzsche, where the issue is that of making a choice without the help of any primary consensus, a consensus expressed in a standardized and accepted critical vocabulary. As Rorty points out, both Nietzsche and James believed that the idea of such a vocabulary was a myth.[12] This turns someone like James into what Rorty calls a "strong textualist," someone who lives without the "comfort" of working with a vocabulary that pretends to get to the essence of the object. Perhaps Rorty is overemphasizing his point slightly, but

[12] See Richard Rorty, *Consequences of Pragmatism* (Minneapolis, 1982), esp. pp. 152–53.

interestingly enough he comes to the conclusion that "Romanticism was *aufgehoben* in pragmatism." I take it that he uses the German word *aufgehoben* in a Hegelian sense as he comes to the following conclusion: "Pragmatism is the philosophical counterpart of literary modernism, the kind of literature which prides itself on its autonomy and novelty rather than its truthfulness to experience or its discovery of preexisting significance. Strong textualism draws the moral of modernist literature and thus creates genuinely modernist criticism."[13]

Without going into the implied value-judgments of Rorty's statement, we can follow the lead given us by emphasizing the ideas of autonomy and novelty. The very best, as Emerson has said, is usually new, and in this sense it must also be autonomous. James's speculative force would always claim a certain autonomy; it tried in fact by representing ideas in a certain style to give back to the individual a kind of autonomy which he or she seemed likely only too willingly to give up. The man of letters frequently makes a heavy demand on his audience, asking them to accept the consequences of practical intellect offered in the guise of aesthetic individualism. Allegory as a mode of thought, as we have tried to show, must combine the two components in the process of reality construction with only the choice of where to put the emphasis.

William James, like Emerson, wrote from the point of view both of a hope for the future and of some larger skepticism about the individual's ability to control or secure its outcome. As we have seen in the examples of Thoreau and Adams there were various ways of dealing with the problems involved when the question about the validity of pretheoretical experience was raised. The common solution was that the acceptance of life without theory was a necessity. They justified this necessity in different ways, but all of them would have agreed that such an acceptance implied a moral choice. Something had to be gained by this choice! Allegory as a mode of thought gains something for the future by seeing it through the past. The future is not a carte blanche but a continuation, not simply of chronological time, but of a past which even to remember involved work. It is the work not only of rediscovery and reconstruction, but the work of starting over. The mere act of starting over requires a point of departure and it makes no real difference whether this point of departure is simply referred to as "Myself," as in the case of Emerson, or whether it is called "temperament," as James liked to have it.

[13] Ibid., p. 153.

CHAPTER 6

> The history of philosophy is to a great extent that of a certain clash of human temperaments. Undignified as such a treatment may seem to some of my colleagues I shall have to account of this clash and explain a good many of the divergencies of philosophers by it. Of whatever temperament a professional philosopher is, he tries when philosophizing to sink the fact of his temperament. Temperament is no conventionally recognized reason, so he urges impersonal reasons only for his conclusions. Yet his temperament really gives him a stronger bias than any of his more strictly objective premises. It loads the evidence for him one way or another, making for a more sentimental or hardhearted view of the universe, just as this fact or that principle would. He *trunks* his temperament. (James, *Pragmatism*, p. 11)

"Trust thyself," one feels tempted to add, if only to show that a continuity exists where the idea of selfhood is concerned, a tradition which managed to maintain certain essentials like the autonomy *and* the legitimacy of the individual's thought in a world of increasing conformity. William James did not have to invent the idea of the autonomous self; his task was to demonstrate the limits of professionalized philosophy and its dangerous impact on traditional notions of selfhood. Emerson had done the first step; in many ways the position of William James was a much more defensive one. To put it differently: Emerson had the freedom to attack where James was bound to a more rational form of explanatory discourse. And yet, we cannot overlook the similarities of their concerns.

As participants in the allegorical tradition they both had to dismantle established belief systems and in doing so they had to invent their own, expedient rhetoric. James's style is often deceptively simple; he would not and could not keep his own temperament under a steadfast control. Like Emerson he has suffered, therefore, in the past from a high degree of quotability, a fact which has often blurred what he really tried to say. Like Emerson, James frequently advised his audience not to expect an immediate conclusion from a point made, but to wait until a later stage of the argument, only to return to the point from which he had begun, instead of finishing his argument with the promised conclusions. There is of course a method behind this: namely to demonstrate that you can look at a given subject from many perspectives, but never from all of them at once. It is the allegorist's way of representing reality, always pointing out that a particular view *also* involves a *locus standi* and that both what we see and our perspective are subject to change.

As we have pointed out at the beginning of our argument, the prospect of change is frequently associated with feelings of anxiety and even dread. It is the great achievement of William James that he has managed to demonstrate that the very act of philosophizing involves such risks. It is he, therefore, who also provides at least a part of the answer to the question of where the philosophical energies of America were spent in the nineteenth century. Looking over the threshold of the twentieth century, with his assertion that risk and selfhood are inextricably linked, he seems to say that *this knowledge* was the intellectual wisdom of the previous generation. James wanted to preserve this knowledge and it would be a hard case to argue that he was successful. He can be said to be successful only to the extent that *we* manage to reclaim him as part of the tradition which he tried to defend. This, of course, we can do only if we ourselves let go of certain creeds and canonized opinions which we have become used to and which we have come to like.

Temperament! Stressing allegory as a mode of thought and as a tradition in its own right in the American nineteenth century cannot, of course, be discussed without acknowledging the role of religion as a driving force behind the changes within this tradition. William James in his chapter "Pragmatism and Religion" in *Pragmatism* wondered whether the pluralistic "tough-minded" would not be criticized by the "tender-minded" as a merely moralistic scheme of thought. His own candid answer to this hypothetical criticism demonstrates the stability through change, of the allegorical way of perceiving reality.

> I cannot speak officially as a pragmatist here; all I can say is that my own pragmatism offers no objection to my taking sides with this more moralistic view, and giving up the claim of total reconciliation. The possibility of this is involved in the pragmatistic willingness to treat pluralism as a serious hypothesis. In the end it is our faith and not our logic that decides such questions, and I deny the right of any pretended logic to veto my own faith. I find myself willing to take the universe really to be dangerous and adventurous, without therefore backing out and crying "no play." (James, *Pragmatism*, pp. 141–42)

This is the same self-confidence which Emerson had to acquire and a view of the universe which Thoreau and Adams shared. Neither of them was willing to back out, but they found different ways of playing the game. In all cases the moralistic element prevailed, and that is another gain that arose from the choice mentioned earlier on. Morals are principally a contribution *to* the world, and it is in this sense that we can see such masters of withdrawal as Adams and Thoreau as contributors. The allegorical tradition in American thought has played a vital role in the process of secularization by keeping the religious legacy of a Puritan past accessible within the nineteenth century's development of a moral temper. It prevented, by means of aesthetic individualism, the brute dominance of materialistic expediency. Practical intellect needed such a slow transformation. We cannot be seriously surprised, therefore, by how preoccupied William James was with questions touching upon religious subjects. We need only remember that within the context of the allegorical tradition, aesthetic individualism, as in the case of *Mont-Saint-Michel and Chartres*, served a practical purpose for the present and the future.

The art of "learning backwards" was indeed an art that William James had come to master, just as his predecessors had. And again, just as in the works of Emerson, Thoreau, and Adams, there is a prophetic tone in the voice of William James, a tone that addresses what Emerson had called "the party of hope." It is not a prophetic tone of blind optimism and far-fetched hopes but a serene tone of limited expectations that points out how things could be. The allegorical tradition of which James is a part is after all characterized by a careful balancing of skepticism and optimistic moralism. James, in *Pragmatism*, has vividly described the sense of accepting what he calls a "moralistic universe."

> As a matter of fact countless human imaginations live in this moralistic and epic kind of universe, and find its disseminated and strung-along successes sufficient for their rational needs. There is a finely translated epigram in the Greek Anthology which admirably expresses this state of mind, this acceptance of loss as unatoned for, even though the lost element might be one's self:
>
> A shipwrecked sailor, buried on this coast
> Bids you set sail
> Full many a gallant bark, when we were lost
> Wheathered the gale.
>
> Those puritans who answered 'yes' to the question: Are you willing to be damned for God's glory? were in this objective and magnanimous condition. . . . It is then perfectly possible to accept sincerely a drastic kind of universe from which the element of 'seriousness' is not to be expelled. Whoever does so is, it seems to me, a genuine pragmatist. He is willing to live in a scheme of uncertified possibilities which he trusts; willing, to pay with his own

person, if need be, for the realization of the ideals which he frames. (James, *Pragmatism*, p. 142)

Thoreau and Henry Adams could hardly have found a better justification for the lives they lived and for the work they accomplished. Traditions can be read backwards and it is when we read James that we realize that the legacy of American transcendentalism went beyond the brief golden days of its romantic phase. But the romantic interpretation of transcendentalism has been an understandable misreading from the very beginning, as we have pointed out, just as the ideas of James's pragmatism would soon be misinterpreted. We have mentioned at the beginning of our argument that William James's *The Varieties of Religious Experience* seems a proper ending of the era that we have tried to discuss. I do not think that this statement needs to be qualified. Emerson, who first broke away from the safeguards of a theoretically, which in his days meant a theologically, justified universe took a great risk. *The Varieties* is not an exercise in theology but a book about the "life" of religious experience. As if in answer to Emerson's leaving the ministry, James concludes his book with the following remarks: "I think in fact that a final philosophy of religion will have to consider the pluralistic hypothesis more seriously than it has hitherto been willing to consider it. For practical life at any rate, the *chance* of salvation is enough. No fact in human nature is more characteristic than its willingness to live on chance."[14]

Thus they all took their chance, Emerson, Thoreau, Adams, and William James: the chance they took was to follow their will to *make sense*. If *we* see the sense, *they* were successful.

If James's highly accessible works on "Pragmatism" were so soon misread and the philosophy itself became trivialized even during his own lifetime, how great must the chance be to misunderstand Emerson, Thoreau, and Henry Adams. In his last public lecture, the old Emerson—too old at least to lecture—allegedly made a self-ironic remark that a confused speaker was addressing an equally puzzled audience. In the light of this anecdote, how are we to construe a sense of tradition, or even a structure of tradition, if we are the audience listening to many speakers from a considerable distance? Obviously no kind of teleological explanation will do. Irrationalism offers no solution, either. If, in the preface, we mentioned that Husserl had implicitly suggested to us a teleology of the middle range, we can now qualify this statement by adding that what we mean is a teleology of conflict. By seeing tradition as an ongoing argument we can make ourselves par-

[14] William James, *The Varieties of Religious Experience* (London, 1902), p. 526.

ticipants, and as such we may raise *our* questions. We will demand further distinctions, because we already know the old answers. The American nineteenth century has addressed many problems that are still unsolved. Our task is not so much to find solutions as to formulate a question that allows a restatement of the original problem. In the end, where this task is concerned, we, the audience, like our speakers, stand alone and have to speak for ourselves.

CHAPTER 7

American Allegory

Here we drift, like white sails across the wild ocean, now bright on the wave, now darkling in the trough of the sea;—but from what port did we sail? Who knows? Or to what port are we bound? Who knows! There is no one to tell us but such poor weather-tossed mariners as ourselves, to whom we speak as we pass, or who have hoisted some signal, or floated to us some letter in a bottle from far. But what know they more than we?

—RALPH WALDO EMERSON

The axis of reality runs solely through the egotistic places, —they are strung upon it like so many beads. To describe the world with all the various feelings of the individual pinch of destiny, all the various spiritual attitudes, left out from the description—they being as describable as anything else—would be something like offering a printed bill of fare as the equivalent for a solid meal.

—WILLIAM JAMES

Finding meaning in the flux of time is the work of tradition and when the result of such work assumes form, it is the configurative and involved, epistemologically charged shape of allegory which arises.

By allegory we customarily mean a particular form of artistic expression, which, above all, is known to us as one which has had a history of declining literary importance. Its main fault, so it seems, is that allegory as opposed to other symbolic art forms seemed to have missed the road to modernism. In many ways the fate of allegory was sealed by the influential Goethean distinction, later popularized by Coleridge according to which: "Allegory changes a phenomenon into a concept, a concept into an image, but in such a way that the concept is still limited and completely kept and held in the image and expressed by it [whereas symbolism] changes the phenomenon into the idea, the idea into the Image, in such a way that the idea remains always infinitely active and approachable in the image, and will remain inexpressible even though expressed in all languages."[1]

Always out-of-date and didactically rigid, the allegorical poem—to name just one example—never seems to reach the depth of true symbolism. Sometimes, though, in its history of diminishing returns, as in the case of Charles Baudelaire (*un genre si spirituelle*) or of Walter Benjamin, allegorical expression has been both defended against its detractors and in the end redeemed as a legitimate mode.[2] That such instances of sudden historical reversals are at all possible lies in the very nature of allegorical expression, in the nature, that is, of its relationship to time. Allegory, as it will be discussed here, namely as a mode of thought, is the result of a conflict, of a crisis, which owes its

[1] Fletcher, *Allegory*, p. 17.

[2] Walter Benjamin, *Ursprung des deutschen Trauerspiels* (Frankfurt, 1974); see especially "Allegorie und Trauerspiel" in Walter Benjamin, *Gesammelte Schriften*, vol. 1, pt. 1 (Frankfurt/Main, 1985), pp. 336–71.

characteristics to a specific constellation of cultural contradictions. Allegory, in short, becomes a viable form of expression whenever its cognitive qualities are needed as part of a solution to a cultural crisis, which is best defined as a *question from within* of the symbolic character of reality. If we see the internalization of Nature as a process of enculturation which repeats itself again and again only to break down at regular intervals because what seems so successfully internalized and hence under control starts to assert itself, we may understand the function of allegory as a defense mechanism in the name of and for the sake of realism.[3]

Allegory as a mode of thought not only acknowledges the fact that the symbolic character of reality is fictitious, it also works with this realization. There is something highly applicable or practical about allegory upon which its specific characteristics depend. These characteristics change, however, even if a look at the long history of allegory and at the attempts to find an adequate definition shows a remarkable stability in such a formulation. "The difficulty of allegory is rather that this emphatic clarity of representation does not stand in the service of something that can be represented."[4] How much, in fact, depends on this element of "public persuasion," becomes obvious if we refer to Jean Pépin's seminal book *Mythe Et Allégorie* and take a look at his brief chapter "De L'Allégorie A Topologie," where he discusses the differences between ancient and Christian allegory.

> D'un ensemble de récits tenus très généralement pour imaginaires, l'allégorie hellénistique dégageait un enseignement sans âge qu'elle considérait *sub specie aeternitatis*, sans soupçonner la notion d'un développement irréversible. L'allégorie chrétienne au contraire discerne, dans la trame d'un tissu historique, une signification qui est elle-même une histoire; au didacticisme, elle substitue le prophétisme; à l'interprétation éterniste, le souci du temps historique et de l'avènement du salut.[5]

It does not take a far stretch of the imagination to realize that the American allegory of the nineteenth century must have had its "Greek" moment and that once emerging as an acknowledgment of a nonsymmetrical relationship between meaning and event, between the individual and the world, it would become incorporated into the movement of nineteenth-century realism. Coming out of the transcen-

[3] This accounts for the skeptical element in allegorical thought.

[4] Paul de Man, "Pascal's Allegory of Persuasion," in Stephen J. Greenblatt, ed., *Allegory and Representation* (Baltimore, 1981), p. 1.

[5] Jean Pépin, *Mythe et Allégorie* (Paris, 1976), pp. 500–501.

dental movement, the American allegorical expression would, of course, serve a *counterfactual* purpose within the realistic tradition proper: but this exactly was its service to the legacy of the American Enlightenment.

If earlier we mentioned that allegory moves into a decisive place in the order of tradition whenever a specific cultural constellation produces a sense of crisis, we can now safely add that whatever became manifest in the era of transcendentalism had, of course, a latent history reaching much further back. American allegory, represented as a mode of thought in such men as Emerson, Thoreau, Adams, and James, never lost the essential traces of its Puritan origins. We have to bear this simple, but extremely important, fact in mind if we want to understand the role of the American allegory in the shaping of the American culture as a whole. Nineteenth century allegorical thought was the last resort of intellectual resistance against a kind of willful and violent act of replacement of the Puritan's paradoxical world view which had tried to reconcile the sacred and the profane. American allegory, to be more precise, tried to resist a replacement which would have worked above all as the avoidance of a solution to a paradox, at the heart of which lay the old problem of self-reference. It is only when we look at the ease with which the generation of the early years after the turn of the century referred to "themselves" that we understand the whole content of the problem which the idea of self-reference represented for men like Emerson, Thoreau, Adams, and James. Allegory forced them to occupy auctorial authority, and at the same time informed them about the fragility of their stance. Hence we find in these men, safely allied, ideas of grandiosity and feelings of extreme vulnerability, a sense of being masters of their sense of life and notions of great futility. In this sense, then, American allegory is not a capricious or whimsical twist of mind in the intellectual disposition of a few privileged, though somewhat disenchanted, gentlemen of refined and easily offended cultural taste, but a structurally essential part of the movement of tradition. Without the allegorical mode of expression as a vital link in the axis of tradition, transformation would not have been possible: the cultural mainstream rolls along on its very own undertow.

It is in this specific way of thinking about the world which we have identified as American allegory that we find the modern, that is, the nineteenth-century counterpart to the Puritan's idea of the errand.

American allegory as part of the nineteenth-century intellectual history, and as exemplified in the writing of the men of letters under discussion, emerges as a thoroughly modern device in the shaping of the structure of a tradition: modern by virtue of its actuality and classical at the same time by virtue of its descent.

Some of the main characteristics of American allegory as an integral part of the nineteenth-century intellectual history are worth mentioning in order to emphasize its ability to serve as functional part in the cultural process. There is, first of all, the overall and pervasive conviction that the allegorical view of history perceives it as being transitory to the point where it annihilates any kind of stable time span, with the possible exception of the brief, single, epiphanic instant. Next, there is a language which tries to deal with this sense of time's lack of substance by deciphering the signature of this decaying existence in time, by way of projection. Emerson, Thoreau, Adams, and James *saw* the world through allegoresis. The strong visual and emblematic sense of perception which we find in the writing of Emerson, Thoreau, Adams, and James invites extremely radical readings of their texts. To a certain extent the Puritan origins of the allegorical tradition has provoked criticism from some of the radical critics of culture after 1900. But we simply cannot overlook, even if such criticism turned into devastating denunciation, that there were a great number of latent affinities between the critics and their victims. The idea of a usable past had already been dealt with in the form of the quest for a usable present.

Besides being pictorial and emblematic, and besides the generally tragic world view, it was the extremely subjective perception of the world which American allegory carried into the realm of cognitive and artistic realism. Such subjectivity demands a point of view—a firm *locus standi*—and a kind of passionate attention which takes its task seriously, namely to attend, to wait. American allegory, gaining shape, intricate form, and great subtlety at a time of enormous social changes, became, to borrow a phrase from Sacvan Bercovitch, the stoic equivalent to the American jeremiad. This kind of allegory presents a series of frozen moments of arrested time. It is always the work of the outside observer, as Henry Adams emphasizes explicitly in his *Education*. Instead of hoping for a final revelation which is going to end progress, apocalyptically or otherwise, the allegorical disposition turns towards nature in order to be reminded of the limitations of the mind's place in the world. And in the end it accepts the limitations as the only viable answer to the question of why one should go on asking questions.

Allegory appeals to both intellect and emotion, never promising the achievement of synthesis. In a philosophical sense, then, allegory is the expression of an enlightened mind which seeks freedom from historical constraint by *remembering* the manifold ways such constraint had found to exercise its control in the past.

Both the abrupt and unfulfilled end of American enlightenment and the warped, distorted history of American romanticism suggest a rethinking of their relationship. In fact, the allegorical tradition in America since the mid-nineteenth century is exactly this kind of process: it correlates the idea of emancipation with the idea of organic growth into a configuration of thought and artistic expression which diminishes the overwhelming powers of infinite possibilities. If the American myth has consistently been interpreted as a bipolar structure of promise and disappointment, of endless potential and meager reapings, we can rightfully claim that the allegorical tradition has resisted such tendencies. And just as the relationship between promise and unfulfillment eventually develops towards some form of identity, such as the *one*, single point of original fall or rise, or simply of misplaced hopes, so the achievement of allegory lies in the capacity to sustain complexity by making successful changes.

American allegory, therefore, is a mode of thought in which transformation takes place. It is a setting not of rest and eternal Sunday, but one where work is in progress. Furthermore, allegory questions the authority of the canon. So it is not really surprising that often, in the middle of the transformative effort, the threat to tradition suddenly takes shape and leaps up as a reminder that the successful overcoming of tradition, however potential it may seem to be, will necessarily entail the fact of succession. What the consequences of abolishing the power of the existing tradition will be is a question which, either as a threat or as a promise, accompanies the effort of letting the traditional constellation of meaningful choices go—long before such an effort has achieved its goal.

William James, whose work *The Varieties of Religious Experience* seems so proper an ending to the tradition of the era we have discussed, could not avoid (even if he seriously thought of resisting) referring to the heart of the matter.

> Whilst in this state of philosophical pessimism and general depression of spirits about my prospects, I went one evening into a dressing-room in the twilight to procure some article that was there; when suddenly there fell upon me without any warning, just as if it came out of the darkness, a horrible fear of my own existence. Simultaneously there arose in my mind the image of an epileptic patient whom I had seen in the asylum, a blackhaired youth with greenish skin, entirely idiotic who used to sit all day on

> one of the benches, or rather shelves against the wall, with his knees drawn up against his chin, and the coarse gray undershirt, which was his only garment drawn over them enclosing his entire figure. He sat there like a sort of sculptured Egyptian cat or Peruvian mummy, and looking absolutely non-human. The image and my fear entered into a species of combination with each other. *That shape I am*, I felt, potentially.[6]

William James, hiding behind an invented French source, a correspondent whom he thanks for the permission that allowed him to publish the experience described, is in fact telling his audience about one of his own lapses into a state of sudden fear. Against such overpowering emotions the idea of a monolithic universe must have been extremely tempting. How dangerous to work out the system of a pluralistic universe, against the power of the time as represented in the Egyptian cat and the Peruvian mummy! To abandon the world as it has been represented over the ages, involves the risk of losing one's self.

Just as in Nick Carraway's fantasy of the Dutch sailor, the feeling of fear is associated with visions of metamorphosis, represented by the abyss of the self's introspective powers. Ralph Waldo Emerson very early on saw metamorphosis as an elementary part of nature to which humankind was bound: he probed both the threatening and the promising aspects of this idea. He also anticipated, in vain, the reaction of his readers who would readily admit that "nature ever flows," simply because they did not see themselves as part of nature. William James, whose ability to endure stress and to accept it in many ways resembled Emerson's, allowed no doubts about the individual's involvement.

> Nothing that I possess can defend me against the fate, if the hour for it should strike for me as it struck for him. There was such a horror of him, and such a perception of my own merely momentary discrepancy from him, that it was as if something hitherto solid within my breast gave way entirely, and I became a mass of quivering fear. After this the universe was changed for me altogether. I awoke morning after morning with a horrible dread at the pit of my stomach, and with a sense of the insecurity of life that I never knew before and that I have never felt since. (James, *Varieties*, p. 160)

[6] James, *Varieties*, p. 160. Hereafter cited in text as James, *Varieties*.

He finally sums up his examples of states of "the sick soul" in the following way: "The cases we have looked at are enough. One of them gives us the vanity of mortal things; another the sense of sin; and the remaining one describes the fear of the universe;—and in one or other of these three ways it always is that man's original optimism and self-satisfaction get leveled with the dust. —In none of these cases was there any intellectual insanity or delusion about matters of fact" (p. 161).

William James goes far out of his way to impress his message upon his audience: "The lunatic's visions of horror are all drawn from the material of daily fact. Our civilization is founded on the shambles, and every individual existence goes out in a lonely spasm of helpless agony. If you protest, my friend, wait till you arrive there yourself" (p. 163).

In a rather defensive postscript to the publication of his Gifford lectures, William James explained why he preferred "piecemeal supernaturalism" to any other version of philosophical reasoning, and the reader can hardly miss the strong negation of both dualistic philosophies and those based on versions of the Absolute. *Too late*, William James seems to say in a footnote which must have seemed utterly blasphemous to a genteel reading audience, "We should have spoken earlier, prayed for another world absolutely, before this world was born" (James, *Varieties*, p. 522).

It was the old William James who delivered the lecture in Edinburgh and what he meant to demonstrate was simply that the work of acceptance, which is a prerequisite to any motion beyond a given cultural context, is hard, slow, and often invites despair. But the rewards are there too: accepting the discrepancy between the facts, such as they may be, and their appearance as experienced by the individual involves casting off the sad necessity of mythic dualism. Choice at least becomes a possibility, even if it involves a certain amount of indifference towards the powers of reality. Nobody, as yet, this is what William James tells us, has proof that the heterogeneous is not as inhabitable a space as the homogeneous. It therefore remains an open question whether America is a symbol of identity or a metaphor of potential self: *practical intellect* will always claim and celebrate, even by way of criticism, the existence and historical power of America as a symbol of identity. *Aesthetic individualism* will always point out that America is bound to an uncertain future, hence its frequent preoccupation with the legitimacy of the past. As William James managed to evoke so vividly, there is always the possibility that our whole sense of being will suddenly turn out to be based on illusion. It is therefore sensible and rational to limit the powers of illusion by allowing at least for the existence of discrepancy as a change. Merlin's laughter, after all, is still with us.

If the final metaphor, incorporating the wealth of the American cultural tradition, is that of the journey, it has become for the American experience what Hans Blumenberg has called an "absolute metaphor." As a point of eternal departure it only takes shape in the form of deviations which *we* define. Whether it is in the final sentence of F. Scott Fitzgerald's novel *The Great Gatsby*: "So we beat on, boats against the current, borne back ceaselessly into the past," or whether it is Perry Miller's question about the length of the errand into the wilderness: the lesson we learn is the same. We shall never know what the Dutch sailor really saw, just as we cannot answer Perry Miller's question, even if it seems to imply the answer. Like Emerson in his statement in "The Natural History of Intellect," which suggests to be content with "dotting a fragmentary curve," we must learn to work with clues.

> And as the moon rose higher, the inessential houses began to melt away until gradually I became aware of the old island here that flowered once for Dutch sailors' eyes—a fresh, green breast of the new world. Its vanished trees, the trees that had made way for Gatsby's house, had once pondered in whispers to the last and greatest of all human dreams; for a transitory enchanted moment man must have held his breath in the presence of this continent, compelled into an aesthetic contemplation he neither understood nor desired, face to face for the last time in history with something commensurate to his capacity for wonder.[7]

The dominant theme again is one of fear, of anxiety, and of loneliness. The drama of experience is structured by the sheer force of our "capacity to wonder," from which our conscious self tries to escape. Discovery turns into self-discovery; the fear is produced by the powers of recollection and by the insight that this is the only way of knowing. Such knowledge, in essence, is the wisdom of allegory. In a less poetic way than F. Scott Fitzgerald, Perry Miller makes a similar observation: "Can a culture, which chances to embody itself in a nation, push itself to such remorseless exertion without ever learning whether it has been sent on its business at some incomprehensible behest, or is it obligated to discover the meaning for its dynamism in the very act of running?"[8]

[7] F. Scott Fitzgerald, *The Great Gatsby* (New York, 1925), p. 182.

[8] Perry Miller, *Errand into the Wilderness* (Cambridge, Mass., 1976), p. 217.

It is revealing that Perry Miller asks this question at the beginning of an essay to which he gave the title "The End of the World," an essay which he finished with the simple statement: "Catastrophe, by and for itself, is not enough."[9] What if, however, this is *all* which we can expect if we interrupt the "very act of running?"

The strength of the allegorical effort lies in the fact that it allows no interruption; the work goes on because any concentration of meaning in one place of the configuration leaves an open space elsewhere. Rather than avoiding or denying it, the allegorical tradition admits what Bacon called the "contract of error." The allegorical tradition invites criticism of and participation in its making, hence its reliance on the fragmentary and dark forms of expression, and its antisystematic bias. We must keep in mind that absolute metaphors guide theoretical discourse by stretching its credibility beyond the realm of logic into the legitimate sphere of imagination. The Conradian element in Perry Miller's description of how he conceived of his mission is overshadowed by his reference to Edward Gibbon. Obviously, though, Perry Miller had something else in mind, his bold rhetoric giving away the affinities he wants to establish.

> It was given to me, equally disconsolate on the edge of a jungle of central Africa, to have thrust upon me the mission of expounding what I took to be the innermost propulsion of the United States, while surprisingly, in that barbaric tropic, the unloading of drums of case-oil flowing out of the inexhaustible wilderness of America. However it came about, the vision demanded of me that I begin at the beginning, not at the beginning of a fall (wherein Gibbon had an artistic advantage, which he improved to the utmost), but at the beginning of a beginning.[10]

The demanding vision, it seems, was not really interested in the finer points of theory and method, but this lack of interest lies, of course, in the very nature of visions. For the historian of culture there is no such thing as the beginning of a beginning. Such a point of departure simply does not exist. This is why the original nature of the vision will eventually be translated into a *style* of acquiring knowledge. Indeed, where beginnings are concerned, theory, even when seen in the role of a handmaid serving the argument, avails to nothing. We can neither avoid nor solve the question of origin, however great the delight about our particular handmaid's availability may be.

[9] Ibid., p. 239.
[10] Ibid., p. viii.

Our *real* problem, then, is that we know at the same time too much and yet not enough about the culture which we call our own. The time and the people which, as intellectual historians, we try to portray, exist as parts of more than just one tradition, and unless we are content with the role of the annalist or the collector, we are forced to admit that by culling meaning from information we are putting the idea of truth to a severe test. Nothing *applies* to this problem in the sense of a pithy solution, which only needs to be unfolded for the sake of a more general understanding. The use of a theoretical framework, to put it bluntly, is extremely limited: theories, after all, have their very own and specific history. Theories, simply because of their very availability, cannot be employed in the name of historical truth. Theories are themselves a part of history. They help to solve problems—if we know what exactly the nature of our problem is. Thus, the problem of finding the right kind of knowledge, a kind of knowledge which is adequately situated within our paradoxical situation of knowing too much and yet not enough about a subject, can only be solved by acknowledging the kind of *need to know* which this paradox generates.

The anthropogenetic nature of the paradox in question is as obvious as are its transcendental qualities—there is, in a literal sense, nothing beyond it. Just as in Emerson's famous image of the stairs, we find ourselves somewhere between impossible extremes, neither inside nor totally outside of the paradox which constitutes the kind of knowledge about the world which we call acquired culture. Beyond this kind of knowledge there is only what Henry Adams referred to as "true ignorance."

Once we accept the paradox as a beginning and the need to know as its logical result, culture can be defined as an unending process of shaping all our knowledge and the act of reinterpreting a given period of the American nineteenth century can be seen as part of this process. The idea of meaning in the historical flux and the sense of our own self and identity are inextricably related, intertwined, and we have to conjecture what Stephen C. Pepper calls a world hypothesis in order to assert our notion of reinterpretation as a kind of sensible and necessary repetition.

The first points to bear in mind, then, are that it does not make much sense to write "against" previous interpretations (unless, of course, they are foolishly biased and wrongheaded) and that we cannot take refuge in a theoretical niche, which we call "our perspective," and from which we pretend to look at "our part of the century." The argument, in short, is directed against the idea of reinterpretation as a kind of linear progression. What we have to cope with in a plausible manner, instead, is *the necessity of repetition.* The historian of culture—for obvious reasons—tends to dislike the idea of repetition, associating it with a lack of originality, of progress, and of increase of knowledge. Rational skepticism, however, seems the appropriate attitude once we are forced to define what we need to know: and this we know indeed—definitions always need a supporting argument.

The most supportive argument will also have to be the most tentative. In the long run, however, the fact that our argument is open for criticism will turn out to be its essential source of strength. By eliminating a fixed theory, as a point of departure, we also eliminate the harrassing problem of easy confirmation or negation. It is, in other words, a simple and perfectly acceptable procedure not to subscribe to any given theory. Defined points of views in our preparadigmatic discipline may or may not be shared on the basis of belief-systems. It is an altogether different affair once we have to deal with the problem of following or disregarding a hypothetical beginning: waiting for failure or success is the name of the game. Ralph Waldo Emerson, who in his meandering fashion so frankly invented himself, played the game well, so well indeed that he more or less spelled out the rules for future players.

The fact that F. Nietzsche recognized these qualities in Emerson's thought, qualities which he tried to defend *against* Carlyle's praise of Emerson, demonstrates the existence of a hidden continuity which the second half of the nineteenth century provides. Nietzsche saw in Emerson a kind of kindred spirit, an intellectural brother in arms against the tendency of the nineteenth century to demoralize the idea of truth, and professing instead ideas about life. Nietzsche quoted approvingly from Emerson's essay "Circles" condensing two passages into one:

> Ein Amerikaner mag ihnen sagen, was ein grosser Denker, der auf die Erde kommt, als neues Centrum ungeheurer Kräfte zu bedeuten hat. "Seht euch vor," sagt Emerson, "wenn der grosse Gott einen Denker auf unsern Planeten kommen lässt. Alles ist dann in Gefahr. Es ist wie wenn in einer grossen Stadt eine Feuersbrunst ausgebrochen ist, wo keiner weiss, was eigentlich noch sicher ist und wo es enden wird. Da ist nichts in der Wissenschaft, was nicht morgen eine Umdrehung erfahren haben möchte, da gilt kein literarisches Ansehn mehr, noch die sogenannten Berühmtheiten; alle Dinge, die dem Menschen zu dieser Stunde theuer und werth sind, sind dies nur auf Rechnung der Ideen, die an ihrem geistigen Horizonte aufgestiegen sind und

welche die gegenwärtige Ordnung der Dinge ebenso verursachen, wie ein Baum seine Äpfel trägt. *Ein neuer Grad der Kultur würde augenblicklich das ganze System menschlicher Bestrebungen einer Umwälzung unterwerfen.*"[11]

As I have suggested earlier, the chance exists that the "new degree of culture" which Nietzsche mentions has been with us, going along like a waiting friend, taking his time unobtrusively helping us along while patiently expecting to be asked for the reason of his presence. Instead of looking for one single source, we ought to reckon with the presence of several traditions. If, in the preceding pages, the previous allegorical tradition in American culture has received more attention than it seems at first glance to deserve, one must bear in mind that it has been neglected for a long time—if in fact it ever has been acknowledged as a major force in the shaping of American culture. Only by emphasizing the role of allegory as a way of cognition in both its literary and in its visual form, can we answer the question which Stanley Cavell has phrased as follows: "Why has America never expressed itself philosophically? Or has it—in the metaphysical riot of its greatest literature? Has the impulse to philosophical speculation been absorbed, or exhausted, by speculation or in territory, as in such thoughts as Manifest Destiny? Or are such questions not really intelligible? They are, at any rate, disturbingly like the questions that were asked about American literature before it established itself."[12]

In short, then, what we shall have tried to present as a kind of answer to a disturbing question is the establishment of an American allegorical tradition in its own right. That such a tradition would indeed absorb material traditionally left for philosophers to work with will have, I hope, become evident.

Plato's light and Newton's optics: as if seen through a magnifying glass, the fragility of America as a symbol of identity, with all its cracks and fissures, has become clearly visible by the mid-thirties of the nine-

[11] An American may tell them what a center of mighty forces a great thinker can prove on this earth. "Beware when the great God lets loose a thinker on this planet," says Emerson. "Then all things are at a risk. It is as when a conflagration has broken out in a great city, and no man knows what is safe, or where it will end. There is not a piece of science, but its flank may be turned tomorrow; there is not any literary reputation, not the so-called eternal names of fame, that may not be revised and condemned. . . . The things which are dear to men at this hour are so on account of the ideas which have emerged on their mental horizon, and which cause the present order of things as a tree bears its apples. *A new degree of culture would instantly revolutionize the entire system of human pursuits*" (Friedrich Nietzsche, *Thoughts out of Season* [New York, 1964] 2: 200).

[12] Stanley Cavell, *The Senses of Walden* (San Francisco, 1981), p. 33.

teenth century. For those who cared, America as a symbol of unity and reconciliation had become questionable, and with it the very idea of the American myth. Deprived of its mythical force, American history could only lead towards chaos or towards something very close to it, namely a social equilibirium, always on the brink of unbalance or total anomie. If one needs a periodization and the limited orientation it affords, it seems a reasonable choice among several others to claim that the era we have dealt with can be qualified as having taken shape structurally either *after* W. E. Channing or *before* John Dewey. The diagnostic potential of the second choice is, of course, intriguing. The issue of intrigue, here, is one of explanatory value. Looking at the time in question as one which is essentially being defined as a period before, allows us by the sheer force of John Dewey's optimism, to emphasize the waning of telos-consciousness in the nineteenth century. The loss of the authority of the future accompanies the course of the nineteenth century towards the point where the vexing skepticism of its beginning finds its logical transformation. At a time when reality itself had become unreal to those who had their roots deeply imbedded in the nineteenth century, like Henry Adams, others abolished by means of daring and dazzling mental operation the distinctions between the knower and the known, thus opening the gate into a future of hitherto unknown possibilities. Cultural transformations of such enormous consequences are hardly ever brought about by one single major achievement. The opposite is the case: many voices, though heard individually, articulate the same idea. As if by incantation everything suddenly seems new. The enchantment of a fresh, unspoiled beginning carries over into the rhetoric of those who stake their claim unto the future.

We need not turn to such an obvious voice as Waldo Frank's in *Our America* in order to make our point. John Dewey, in his short essay of the year 1905, "Philosophy and American National Life," has provided us with an exemplary specimen of the rhetoric of a new beginning. Invariably it deals with fundamental issues first and ends with an appeal for action.

> It is today generally recognized that systems of philosophy, however abstract in conception and technical in exposition, lie, after all, much nearer to the heart of social and of national life than superficially appears. . . . It is, then, to the needs of democracy in America that we turn to find the fundamental problems of philosophy; and to its tendencies, its working forces, that we look for the points of view and the terms in which philosophy will envisage

> and solve these problems. . . . Such a conception of the aim and worth of philosophy is alone, I take it appropriate enough to the inherent logic of *our America* [my emphasis]. Philosophers are not to be a separate and monopolistic priesthood set apart to guard, and under certain conditions, to reveal, an isolated treasure of truths. It is theirs to organize—such organization involving, of course, criticism, rejection, transformation—the highest and wisest ideas of humanity, past and present, in such fashion that they may become most effective in the interpretation of certain recurrent and fundamental problems, which humanity, collectively and individually, has to face.[13]

This is the all-encompassing rhetoric of infinite possibilities: the future can be appropriated because it is only vaguely preceived—it is a future without authority.

The authority of the past is a different matter altogether. Between W. E. Channing's famous address "Self-Culture" of 1838 and John Dewey's *Human Nature and Conduct*, which appeared almost a hundred years later, there lies an era which the two texts help to qualify as points of extreme equidistance—without yielding, however, a plausible center. We are dealing with a time where pure chronology means very little! Neither can we claim that the substance of the era we have discussed lies hidden under some kind of metaphysical cloud marking the dividing line between light and darkness. Nor are we dealing with the life and death of a certain typology of thought, allowing us to put our finger on a decisive moment of gestalt-switch, or paradigm change. In fact, the very chiaroscuro qualities of our period make it a necessary strategic choice to look at it from the perspective of its replacement.

It is a perspective of diminution: the hundred years outlined before shrink at closer scrutiny, so there is no need to worry about symmetry. If then, as we claim, the loss of the authority of the future is best described with the optimism in mind which replaces it, obviously the attraction of such slogans as Van Wyck Brooks's familiar one of the "usable past" was not exactly the result of revealing fresh and convincing insights into the making of an American tradition sui generis. Its popularity owed itself mainly to what it insinuated about the potential of the future. In terms of what has been pointed out previously, the success, for example of the Seven-Arts-Group, was above all due to its replacement of the nineteenth-century burden of skepticism and doubt.

[13] John Dewey, "Philosophy and American National Life," in John Dewey, ed., *Essays on the New Empiricism 1903–1906* (Carbondale, Ill., 1977), pp. 73–78.

Managing to cast off that legacy and claiming, one is tempted to say, a new deal on the future, they deemphasize, however, at the same time and without intent, the critical potential of culture. Odd enough as it may seem at first glance, the critics of culture, and Van Wyck Brooks above all, safely managed to institutionalize the idea of culture as criticism; the bees of the nineteenth century had been transformed into wasps. Where the first were allowed only one sting in a lifetime of gathering honey, the critical intellectuals after the turn of the century were allowed many attacks. This is not to say that their criticism was not valid; the contrary is true. But we are looking at their function as a force of replacement, and if we want to make an estimate of how strong the currents of doubts and uncertainty really were to which they had managed to deny recognition, we must take a critical look at what they seemed to have gained. From the turn of the century straight into the thirties of the depression and into the New Deal, the idea prevailed that the future could be "engineered." The impact of the idea of beneficial cultural and social engineering with the purpose of reform and uplift has been so massive that it continues to express itself in academic writing, where the familiar triad of twentieth-century optimism qua criticism still prevails: society—individual—culture.

It would hardly be an undue exaggeration if one were to say that with the exception of F. O. Matthiessen, whose Emersonian sense of tragedy as fate (and therefore *not* as failure) allowed him to work with nonsymmetrical forms of analysis, most of the academic cultural criticism in the twentieth century has woven its argument in the triangular pattern.[14] Even if figures like V. L. Parrington did cast a mighty shadow, obscuring the indispensable realm of the aesthetic, the formidable triad "individual, culture, and society" served as a useful frame of reference for critics of the left, of the liberal persuasion, and for conservatives as well. If the coinciding interest and implicit companionship of opposing critical schools has gone unnoticed so far and becomes remarkably clear today, we should not assume that such a development is the result of a better and more refined critical theory. The fact that we now see an underlying structure which we previously did not notice must be attributed mainly to one major factor: the absence of struggle. So the cultural transformation which began after the turn of the century and was implemented in the following decades was successful. That is why we now can reconsider and make an estimate of what this success really means and at what cost it was achieved.

Two observations can be made and put forward as preliminary find-

[14] For F. O. Matthiessen's specific blend of literary and social criticism see Frederick C. Stern, *F. O. Matthiessen: Christian Socialist as Critic* (Chapel Hill, N.C., 1981).

ings. First, the intellectual maturity of the nineteenth-century America which we discuss is more than merely equal to the intellectual life of the twentieth century. In many ways educated men and women in the second half of the nineteenth century were better educated and more internationally oriented than most of their successors after the turn of the century. The second observation simply concerns itself with the fact that by being cosmopolitan in education, interest, and in outlook, American intellectuals of the nineteenth century did not cease to be American. For men and women like Emerson, Thoreau, Margaret Fuller, Adams, and William James, as well as for the later nineteenth-century historians and social scientists, the opposite is true. The more they immersed themselves in continental thought the better they understood what it meant to be an American.

If we claim that the severe criticism of American culture, as it was pronounced by Van Wyck Brooks and those who followed his track even while disavowing his ancestry, dominated the following decades, we must also say that in terms of replacement the American nineteenth century had become a particular kind of cultural moment in the life of the twentieth century. "[H]e had heard his father whistle. That was the end of the old faith for Channing. If his father did not believe in it, life was not so dismal, after all." This is the brief account Van Wyck Brooks gave us in *The Flowering of New England.*[15] And simply because the course of the history of consciousness must follow a logical sequence, he had to emphasize the nearly all-embracing powers of Unitarianism. But such is the order of construction.

Had Van Wyck Brooks, instead of emphasizing the terrible dominance of Unitarian culture and genteel Victorianism, dwelt on the heathenish broodings contained within the legacy of transcendentalism, it would have been somewhat more difficult for him to canonize his own iconoclasms. The strategic choice of looking at the second half of the American nineteenth century as the time *before* John Dewey therefore allows us to posit the idea of selfhood, as opposed to the role of the individual, at the center of gravity, or more precisely, as the strange fixed point in the field of a seemingly coherent order of tradition.

Indeed, the most immediate answer to the exhaustion of America's function as a symbol of identity in the twentieth century must be seen in the emergence of a new philosophy of self in the nineteenth century. The rise of a genuinely new idea of the self, by the very consciousness of its own authenticity, threatened any conceivable course

[15] *The Flowering of New England* (New York, 1941), p. 54.

of ordained history, whether in a secular or nonsecular sense. It was as if in imitation of the well-known Augustinian formula, the new emerging self seemed to have its center everywhere and its circumference nowhere, thoroughly confusing the stable order of Unitarianism. The most troubling aspect about the transformation of the traditional idea of selfhood was not, however, as might be expected, its rebellious and anarchic character, but its certainty of belonging. By looking for a place beyond it, each of the men whose thoughts we have been discussing, in their individual and idiosyncratic way, represented continuity. The continuity—not to be tedious—of allegory, as opposed to that of history. This last statement is a shortcut, but in their most profound and stunning statements it becomes obvious that each of them, in his own way, had realized that metamorphosis has always been an essential quality of allegory. To the extent that they saw themselves as going beyond the established forms of knowledge, American history, in their eyes, had become dangerously predictable—long before it had been established, in any but the most superficial sense, what the sense of American history was all about.

Plato's light and Newton's optics, at the risk of repeating myself, were essential ingredients of a variety of metaphorical references to a self which found its singularity guaranteed and justified by the act of self-reflection. Singularity: each of the four men whose work we have taken to be representative of the allegorical tradition in question possessed a highly developed gift of formulating universal questions within the limits of self-reflection. They were masters, to be more precise, in the art of expressing the sense of their time in a specific style, reflecting the aporetic viewpoint they had chosen to work with.

Self-knowledge as an anthropological paradox became the obsession of many nineteenth-century thinkers. Their search for a style and an adequate form for what they felt to be humankind's fate accounts for the enduring attraction of the nineteenth century. Rhetoric, as I have tried to show, by having been reinstated and rehabilitated as a domain of natural metaphysics, rather than being cast in the traditional role as an embellishing ornament or as a quasi-scientific tool of persuasion, is the primary drawing force behind this attraction. The insight that all possible achievements of subjectivity are defined by acknowledging its limitations through self-reflection is the second major force behind an attraction which has a powerful appeal to the modern mind.

Emerson, who greatly valued Montaigne, may well have seen the truth in the French philosopher's statement "la pire place, que nous puissions prendre, c'est en nous," and he accordingly cultivated a deep antipathy against ideas of unrestrained subjectivity. Restraint and a sense of limit, these qualifications of the self were the preconditions to go beyond the American myth, if we accept that the essence, or at least the final characteristic of the American myth which we can name is the fear that America might not exist. That we should be "but a *thought*—a vagrant thought, a useless thought, a homeless thought, wandering forlorn among the empty eternities," as Mark Twain has Satan say in *The Mysterious Stranger* would have been the discovery of unrestrained self-constitution. As a countermeasure the emergence of a new philosophy of the self, differing dramatically from the technically future-oriented self designed by Channing was involved, from the very beginning, with the infinite abundance of concrete things, objects, forms of life, customs, and habits. A great respect for the fantastic of the real was accompanied by a latent suspicion that the yields of pure speculation would probably turn out to be meager. Evolution, in short, was our finest epos. Only in bits and pieces would we ever know the whole tale. As Emerson liked to point out: if one knew the whole history of nature, the result would probably be extremely disappointing. So the self in question, the subjectivity facing nature both inside and outside of itself, not only learned to see the merits of limited truth but also developed a rhetoric of probabilities. Emerson's essays express states of being which are *also* possible, they do not primarily advocate. If a quick and fundamental assessment is needed concerning the novelty of transcendent subjectivity, one needs only compare its modes of speech with the rhetoric rules taught at Harvard by the other Channing, Edward Tyrell, Boylston professor of rhetoric and oratory.[16]

So there is something about the nineteenth century, a kind of urgency and presence, which makes it difficult to keep one's distance. It is in many ways *our* century, as we soon realize when we consider some of its more disturbing qualities; its sense of grandiosity—frequently expressed by involved and elaborated ways of identification; its inevitable moments of profound disillusionment; and last but not least, its sense of unreality. The age of competing realisms rested upon uncertainties. Towards the end of the century many suspicions were confirmed: "It is true, that which I have revealed to you: there is no God, no universe, no human race, no earthly life, no heaven, no hell. It is all a dream—a grotesque and foolish dream."[17]

The nineteenth century is *ours* to the extent of our refusal to be

[16] See Daniel Walker Howe, *The Unitarian Conscience: Harvard Moral Philosophy 1805–1861* (Cambridge, Mass., 1970).

[17] Mark Twain, *No. 44, The Mysterious Stranger* (Berkeley, 1969), p. 187.

complacent inhabitants of a globalized Eseldorf. Even if the postmodern attitude tells us not to resist and to avoid the trap of logocentric reasoning, we sense the futility of such instructions. They have about them distinct features of anxiety and subdued hysteria. Philosophical criticism within the humanities today betrays its lack of *sophia* in its exhibitionist, unrestrained posturing. The plight of the postmodern mind, it seems, lies in the easy access it has to virtually *all* the answers, while at the same time it seems to be unable to formulate a singly satisfying question. Saying this, of course, is just another way of pointing out to what an extent the postmodern mode of thinking is part of a tradition which it tries to negate. Ignoring tradition often results in missing the present as well: the times *have* changed, and the flâneur today walks on a tightrope; his choice of pace, in other words, is limited to the right balance between going either too slowly or too fast. There is no turtle to help him to measure the correct pace: this being an extremely late consequence of the almost *given* fact that the pace of the turtle has always been a paradigm of deception. We therefore *need* the nineteenth century. It does provide questions which have remained open until today.

Mark Twain was not the only one to wonder about the reality of the real. Henry Adams, at about the same time when Mark Twain was tentatively "dipping his pen into hell," took a final, long glance at our ability to identify our place in the cosmic order—and remained unconvinced. Both men, incidentally, had to violate established rules of their profession in order to articulate their misgivings. Henry Adams, among other achievements, managed, however, to outline the poetics of allegory. He clearly pointed out what one could rightfully be expected to live up to. He also, and in this respect he was much more of a philosopher *au fond* than most people realized, left no doubt that it was part of humankind's future to live within the boundaries of allegory by looking for a place beyond it.

> The problem to the anthropoid ape a hundred thousand years ago was the same as that addressed to the physicist-historian of 1900:—How long could he go on developing indefinite new phases in response to the occult attractions of an infinitely extended universe? What new directions could his genius take? . . . The figure used for illustration is immaterial except so far as it limits the nature of the attractive force. In any case the theory will have to assume that the mind has always figured its motives as reflections of itself, and that this is as true in its conception of electricity as in its instinctive imitation of a God. Always and ev-

> erywhere the mind creates its own universe, and pursues its own phantoms; but the force behind the image is always a reality,—the attractions of occult power. . . . If the physicist-historian is satisfied with neither of the known laws of mass,—astronomical or electric,—and cannot arrange his variables in any combination that will conform with a phase-sequence, no resource seems to remain but that of waiting until his physical problems shall be solved, and he shall be able to explain what Force is. As yet he knows almost as little of material as of immaterial substance. He is as perplexed before the phenomena of Heat, Light, Magnetism, Electricity, Gravitation, Attraction, Repulsion, Pressure, and the whole schedule of names used to indicate unknown elements, as his own Thought whose action is so astounding on the direction of his energies. Probably the solution of any one of the problems will give the solution for them all.[18]

We have examined Henry Adams's rhetoric more closely and may now safely assume that both, a dim view of progress and the growing insights into the essentially elusive character of nature, guided the current and the undertow of the American nineteenth-century stream of consciousness.

At the end of the epoch it was obvious that the choices were limited and that tradition was not a storehouse of possibilities but rather a necessary force at work. History of consciousness cannot be written in other terms than in those which it produces for purposes of self-reflection: allegory as a mode of thought.

A final word on the problem of allegory. By treating it above all as a mode of cognition, we are emphasizing the Platonic side of the neo-Platonic tradition, favoring the truth-status over the idea of revelation. The Greco-Roman heritage in the history of the perception and criticism of allegory has been overshadowed for a long time by the Judeo-Christian hostility against what seemed to be above all a remnant of anthropocentric paganism. The allegorical mode of cognition and expression openly invites the discussion of intention and auctorial authority. The author's right to speak about the world, to describe and analyze it, is being judged with the idea in mind that we are looking at a conscious design of representation. We are invited to analyze the procedure. In our earlier discussions of these matters, we have tried to show why the allegorical mode of expression had such an appeal to troubled minds who tried to deal honestly with their conviction that in

[18] Henry Adams, *The Degradation of the Democratic Dogma*, ed. Brooks Adams (New York, 1949), p. 298.

the end truth will always remain hidden behind surfaces and appearances.

In terms of the traditional distinction between anomalist and analogist modes of thought, we have tried to show that the typologist tradition in the American nineteenth century not only allowed, but in fact invited, the divergent, anomalist view of the world. That language would become the primary issue of concern and its relationship to things the next issue, is not surprising. It is the forceful conceptualization of the relationship between the literal and the visual perception and representation of the world which is the most striking and intellectually revealing phenomenon in the second half of the American nineteenth century. The full force and energy of these conceptualizations emerge only once they are seen as constituents of the allegorical tradition. If the allegorical tradition expresses doubts and skepticism, as well as the will to go beyond the safe grounds of established knowledge, then both the formation of a literary canon and the growing professionalization within a broadly defined field of the humanities work against allegory. Two examples, picked more or less at random, may help us to understand the nature of the disappearance of the allegorical consciousness in the context of American culture after the turn of the century.

If we look at F. O. Matthiessen's great book *American Renaissance*, which appeared in 1941, we are not only struck by the sudden insight that 1941 is indeed a threshold year in the periodization of American literary criticism, but furthermore we have to acknowledge the canonical character of Matthiessen's book. It is, in this sense, the result of a process which began about 1913. If Matthiessen's book, which one often reads paying too much attention to its individualistic format, is now considered a classic, this can only confirm its successful role in the establishment of the canon. In fact, in many ways *American Renaissance* is the logical outcome of the covert complicity between the warring factions of literary intellectuals at work ever since the 1910s, who so often seemed to be at each other's throats. In the end they all translated culture into poetry or fiction as its supreme form of expression, while at the same time they acknowledged, as if in a gesture of repentance, the importance of popular culture. Between these two positions legitimate modes of knowledge, which had been part of the intellectual life of the nineteenth century, quickly disappeared from sight. It is indicative of this process of replacement that F. O. Matthiessen delegated allegory almost exclusively to the realm of fiction. At the same time this very act of reserving the function of allegory for fiction, for Hawthorne's above all, enabled Matthiessen to stick to his own Christian-Socialist beliefs and to the hope which such a creed had to invest in the discursive argument and its access to reality. We must remember, of course, that it took F. O. Matthiessen ten years to write the book, so in many respects it is the product of the thirties as well.

In his decisive chapter on the question of allegory and symbolism, Chapter 7, Matthiessen leaves no doubt, drawing heavily on Coleridge, that symbolism, which "in contrast with allegory, is dynamic," is the more valid form of expression, the one closer to life. Matthiessen, by combining such divergent tendencies as T. S. Eliot's theory of poetry and Van Wyck Brooks's early interest in the democratic character of American literature and culture, forged the canon of literary works and their meaning. Matthiessen's canon is supposed to provide ideas for a usable present. Where in this sense *autonomous* art manages to become *functional*, allegory can only be a disturbance. It interferes with the kind of practical action which the establishment of the canon manages to set free.

Our second example, referring above all to the limits of professionalization, can be presented best if we take another look at the figure of William James. The arsenal of James's thought not only contained the stuff of allegory and metamorphosis, it also incorporated the fundamentals of antiprofessionalism. If we want to put these fundamentals into a nutshell it helps to confront his introduction to *The Literary Revisions of the Late Henry James* with such blunt assertions as William J. Goode's that "An industrializing society is a professionalizing society."[19] William James, in the process of writing the introduction to his father's literary papers, despite certain misgivings concerning his father's views of nature and society, eagerly grasped the chance to work out the latter's view of reality. In a clear case of identification, William James not only describes his father's view of that world as being both "optimistic in one sense, pessimistic in another." He goes even further when he sets out to convey to his readers the difficulties one has to face when writing from such a dualistic, or rather contradictory frame of mind.

> My father's own disgust at any abstract statement of his systems could hardly be excelled by that of the most positivistic reader. I will not say that the logical relations of its terms were with him a mere afterthought; they were more organic than that. But the core and centre of the thing in him was always instinct and attitude, something realized at a stroke, and felt like a fire in his

[19] William J. Goode, "Encroachment, Charlatinism and the Emerging Professions," *American Sociological Review* 25 (1960): 902.

> breast; and all attempts to articulate verbal formulations of it were makeshift of a more or less desparately impotent kind. This is why he despised every formulation he made as soon as it was uttered, and set himself to the Sisyphos labor of producing a new one that should be less irrelevant.[20]

Couched in terms of memory, William James could hardly have described his own troubled self in any better way than he did when describing his father: "I remember hearing him groan when struggling in this way, 'Oh that I might thunder it out in a single interjection that would tell the *whole* of it, and never speak a word again!' But he paid his tribute to necessity; and few writers in the end were more prolix than he."[21]

Sons are not always so generous when they have to account for the work of their fathers. William James's own philosophical position was far removed from that of his father. But then his sympathy is reserved for the man who tried to see—and by writing to create—order in what seemed an oppressingly unstructured universe.

If we want to hear the questions raised in the nineteenth century and addressed to us, because they were left unanswered, we listen to the voices of Walter Benjamin and Friedrich Nietzsche. Their presence in our own times constantly reminds us of the nineteenth-century heritage under discussion here.

What exactly do we gain by looking at the nineteenth century through the eyes of Nietzsche and Benjamin? There are many advantages of such a view—of which only a few need to be mentioned in order to finish our argument. Above all, I think we establish the kind of distance to Hegel, which nineteenth-century studies so badly need. Since the general tendency persists to read Hegel as an absolute idealist of sweeping teleology, much of the architecture of such a reading is imposed upon the nineteenth century. Looking at the nineteenth century from the perspective of Nietzsche and perhaps even Benjamin will immediately reveal one important fact to us: the nineteenth century had no architect. It may have had many architects, but they certainly did not work with the same blueprints in mind. This, of course, is especially true of the American nineteenth century—but we do not need to make a special case here. As a glance at the *North American Review* shows immediately, the American observers were quite aware of the variety of influences which made up the romantic tradition.

[20] James, *Essays*, p. 7.

[21] Ibid., p. 8.

In addition to establishing some distance to Hegel's overpowering image as the archteleologist, by looking at the nineteenth century from the point of view of Nietzsche and Benjamin, we also gain a perspective that allows us to compare two essential cosmological concepts: first, the cyclical image of eternal recurrence of Nietzsche, and second, the linear concept of progression by decay which is Benjamin's. Both of these concepts are related to the very process of secularization as it was interpreted by the protagonists of the allegorical tradition in nineteenth-century America. The striking ahistorical aspect of Nietzsche's theory of eternal recurrence throws a harsh light on the affinity between joy and pain in Emerson's theory of compensation, where he focused on the labor and effort which were necessary to the production of such sublimations.[22] If we were to follow Heidegger's metaphysical interpretation of Nietzsche's "scientific hypothesis" of eternal recurrence, we would immediately have to think of the essential loneliness of those struggling to give shape and meaning to the cultural experience of the American nineteenth century. As if mending their own raft, they added one volume to another, spinning out the rise, fall, and fate of other republics and civilizations, obsessed, of course, with the culture and society which they inhabited.[23] True, the threat of the idea of eternal recurrence is that of having no more questions to ask—but it is equally true that it is the ruin which always invites the next question. Henry Adams exemplified this configuration of ideas in his fanciful comments on the "immorality of Roman history": "Rome was actual; it was England; it was going to be America. Rome could not be fitted into an orderly, middle-class, Bostonian, systematic scheme of evolution. No law of progress applied to it. Not even time-sequences—the last refuge of helpless historians—had value for it."[24]

This is not the final insight. The questions do continue: "Two great experiments of Western civilization had left there the chief monument of their failure, and nothing proved that the city might not still survive to express the failure of a third."[25]

Nietzsche and Benjamin provided the metaphors for such failure which would make its ideas bearable: but their sublime despair was preceded by darker broodings. There are some further advantages in

[22] The fact that Nietzsche admired Emerson is due above all to Nietzsche's recognition of Emerson's antihistorical attitude. This includes Emerson's iconoclasm and his rejections of systematic thought that would fit in a historical mold.

[23] See Levin, *History*, and Richard C. Vitzthum, *The American Compromise* (Norman, Okla., 1974).

[24] Adams, *Education*, p. 91.

[25] Ibid.

accepting Nietzsche and Benjamin as the central witnesses of the nineteenth century's legacy to our own time which should not go unmentioned. Both Benjamin and Nietzsche picked up the essential material which the nineteenth century provided in order to allow the forging of the tools which it took to understand, by dissection, the core of the twentieth century. Both Benjamin and Nietzsche transformed the nineteenth-century preoccupation with truth into a problem of language and its indicative character related to modern humanity's place in nature. Nietzsche outlined what we may regard as the very structure of the bridge which the traveler from the nineteenth century into the twentieth had to cross in his brief essay "On Truth and Falsehood in an Extra-Moral Sense," where, before evoking the potential powers of a philosophy of culture, he deals a hard and precise blow at established theories of truth by stating his own misgivings.

> What then is truth? A mobile army of metaphors, metonymines, anthropomorphisms—in short, a sum of human relations which poetically and rhetorically intensified, became transposed and adorned, and which after long usage by a people seem fixed, canonical and binding on them. Truths are illusions which one has forgotten *are* illusions, worn-out metaphors which have become powerless to affect the senses, coins which have their obverse effaced and are now no longer of account as coins but merely as metal.[26]

Nietzsche, of course, when talking of an "army of metaphors," did not anticipate the aberrations of the so-called postmodern period. By implication, however, he drew attention to the nonmetaphorical realm of life, to the organization of things to which language remains bound. This bind, on which Nietzsche in his essay finally relies, is the real and original source of his well-known statement: "Only as an aesthetic phenomenon is the world and the being of man eternally justified."[27]

The aesthetic attitude, therefore, is first of all a necessity, and furthermore it is the condition preceding one's potential liberation by becoming a creative, acting individual (*künstlerisch, schaffendes Subjekt*). Nietzsche's view that developments in society, in science, and in culture denied nature provides him with the means to emphasize language as a way to work against the "cult of knowledge" which had effected the downfall of culture—and society. We need not go into the details of Nietzsche's dramatization of his ideas on language in order

[26] Friedrich Nietzsche, *Early Greek Philosophy and Other Essays* (New York, 1964), p. 180.

[27] Friedrich Nietzsche, *The Birth of Tragedy* (New York, 1964), p. 50.

to realize that by redeeming rhetoric from the confinements of its ornamental role, Nietzsche elevates the realm of surfaces to the level of having the truth-status which had been traditionally reserved for probings into the realm of being. The crisis, in short of culture and society, cannot be tackled and overcome by means of more penetrating and effective knowledge, but by redefining the very character of the crisis in question.

Nietzsche emphasized two aspects in his essay "On Truth," both of which are directly related to his diagnosis of the crisis of the modern mind. Positive science not only serves as a negative image for the "cult of knowledge," it also pushes philosophy back into the realm of art—and in the end, back into the realm of common experience. Common experience in Nietzsche's sense is antisocial: society is one of the main agents to further the activities of the intellect, *but* society is at the same time and by virtue of exactly the quality mentioned before, a constant reminder of language's inherent debt to nature. Attaching the idea of nature to modern concepts of social crisis via the concept of language and the aesthetic consequences resulting from the useful nature of illusion: these are Nietzsche's main contributions in the process of outlining the allegorical tradition of the nineteenth century to us.

In a not altogether different way it is Walter Benjamin, whose efforts to restore with a naturalistic interpretation of language the sacred dignity of the profane, be it the artifact or the physical fact of our experience, who provides us with a frame of reference which comes out of the twentieth century—drawing its energies from the material offered by the nineteenth. Like two poles of an electric field, Nietzsche and Benjamin order our experience of the nineteenth century. Our debt to both of them has become quite apparent, not only in the long-run discussion of the allegorical tradition in the American nineteenth century, but also as we finally outline the focal points around which we have structured our discussion of the shape and meaning of this tradition. As none of these points of special attention could be chronologically isolated from one another within the context of our argument, it seems sensible enough to present them as *themes* which have pervaded our arguments as a whole—sometimes in the foreground and sometimes less visibly in the background of our discussion. In addition, a brief commentary will accompany them which is best presented as a *thesis*, if only for the obvious lack of a comprehensive, let alone exhaustive, foundation.

Theme: Crisis and modernism—the inflation of a concept.

Thesis: The key term in practically any kind of analysis of contemporary society and culture is that of crisis. To such an extent, indeed, have modernism and crisis become synonymous concepts, that their explanatory value has decreased and in the exact proportion to their rising prominence in sociological, cultural, and literary criticism. As a result, the idea of criticism itself has lost much of its original authority, based on objectivity, enlightenment, and advocacy. If we discard for our present purpose Max Weber's statement that the soteriologically oriented intellectual will always feel a strong sense of crisis, we must in due fairness admit, however, that a disquieting sense of arbitrariness and futility becomes dominant whenever the personal and social experience of modern humanity articulates itself. The question whether the course of history is contributing to the welfare of humanity seems to be as pressing now as it was in the nineteenth century. If the term *crisis* has in fact become inflationary to the extent of explaining nothing, or very little, we have to ask ourselves what we could have sensibly expected as problem-solving answers, given the questions we were asking. Instead of continuing to formulate our set of questions from the perspective of an ill-defined sense of intellectual confusion and dislocation characterizing the present (i.e., committing the postmodernist fallacy), we must clarify what we originally could have rightfully hoped for. If the acquired and accumulated practical and theoretical knowledge of the past has proved to be insufficient for our purposes today, we have to reexamine how and why the potential for truth pertaining to the knowledge available on the one hand and our needs to know on the other hand have continuously grown apart.

How, in other words, can we explain the tendency of the contemporary individual to establish him or herself in the world as a kind of *homo demiurgus* and experience at the same time an overpowering loss of self? If self-preservation (*conservatio sui*) is the fundamental category of modernity, as Hans Blumenberg claims, we have to go back to those points in time when the self in question asserted itself in ways which tell us something about the historical consequences of that act. Two paradigmatic, and genetically consequential, models of self-construction must serve as framework for our topic. Both of them are allegories of ending and beginning; both of them also define the limits of what we might call the historical substance of the nineteenth century.

Theme: Transcendentalism and secularization—cosmogony and the idea of self-limitation.

Thesis: Emerson's concept of an autonomous self was the final and therefore fragile result of a dialectical redefinition of nature, a process which involved the complex movement from *cosmodicy* to *theodicy* and finally to *anthropodicy*. This development of Emerson's thought emerged from a historical consciousness which intended to maintain a sense of those elements which had provided the energy for the dynamics of historical change in the first place. Emerson therefore started a tradition not by replacing one set of ideas by another, but by adding to the traditional transition from the Book of Scripture to the Book of Nature a question about the future which allowed the reemergence from the past, and thus the recovery of some of the tendencies of eighteenth-century enlightenment. (The progress made by Emerson becomes all the more obvious if one compares his restructuring of the relationship between the Book of Scripture and the Book of Nature with Jonathan Edward's famous Image 156 in *Images and Shadows*. Such a comparison will also demonstrate why the typological approach has to be replaced by dialectical hermeneutics when we move into the nineteenth century proper.) Like Kant in his early writings, Emerson used the model of Newtonian science, the idea of empirical science in general, in order to demonstrate humankind's moral responsibilities as part of an unfinished act of creation. The idea of telos implied a paradoxical structure of time, a messianic *and* secular temporality, telos being divided into the notions of a fulfilled life now where the individual was concerned and that of a common *restitutio ad integrum* in the future, with respect to the human race. Redemption in actual time, however, demanded allegorical expression.

Skeptical romanticism, the essential ingredient of transcendentalism, provided an otherwise disunified concept with a theoretical vitality, based on the acceptance of paradox, doubt, uncertainty, conflict, and continuity. Transcendentalism, thus understood, constitutes *the* great American philosophy, carrying its powers of explanation from the context of scripture to nature to culture to politics. Transcendentalism, in other words, became an ongoing dialogue, a continued argument, surviving by virtue of its social adaptability. Adaptability, however, must have its limits, the limit of transcendentalism being the replacement of uncertainty and skepticism, inextricably connected with the idea of telos by a sense of explanatory absolutism and theoretical purity. Transcendentalism and its legacy, which had still been a formative influence on the emergence, development, and substance of pragmatism, began to disintegrate when the *need* to know, and with it the tacit acceptance of life's uncertainty, made way for the cultural consensus that all the knowledge needed to make life meaningful (and empirically predictable) had become generally available. It was not the development of science and professionalization which superseded the legacy of transcendentalism, but a reinterpretation of empirical science.

Where in the case of Emerson and Kant the empirical immediacy of material nature provoked questions about the character of humankind's experience, the later belief in the predictability and empirically controllable production of experience abolished the motive behind the original question.

The history of the tradition outlined so far will have to be written as a dialectical history, in the post-Hegelian sense. The strategy of such historiography would obviously have to stress the Janus-faced quality of the organic metaphor and the elements of conflict, of discontinuity, of negation and fragmentation which had shaped transcendentalism from the very beginning. A dialectical treatment of transcendentalism should not be confused with the general applicability pertaining to deconstructivist or other such efforts. In fact I would like to claim that transcendentalism in its very essence *is* a post-Hegelian philosophy: negatively dialectic, intentionally unsystematic, and very much aware of the problem of defining a beginning. Metaphysical cosmogony having been discredited twice, by Copernicus and by his interpreters, transcendentalism begins with the finite object, the only material evidence of the infinite. The dialectical energy of transcendentalism derived its momentum from the inherent "otherness" which the finite object represents, namely the simultaneously mute and telling concreteness of nature. Transcendentalism, seen as a genetically dialectic system of thought, could in the end only be resolved by either an allegorical or an aesthetic justification of history. From the very beginning the convergence of the ethical and the aesthetic world-construction was therefore implied in its development.

Theme: Nature, culture, politics—the tragic disposition of the American man of letters; the triumph of nature.

Thesis: Kant's theoretical speculation of 1775 about the principally unfinished world and the continuing process of creation set the framework for the central question of the nineteenth century, which Ralph Waldo Emerson pointedly defined as the need for an adequate cosmogony. Emerson's demands for an adequate cosmogony, for a new understanding of mythology and a theory of humankind which would, as he put it, include "the beast and the dream," are the points of departure in the effort to contribute to a better understanding of the nineteenth-century American historical consciousness and its part in the development of modernity.

Transcendentalism as a humanistic political tradition in America has been largely neglected on account of its specific resistance to the centripetal formation of modern consciousness. The process by which the modern mind seemed to branch out into a corporate form of highly diversified and segmented varieties of experience was accomplished by an increasing reduction of historically valid choices. The point, however, is not that Max Weber's version of a tightening bureaucracy is responsible—it was rather the result of a pretheoretical development which itself was part of the general tendency of the nineteenth century to save the idea of theodicy by radicalizing the autonomy of the self. The establishment of the autonomous self for the purpose of maintaining the idea of a just God demanded a specific historical consciousness. To use a variation of a phrase coined by Emerson: the party of memory and and the party of hope had to become dialectically intertwined. Either party would eventually find its representative: one being Friedrich Nietzsche, the other being Walter Benjamin. Both worked towards the end of Kant's speculation, or rather towards its transformation into a different set of questions.

On its way towards these two genuine alternatives, the American historical consciousness of the nineteenth century, as exemplified by Emerson, Thoreau, Adams, and William James developed along the lines of Emerson's theory of subjectivity, which included a kind of prepsychological phenomenology of *human* nature, which he kept well guarded behind a stoic attitude, and which his contemporaries misunderstood and deplored. Emerson's view of nature developed into two distinctly separate conceptual areas, connected, however, in the fact of the body. The area of brute anthropological fact and the realm of the sublime were treated as part and parcel of the human condition. Compensation was Emerson's key term when he had to defend his belief in the harmonious universe against his own skepticism and despair. Emerson accepted facts and there are passages in his essays and journals which betray a resigned attitude towards the facts of nature which remind the reader of Freud, were it not for his allegorical sense of construction and his rhetoric of metamorphosis.[28]

Emerson seemed to know what Walter Benjamin would say more than half a century later: postmythical humanity knows only one way to reconcile its inner self and nature, the way of despair. Everything about this conflict urged for a solution within the realm of art, and it

[28] Emerson's probings into the psychological nature of the individual frequently reveal an uncanny knowledge about psychological mechanisms which he discovered and described on the basis of intuition and which only in a post-Freudian era would become named within a theoretical framework.

was Thoreau who forced the issue by moving into the center of the conflict.

Theme: Thoreau's double consciousness—the languages of Nature and the language of Humankind.

Thesis: In *Walden*, in his travelogues, and in his journals, nature and art drifted apart, and the more this tendency became apparent, the harder Thoreau tried to reconcile the two. Transcendentalism with him had become a kind of hope, an ideal, which he needed to protect himself against the cruelties and the vicissitude of experience.

Nature was *not* an ally—and he knew it, but would not say so and betray his own hopes. As a consequence the medium for hiding and revealing, *language*, became for him more than an ordinary form of expressing these conflicting intentions. Thoreau turned the use of language into a Book on Language. By experiencing the conflict mentioned above vis-à-vis nature, he discovered—more by accident than by design—the nature of Language. *Walden*, to put it in a nutshell, is a book about nature by virtue of being a Book of Nature. Nature, of course, being represented by language. There is a revealing paradox at work here, one which Emerson would undoubtedly have enjoyed. Its importance lies in the change of emphasis from the observation of nature to the analysis of the experience, the form and content of the observation. The essence of Thoreau's work, therefore, lies in his journals, rather than in individual books.

Thoreau, to put it differently, transforms nature into a unified *locus*, unified by the aesthetic effort of the observer. Romanticizing nature, as he does in a Novalis-like manner in several passages in *Walden*, and the factual observation of nature's physiognomy were closely related activities. They both imply the existence of a coherence, based on an organized effort of the human senses like seeing or hearing. They imply, in short, a defined point of view, the knowledge about which will eventually tell us more than we are supposed to be told. Where nature with Emerson often assumed an artificial character, as if set up for study in a museum or laboratory, Thoreau was dealing with nature as the independent "other" which eventually provoked its aesthetic domestication.

In the end the scientist and the artist worked towards the same goal—landscape painting and simple graphic illustration, objectivity and imagination shared a common origin. This common origin became, by necessity, the origin of social and political theories as well. The unification of social and artistic vision, of desire and imagination, shaped the substance of the American nineteenth century as a moral imperative. Like all such constructs it was in need of constant vindication in order to survive as part of a tradition which claimed both moral and political legitimacy.

From nature to culture and from culture to history: these are the basic shifts of focus, which slowly changed the character of the intellectual tradition of the American nineteenth century. Nowhere, of course, will we find a fundamental, airtight separation of concepts; but then this is exactly the reason why American transcendentalism was able to establish itself as a historically vital force at all.

Theme: The stoic solution and the function of an aesthetic cosmodicy.

Thesis: Nature and history, in the work of Henry Adams, added yet another configurative aspect to the formation of an intellectual tradition which kept redefining the rational ground for a public morality (politics) by aesthetically justifying the overwhelming powers of nature. Where Thoreau still needed the geographical and at the same time the symbolic *locus standi* in order to produce an image and find coherence where chaos was always a felt presence, Henry Adams chose the *image itself* as his conceptual point of departure. The shared image, an interactional figure of thought, became his central safeguard against chaos and anarchy. Again the opinions about nature and society are profoundly related, both by convergence and by conflict. The beauty of nature, containing both poetry and terror, its playful cruelty, as it had been observed by Henry Adams at his sister's deathbed in Italy, is not Kant's any longer. It is not the kind of beauty which attracts reason (*sittliche Vernunft*), it is instead the very opposite, a reminding force, displaying its mythical origin and thus destroying the self-certainty of enlightenment and its belief in the natural progress of rationality.

Beauty of nature is also the menacing, categorically different opposite and as such it changes the character of art and its relationship to the idea of history. In essence, the sense of reality as experienced and accepted by Henry Adams destroys two vital assumptions underlying the traditional theory of art as mimesis: (a) reality does not contain realms of self-evident substance, serving as a lasting ontologically safe *exemplum mundi*; (b) reality is no holistic entity, neither as idea nor as a projection of the subjective self.

Instead of being mimetic, aesthetic expression assumes the function of the allegorical counterfactual statement. Its truth is not based on verisimilitude but on the *fact* of its creation by human beings, knowing and understanding their faculty of producing consistent elements of reality, which are their very own—worlds apart and self-contained, worlds of potential and possibilities, aesthetic worlds constructed as patterns of self-reference.

The sense of history, therefore, is according to Adams a highly theoretical concept, at best reminding us of the various possibilities of our existence as a subject and object of history, but hardly telling us much about the essence of history itself. Nature will prevail—and as a consequence art is as *necessary* as it is *doomed.* Obviously this kind of philosophy implies both a nonmimetic idea of art and a theory of reality which concedes that history is a borderline phenomenon, a process of ongoing acts of world-making where little can be said in advance about their success or failure. History, in other words, is the great possibility; experience, on the other hand, is the raw material. Reality therefore has two sides to it: docile and domesticated, serving our desire for self-expression, and volatile, elusive, and highly explosive at the same time.

The allegorical image in the case of Henry Adams, its ultimate manifestation being the architectural monument (the analogy of the *ergon* of Herodotus), served as a political expression of both: of one's memory of unity and of one's existence in an unpredictable world. In sum, monuments must be erected for the survival of the community, even if what they represent is based on illusion. The illusion of unity, standing as an allegory of humankind's emancipation from myth, expresses our condition as historical beings, and defines the limit of political choice. Adams knew this only too well and preferred the theoretical side of wisdom. William James would turn these insights, which go all the way back to Emerson, into a wide-ranging criticism of American civilization and culture. An Emersonian in his own tortured way, William James next to J. J. Chapman represents the last of the great figures who, as men of letters, worked out of an Emersonian tradition. Looking at his work, we are once more confronted with the universalizing effort to combine politics and morals, sociology and ethics, and both scientific and spiritual reality. James, in other words, was not only the last great Emersonian, but keeping the transformation of the Emersonian tradition in mind, he was also the most radical representative of that tradition. As Josiah Royce pointed out, he represents and illuminates the end of an era in the American nineteenth century, an era which left many questions unanswered which played an important role in shaping the self-concept of the twentieth century. The work of William James as both scientist and philosopher reminds us, by the mere scope of its inquiry, that one of the most important questions qualifying the modern sense of the self is the one which we still keep asking through work, politics, and art: what is the meaning of nature? Our own nature after all.

CHAPTER 7

Theme: The American object.

Thesis: If allegory, to borrow a phrase from Paul De Man, involves facing the difficulty that its "emphatic clarity of representation does not stand in the service of something that can be represented,"[29] it will become quite evident that the dilemma which the allegorical tradition faces is characterized by paradox. Concentrating on the concrete, the American artist who worked within the tradition in question almost invariably ended up by giving expression to the *idea* of the concrete. The resulting iconography can best be characterized as a stylistic mixture of scientific verism and idealistic materialism. The paintings of Eakins, especially *The Gross Clinic*, can be taken as nearly perfect instances of this combination.

The language of the American object is moralistic, and like its literary counterpart, it is not moralistic by preaching, but by drawing in the spectator and by shifting some of the responsibility for the existence of the image into the realm of the beholder. The art of establishing the "right distance" is the task of the audience: the identity of the viewer and image establish themselves as parts of one unified process. The demanding and highly involved logic of this procedure has all the qualities of a metadiscourse on the relationship between art and society. In fact, it has for all practical purposes often prevented the establishment of such discourse by its mere presence.

The inclusion of visual material into the context of our discussion can hardly have come as a surprise, even if the choice of these particular images may at first have seemed somewhat capricious. Allegorical cognition has, of course, always included the visual image. The outstanding feature of the visual material that has been discussed in the previous chapters is its dialectical tension created by a stylistic combination of *narration* and *representation*. In effect such images appeal by virtue of their explicit constellation of interior spatial subdivisions to the idea of history. Frequently we recognize this tendency by an immediate feeling of melancholy which we experience when looking at the individual paintings. It is a melancholy of a particular kind: a special claim that a constitutive element of the pictorial expression we are looking at is the shock felt about the reality of the present.

The reaction to the shock of the real is usually transformed into historicism, that is, narration, or into a celebration of the surface, that is, representation. "Every form," Emerson tells us, "is a history of the thing," and the unfolding of this history is the enactment of narration.

[29] Paul de Man, "Pascal's Allegory of Persuasion," in Stephen Greenblatt, ed. *Allegory and Representation* (Baltimore, 1981), p. 1.

Thoreau is more direct about his own position vis-à-vis the exterior or the surface. His representation of the surface changes easily into enthusiasm and eventually into the kind of celebration which effects a strange metamorphosis. The essential otherness of the surface becomes part of a scene. The American object, to try a shortcut, is characterized above all by one particular phenomenon: the theatrical surface.

> Now I sit on the Cliffs and look abroad over the river and Conantum hills, I live so much in my habitual thoughts, a routine of thought, that I forget there is any outside to the globe, and am surprised when I behold it as now,—yonder hills and river in the moonlight, the monsters. Yet it is salutary to deal with the surface of things. What are these rivers and hills, these hieroglyphics which my eyes behold? There is something invigorating in this air, which I am peculiarly sensible is a real wind, blowing from over the surface of a planet. I look out of my eyes, I come to my window, and I feel and breathe the fresh air. It is a fact equally glorious with the most inward experience. Why have we ever slandered the outward? The perception of surfaces will always have the effect of miracle to a sane sense. I can see Nobscot faintly.[30]

Looking backwards! If we regard Coleridge as the major influence on American idealistic thought, we are likely to miss three vital elements in the allegorical shaping of the American cultural identity in the nineteenth century. They are, in order of importance, the dominance of conscious doing over the power of the unconscious; second, the intimate link between allegory and secularization; and third, the importance of memory, of *mnemosyne* as embodied in the *making* of the allegorical expression of thought.

Taking into consideration just these three points, we realize instantly that going back to the Platonic tradition in the miraculous year of 1836 as Higginson did, even if it had to be done by way of some neo-Platonic deviations, meant to pick up an ancient quarrel at a strategically vital point in time. If Christian typology, broadly speaking, was *the* answer to the allegorical provocations embodied in the Platonic cosmology, the insistence on conscious authorship in the process of representation must be seen as an assertion of rationality in the face of a fundamentally tragic self-consciousness. We frequently find the allegorist's preoccupation with cosmological dislocation reflected in

[30] Thoreau, *Journal*, p. 478.

both: a celebration of the organic and an equally strong impulse of dissection. Stoically the allegorical mode of cognition faces the transformation of history and time into a fact of nature, into Nature's event. We need not speculate why Emerson opened his wife's grave one year after her death in order to make our point. Whatever ideas come to mind, when we think of this strange act, in the language of allegory the opening of the coffin becomes the acknowledgment of the veil rather than the discovery of some hidden truth underneath. Hence Emerson's single sentence: "29 March. I visited Ellen's tomb and opened the coffin."[31] There was nothing else to say. The movement towards the dissolution of teleological time into allegorical configuration which was accompanied by a parallel movement from the spiritual towards physical nature is borne out by Bronson Alcott's preoccupation with Bacon's "History of Life and Death." In his "Journal for 1836" he comments on his reading in a way which helps to elucidate the overwhelming transition from spirit to nature which radical idealism produces so frequently. "Bacon admits, throughout the whole of his original disquisition—as indeed throughout all his works—the existence and potency of, what he denominates, *Spirit.* I have not as yet found a distinct expression of the *Idea* as it existed in his mind. Yet this *Spirit* was obviously the *standpoint* of all his *philosophy*; he referred to it, perpetually, in all his *Experiments* on Nature, as the *Ground* and *Cause* of all phenomena."[32]

Although most definitely in search of the spiritual source behind Bacon's writing, Alcott quickly gets carried off in the realm of the physical. Having excerpted a long passage from Bacon which centers on the metaphor of reparation as a description of the process of life, Alcott sees the truth in this metaphor, extending such meaning as there is to be found, far beyond its original sense. The movement of language and thought betray the violence involved, when Alcott practically wrests *his sense* of the original text from it, looking for the meaning of the Spirit and being forced into the detail of the body: "But this is the truth of it . . . that the living die in the embrace of the dead, and the parts easily reparable through their conjunction with the parts hardly reparable do decay—for the spirits, blood, flesh and fat are, even after the decline of years easily repaired—but the drier and more porous parts (as the membranes, all tunicles, the sinews, the arteries,

[31] Emerson, *Journals* 4: 7.

[32] Quoted from Joel Myerson, ed., *Studies in the American Renaissance, 1978* (Boston, 1978), p. 52.

veins, bones, cartilages, most of the bowels—in a word, almost all organical parts) are hardly reparable and to their loss."[33]

Plotinus, we remember, deplored the fact that he had a body, something to bear in mind if we want to understand the true extent to which the emergence of physical detail indicates a breaking away—against the conscious intentions of the author—from the neo-Platonist tradition. As an eloquent example of high idealism's tendency to reinstate material nature, Alcott sums up the ancient conflict between the Christian and the Greek traditions of the mind-body controversy, positing human nature somewhere near the middle—only to shift his emphasis, in the end, in the direction of the spirit. He does so by conviction and by will, not by following the logic of his own argument: "Therefore, the inquisition ought to be two-fold—the *one* touching the consumption or dissolution of the body of man—the other touching the reparation and renovation of the same; to the end that the former may, as much as possible, be forbidden and restrained, and the latter comforted."[34]

Emerson would, and in fact did, see through the strategies of such interpretations. He was prepared to face the paradox on which advanced idealism is based. In fact, he recognized the paradox very much in the way in which Kierkegaard would acknowledge its existence as an "absolute paradox." When we look at Alcott's struggle, it is easy to understand Emerson's sympathies, because it was a struggle which he had barely managed to avoid. At the same time we understand Emerson's reaction, when he read Alcott's *Psyche*, which Alcott had given to him in manuscript, hoping for some advice on the possibility of its publication. Emerson's criticism made the point that the major flaw of the text was its exclusive reliance on one idea. This was exactly the kind of fault which someone like Emerson could be expected to find. Emerson after all had himself been preoccupied with the problems and advantages of paradoxical expression for a long time.

The contrapuntal function of Alcott's "Journal for 1836" and Emerson's *Nature* of the same year is to highlight the revival of allegorical intention. The sense of purpose which Emerson was going to display so magnificently first in *Nature* and then, fully developed, in his essays is a latent element in his appraisal of Alcott, which, if it had become manifest, would have turned into criticism. As it stands, the criticism

33 Ibid., pp. 52–53.

34 Ibid., p. 53.

is implicit in his judgment of Alcott, which Emerson entered into his journal on the twenty second of June, 1836.

> Mr. Alcott has been here with his Olympian dreams. He is a world-builder. Ever more he toils to solve the problem, whence is the world? The point at which he prefers to begin is the Mystery of the Birth of a child. I tell him it is ideal for him to affect an interest in the (thoughts) composition of any one else. . . . But he loses like other sovereigns great pleasure by reason of his grandeur. I go to Shakespeare, Goethe, Swift, even to Tennyson, submit myself to them, become merely an organ of hearing, and yield to the law of their being. . . . But Alcott cannot delight in Shakespeare/,/ cannot get near him. And so with all things. What is characteristic also, he cannot recall one word or part of his own conversation or of any one's let the expression be ever so happy. He made here some majestic utterances but so inspired me that even I forget the words often.[35]

If we go back for a moment to Bartlett's remark on becoming "classical to oneself," Emerson's observation that Alcott could not recall his own conversation can be taken as an unintentionally ironic reconstruction of exactly the paradox involved in Bartlett's statement. The solipsism and repetition which such a concept of eternal originality involved held little appeal for someone like Emerson.

The example of Alcott, however, and especially his "Journal for 1836," should demonstrate two major points that ought to be kept in mind whenever we speak of transcendentalism or the allegorical tradition in America. The first and most obvious reservation to be made concerns the unity, or the lack thereof, which has been the issue of critical debates about the transcendentalist movement for a long time. Certainly a critical issue, the crucial point has frequently been missed when the unity or diversity of the movement has been under discussion.

Any horizontal structuring of the group must in the end come to contradictory results, describing the question of unity or diversity of the group in terms of distance or proximity to a center which did not exist. If, however, the group such as it existed is taken as the source of the allegorical tradition, it is easy to avoid not only a description of the obvious, namely the well-known differences which existed among members of the movement. Beyond that, it makes sense to emphasize the role of the group as the origin of the allegorical tradition *by virtue*

[35] Emerson, *Journals* 5: 178.

of the tensions which it produced. In fact, it was the tension rather than the absence of it which allowed the group to have the impact that it did on the particular strain of American culture which preferred the allegorical mode of thought to both the grand idealistic system and to the rigid empiricism of the Lockean kind.

If the intellectual tension which characterized the group of New England transcendentalists can be traced back to one single major force, leaving aside the normal, everyday differences in the theology, politics, and literary taste which one could rightfully expect to exist, it is the figure of Sir Francis Bacon which has to be considered.

Alcott's "Journal for 1836" in general, and his reading and interpretation of Bacon in particular, draw upon the force of allegory as a reminder of separation. Hidden meaning is the designation of allegory and it is therefore constantly referring those who try to find something *beneath* back to the surface in search for clues. The "suggestive incompleteness," to borrow a phrase from James A. Coulter, of the text or the images becomes a scandal to teleological thought once it is installed as the ultimate state.[36] As such, allegory is not a simple trope but the expression of a specific view of the world. It is the result of an act of ordering the cosmos. Epistemologically it means that truth is hidden; ontologically it is a statement about the fact that truth will always remain hidden. Christian typology was *the* answer to the allegorical provocation. Going back to the Platonic tradition, even through the neo-Platonists, meant in short to pick up an ancient quarrel at a strategically highly important point in time. Above all it emphasized the factor of authorial intention, which has been in practice part of the Platonic tradition. Finally, as J. Pépin has shown, Platonism turns the world into an allegory by insisting on its essential exteriority. This instance, renewed and reformulated as a doctrine for the nineteenth century world view is one of the major forces behind the growth and development of the American Renaissance. The allegorical tradition allowed us, once more, to wonder about the meaning of reality, and about our place in a realm of appearances.

[36] James A. Coulter, *The Literary Microcosm: Theories of Interpretation of the Later Neoplatonists* (Leiden, Holland, 1976).

SELECT BIBLIOGRAPHY

Primary Sources

Adams, Henry. *The Degradation of the Democratic Dogma*. Edited by Brooks Adams. New York, 1949.

———. *The Education of Henry Adams*. Edited by Ernest Samuels. Boston, 19.

———. *The Great Secession Winter of 1860–61*. Edited by George Hochfield. New York, 1958.

———. *History of the United States*. New York, 1890.

———. *The Letters of Henry Adams*. Edited by J. C. Levenson, Ernest Samuels, Charles Vandersee, and Viola Hopkins Winner. 3 vols. Cambridge, Mass., 1982.

———. *Mont-Saint-Michel and Chartres*. London, 1950.

Emerson, Ralph Waldo. *The Complete Works of Ralph Waldo Emerson*. 10 vols. Boston, 1885.

———. *The Early Lectures of Ralph Waldo Emerson*. Edited by Robert E. Spiller and Wallace E. Williams. Cambridge, Mass., 1972.

———. *The Journals of Ralph Waldo Emerson*. Edited by William H. Gilman et al. Cambridge, Mass., 1960.

———. *The Letters of Ralph Waldo Emerson*. Edited by Ralph L. Rusk. New York, 1939.

James, William. *Essays in Religion and Morality*. Cambridge, Mass., 1982.

———. *A Pluralistic Universe*. Cambridge, Mass., 1977.

———. *Pragmatism: A New Name for Some Old Ways of Thinking*. New York, 1908.

———. *Pragmatism and the Meaning of Truth*. Cambridge, Mass., 1981.

———. *The Principles of Psychology*. Cambridge, Mass., 1981.

———. *The Varieties of Religious Experience*. London, 1902.

Thoreau, Henry David. *The Journal of Henry David Thoreau*. New York, 1962.

———. *Walden and Civil Disobedience*, ed. Owen Thomas (New York, 1966).

———. *The Writings of Henry David Thoreau* (Manuscript Edition). New York, 1906.

———. *The Writings of Henry D. Thoreau*. Edited by Wendell Glick. Princeton, N.J., 1973

Secondary Sources

Books

Aaron, Daniel. *Men of Good Hope.* New York, 1951.

———. *The Unwritten War.* New York, 1973.

Adorno, Theodor W. *Kierkegaard*; Konstruktion des Ästhetischen. Frankfurt am Main, 1962.

———. *Negative Dialektik.* Frankfurt am Main, 1966.

Alcott, Amos Bronson. *Tablets.* Boston, 1868.

Allen, Don Cameron. *Mysteriously Meant; The Rediscovery of Pagan Symbolism and Allegorical Interpretation in the Renaissance.* Baltimore, 1970.

Allen, Gay Wilson. *Waldo Emerson.* Harmondsworth, 1981.

Allison, David B., ed. *The New Nietzsche.* New York, 1977.

Alpers, Svetlana. *The Art of Describing: Dutch Art in the Seventeenth Century.* Chicago, 1983.

Bacon, Francis. *The Works of Francis Bacon.* Stuttgart, 1963.

Barbour, Brian M., ed. *American Transcendentalism: An Anthology of Criticism.* London, 1973.

Barney, Stephen A. *Allegories of History, Allegories of Love.* Hamden, Conn., 1979.

Barzun, Jacques. *A Stroll With William James.* New York, 1983.

Bates, Ralph S. *Scientific Societies in the United States.* New York, 1945.

Baym, Max Isaac. *The French Education of Henry Adams.* New York, 1951.

Bell, Whitfield J. *Early American Science.* Williamsburg, Va., 1955.

Benjamin, Walter. *Gesammelte Schriften.* 6 vols. Frankfurt/Main, 1985.

Bercovitch, Sacvan. *The American Jeremiad.* Madison, Wis., 1978.

———, ed. *Typology and Early American Literature.* Amherst, Mass., 1972.

Berthoff, Warner. *The Ferment of Realism.* London, 1981.

Blackmur, R. P. *Henry Adams.* New York, 1980.

Bloom, David. *Knowledge and Social Imagery.* London, 1976.

Blumenberg, Hans. *Die Lesbarkeit der Welt.* Frankfurt/Main, 1981.

———. *The Legitimacy of the Modern Age.* Cambridge, Mass., 1983.

Boller, Paul F., Jr. *American Transcendentalism 1830–1860: An Intellectual Inquiry.* New York, 1974.

Bowen, Francis. *Critical Essays on a Few Subjects Connected with the History and Present Condition of Speculative Philosophy.* Boston, 1842.

———. *The Principles of Political Economy.* 1856; New York, 1974.

Bowman, Sylvia E. *The Year 2000: A Critical Biography of Edward Bellamy.* New York, 1958.

Buell, Lawrence. *Literary Transcendentalism.* Ithaca, N.Y., 1979.

Burnham, John C. *Lester Frank Ward in American Thought.* Washington, D.C., 1956.

Caldwell, Patricia. *The Puritan Conversion Narrative.* Cambridge, Mass., 1983.

Cameron, Kenneth Walter. *Ralph Waldo Emerson's Reading.* New York, 1966.

Carafiol, Peter. *Transcendent Reason.* Tallahassee, 1982.

Castelli, Enrico, ed. *Hermeneutique de la Secularisation.* Rome, 1976.

Cavell, Stanley. *The Senses of Walden.* San Francisco, 1981.
Channing, William Ellery. *The Works.* Boston, 1890.
Christakes, George. *Albion W. Small.* Boston, 1978.
Clark, Henry Hayden, ed. *Transitions in American Literary History.* Durham, N.C., 1953.
Clifford, Gay. *The Transformations of Allegory.* London, 1974.
Cohen, Marshall J. *Charles Horton Cooley and the Social Self in American Thought.* New York, 1982.
Conder, John. *A Formula of His Own.* Chicago, 1970.
Cook, Reginald Lansing. *Passage to Walden.* New York, 1966.
Coulter, James A. *The Literary Microcosm: Theories of Interpretation of the Later Neoplatonists.* Leiden, Holland, 1976.
Dahlstrand, Frederick C. *Amos Bronson Alcott.* London, 1982.
Daniels, George H., ed. *Nineteenth-Century American Science.* Evanston, Ill., 1972.
Delbanco, Andrew. *William Ellery Channing.* Cambridge, Mass., 1981.
Demetz, Peter, ed. *Walter Benjamin: Reflections.* New York, 1978.
Dewey, John, ed. *Essays on the New Empiricism.* Carbondale, Ill., 1977.
Dibble, Vernon K. *The Legacy of Albion Small.* Chicago, 1975.
Ebeling, Hans, ed. *Subjektivität und Selbsterhaltung.* Frankfurt/Main, 1976.
Eisely, Loren. *The Unexpected Universe.* New York, 1969.
Elvee, Richard Q., ed. *Mind in Nature.* San Francisco, 1982.
Farrington, Benjamin. *The Philosophy of Francis Bacon.* Liverpool, 1964.
Feinstein, Howard M. *Becoming William James.* Ithaca, N.Y., 1984.
Ferguson, Arthur B. *The Articulate Citizen and the English Renaissance.* Durham, N.C., 1965.
Fine, William F. *Progressive Evolutionism and American Sociology, 1890–1920.* Ann Arbor, Mich., 1976.
Fitzgerald, F. Scott. *The Great Gatsby.* New York, 1925.
Fletcher, Angus. *Allegory: The Theory of a Symbolic Mode.* Ithaca, N.Y., 1964.
Furner, Mary O. *Advocacy and Objectivity.* Lexington, Ky., 1975.
Garber, Frederick. *Thoreau's Redemptive Imagination.* New York, 1977.
Gebhard, Walter. *Nietzsches Totalismus.* Berlin, 1983.
Gérando, Joseph Marie de. *Histoire comparée des systèmes de Philosophie.* Paris, 1804.
Girard, René. *Violence and the Sacred.* Baltimore, 1977.
Goodrich, Lloyd. *Thomas Eakins: His Life and Work.* New York, 1933.
Grave, S. A. *The Scottish Philosophy of Common Sense.* Oxford, 1960.
Greenblatt, Stephen J. *Allegory and Representation.* Baltimore, 1981.
Harbert, Earl N. *Henry Adams: A Reference Guide.* Boston, 1978.
Harding, Walter, and Meyer, Michael. *The New Thoreau Handbook.* New York, 1980.
Harrington, John Beattle. *William James' Theory of Religious Knowledge.* University Microfilms, pub. no. 6810. Ann Arbor, Mich. 1954.
Hartman, Geoffrey H. *Criticism in the Wilderness.* New Haven, Conn., 1980.

Haskell, Thomas L. *The Emergence of Professional Social Science*. Urbana, Ill., 1977.

Heidegger, Martin. *Nietzsche*. Vols. 1 and 2. Pfullingen, 1961.

Henderson, Henry B. III. *Versions of the Past*. New York, 1974.

Hendricks, Gordon. *The Life and Work of Thomas Eakins*. New York, 1974.

Henri, Robert. *The Art Spirit*. New York, 1922.

Herbst, Jurgen. *The German Historical School in American Scholarship*. Ithaca, N.Y., 1965.

Herschel, John Frederick William. *Outlines of Astronomy*. London, 1849.

———. *A Preliminary Discourse on the Study of Natural Philosophy*. New York, 1966.

Hicks, Philip M. *The Development of the Natural History Essay in American Literature*. Philadelphia, 1924.

Higginson, Thomas Wentworth. *Margaret Fuller Ossoli*. New York, 1968.

Hochfield, George, ed. *The Great Secession Winter of 1860–61*. New York, 1958.

Holmes, Oliver Wendell. *Ralph Waldo Emerson*. New York, 1980.

Honig, Edwin. *Dark Conceit: The Making of Allegory*. Evanston, Ill., 1959.

Hopkins, Vivian. *Spires of Form: A Study of Emerson's Aesthetic Theory*. Cambridge, Mass., 1951.

Howe, Daniel Walker. *The Unitarian Conscience: Harvard Moral Philosophy 1805–1861*. Cambridge, Mass., 1970.

Howe, M. A. DeWolfe. *John Jay Chapman and His Letters*. Boston, 1937.

Husserl, Edmund. *The Crisis of European Sciences and Transcendental Phenomenology*. Evanston, Ill., 1970.

Irwin, John T. *American Hieroglyphics*. New Haven, Conn., 1980.

Jardine, Lisa. *Francis Bacon: Discovery and the Art of Discourse*. Cambridge, Mass., 1974.

Jarves, James Jackson. *The Art-Idea*. New York, 1877.

Johns, Elizabeth. *Thomas Eakins*. Princeton, N.J., 1983.

Jordy, William H. *Henry Adams: Scientific Historian*. New Haven, Conn., 1952.

Kammen, Michael. *People of Paradox*. New York, 1980.

Kierkegaard, Søren. *Fear and Trembling and the Sickness unto Death*. Princeton, N.J., 1954.

———. *For Self-Examination and Judge for Yourselves and Three Discourses*. Princeton, N.J., 1974.

Kohlstedt, Sally Gregory. *The Formation of the American Scientific Community*. Chicago, Ill., 1976.

Konvitz, Milton R. *The Recognition of Ralph Waldo Emerson*. Ann Arbor, Mich., 1972.

Konvitz, Milton R., and Whicher, Stephen E., eds. *Emerson: A Collection of Critical Essays*. Englewood Cliffs, N.J., 1962.

Kwiat, Joseph J., and Turpie, Mary C., ed. *Studies in American Culture*. Minneapolis, 1960.

LaCapra, Dominick, and Kaplan, Steven L., ed. *Modern European Intellectual History*. Ithaca, N.Y., 1982.

Larkin, Oliver W. *Art and Life in America.* New York, 1949.
Lears, T. J. Jackson. *No Place of Grace.* New York, 1981.
Levenson, J. C. *The Mind and Art of Henry James.* Boston, Mass., 1957.
Levin, David, ed. *Emerson: Prophecy, Metamorphosis, and Influence.* New York, 1975.
———. *History as Romantic Art.* Stanford, Calif., 1959.
Lewis, C. S. *The Allegory of Love: A Study in Medieval Tradition.* London, 1936.
Leyburn, Ellen Douglas. *Satiric Allegory: Mirror of Man.* New Haven, Conn., 1956.
Loewenberg, Bert James. *American History in American Thought.* New York, 1972.
Lowell, James Russell. *The Writings of James Russell Lowell in Prose and Poetry.* Boston, 1864.
Lynn, Kenneth, ed. *The Professions in America.* Boston, 1965.
Lyon, Melvin. *Symbol and Idea in Henry Adams.* Lincoln, Neb., 1970.
McCoubrey, John W. *American Art 1700–1960.* Englewood Cliffs, N.J., 1965.
McIntosh, James. *Thoreau as Romantic Naturalist.* Ithaca, N.Y., 1974.
MacIntyre, Alasdair. *After Virtue.* Notre Dame, Ind., 1981.
McKenney, Ruth. *Industrial Valley.* New York, 1939.
Man, Paul De. *Allegories of Reading.* New Haven, Conn., 1979.
———. *Blindness and Insight.* Minneapolis, 1971.
Mane, Robert. *Henry Adams on the Road to Chartres.* Cambridge, Mass., 1971.
Marini, Stephen. *Radical Sects of Revolutionary New England.* Cambridge, Mass., 1982, pp. 172–76.
Martland, Thomas R. *The Metaphysics of William James and John Dewey.* New York, 1963.
Matthiessen, F. O. *American Renaissance.* London, 1968.
Mead, David C., ed. *The American Scholar Today.* New York, 1970.
Meisel, Max. *A Bibliography of American Natural History.* New York, 1967.
Mendelsohn, Jack. *Channing the Reluctant Radical.* Boston, 1971.
Metzger, Charles. *Emerson and Greenough.* Berkeley, Calif., 1954.
———. *Thoreau and Whitman: A Study of the Aesthetics.* Hamden, Conn., 1968.
Meyer, Michael. *Several More Lives to Live.* Westport, Conn., 1977.
Miller, Perry. *Errand into the Wilderness.* Cambridge, Mass., 1976.
Minter, David L. *The Interpreted Design as a Structural Principle in American Prose.* New Haven, Conn., 1969.
Moore, Wilbert E. *The Professions: Roles and Rules.* New York, n.d.
Murrin, Michael. *The Veil of Allegory: Some Notes toward a Theory of Allegorical Rhetoric in the English Renaissance.* Chicago, 1969.
Myerson, Joel, ed. *Studies in the American Renaissance.* Boston, 1978.
Nietzsche, Friedrich. *Sämtliche Werke.* Munich, 1980.
Nochlin, Linda. *Realism.* Harmondsworth, 1971.
———. *Realism and Tradition in Art, 1848–1900.* Englewood Cliffs, N.J., 1966.
Novak, Barbara. *American Painting of the Nineteenth Century.* New York, 1969.
Novak, Michael, ed. *American Philosophy and the Future.* New York, 1968.

Odum, Howard W. *American Sociology*. New York, 1951.
Packer, B. L. *Emerson's Fall*. New York, 1982.
Padover, Saul K. *The Genius of America*. New York, 1960.
Pasley, Malcolm, ed. *Nietzsche: Imagery and Thought*. London, 1978.
Patterson, Robert Lee. *The Philosophy of William Ellery Channing*. New York, 1952.
Paul, Sherman. *Emerson's Angle of Vision: Man and Nature in American Experience*. Cambridge, Mass., 1952.
———. *The Shores of America*. Urbana, Ill., 1958.
Pépin, Jean. *Mythe et Allégorie*. Paris, 1976.
Persons, Stow. *The Decline of American Gentility*. New York, 1973.
Piehler, Paul. *The Visionary Landscape: A Study in Medieval Allegory*. London, 1971.
Porte, Joel. *Emerson and Thoreau: Transcendentalism in Conflict*. Middletown, Conn., 1965.
———. *Emerson: Prospect and Retrospect*. Cambridge, Mass., 1982.
———. *Representative Man*. New York, 1979.
Porter, Fairfield. *Thomas Eakins*. New York, 1959.
Pritchard, John Paul. *Return to the Fountains*. Durham, N.C., 1942.
Rice, Madeleine Hooke. *Federal Street Pastor: The Life of William Ellery Channing*. New York, 1961.
Richardson, Robert D., Jr. *Myth and Literature in the American Renaissance*. Bloomington, Ind., 1978.
Rollinson, Philip. *Classical Theories of Allegory and Christian Culture*. Pittsburgh, 1981.
Rorty, Richard. *Consequences of Pragmatism*. Minneapolis, 1982.
———. *Philosophy and the Mirror of Nature*. Princeton, N.J., 1979.
Ross, Ralph. *Makers of American Thought*. Minneapolis, 1974.
Rowe, John Carlos. *Henry Adams and Henry James*. Ithaca, N.Y., 1976.
———. *Henry Adams: The Major Phase*. Cambridge, Mass., 1964.
———. *Henry Adams: The Middle Years*. Cambridge, Mass., 1958.
———. *The Young Henry Adams*. Cambridge, Mass., 1948.
Sanborn, F. B. *Recollections of Seventy Years*. 2 vols. Boston, 1909.
Sanborn, F. B., and Harris, William T. A. *Bronson Alcott: His Life and Philosophy*. Boston, 1893.
Sanford, Charles L. *The Quest for Paradise*. Urbana, Ill., 1961.
Scheick, William J. *The Slender Human Word: Emerson's Artistry in Prose*. Knoxville, Tenn., 1978.
Schendler, Sylvan. *Eakins*. Boston, 1967.
Scheyer, Ernst. *The Circle of Henry Adams: Art and Artists*. Detroit, 1970.
Schlüpmann, Heide. *Friedrich Nietzsches Ästhetische Opposition*. Stuttgart, 1977.
Scott, Clifford H. *Lester Frank Ward*. Boston, 1976.
Scott, Donald M. *From Office to Profession: The New England Ministry, 1750–1850*. Philadelphia, 1978.
Sealts, Merton M., and Ferguson, Alfred R., ed. *Emerson's Nature: Origin, Growth, Meaning*. New York, 1969.

Segal, H. *Technological Utopianism and American Culture.* Chicago, 1985.
Sellin, David. *The First Pose.* New York, 1976.
Seven Arts, The. 1 (November 1916–April 1917) and 2 (May 1917–October 1917). AMS Reprint Co., New York.
Sewell, Darrel. *Thomas Eakins.* Philadelphia, 1982.
Sheldon, George William. *American Painters.* New York, 1972.
Shepard, Odell, ed. *The Heart of Thoreau's Journals.* New York, 1961.
Simon, Myron, and Parsons, Thornton H., ed. *Transcendentalism and Its Legacy.* Ann Arbor, Mich., 1969.
Soyer, Raphael. *Homage to Thomas Eakins.* South Brunswick, N.J., 1966.
Stebbins, Theodore E.; Troyes, Carol; and Fairbrother, Trevor J. *A New World: Masterpieces of American Painting 1760–1910.* Boston, 1983.
Steinkraus, Warren E., ed. *New Studies in Hegel's Philosophy.* New York, 1971.
Stephens, James. *Francis Bacon and the Style of Science.* Chicago, Mich., 1975.
Stern, Frederick C. *F. O. Matthiessen, Christian Socialist as Critic.* Chapel Hill, N.C., 1981.
Stoessel, Marleen Aura. *Das vergessene Menschliche, Zu Sprache und Erfahrung bei Walter Benjamin.* Munich, 1983.
Tanner, Tony. *The Reign of Wonder, Naivete and Reality in American Literature.* Cambridge, England, 1977.
Taylor, Mark C. *Journeys to Selfhood: Hegel and Kierkegaard.* Berkeley, Calif., 1980.
Thomas, John L. *Alternative America.* Cambridge, Mass., 1983.
Thomas, Owen, ed. *Walden and Civil Disobedience.* New York, 1966.
Trachtenberg, Alan. *The Incorporation of America.* New York, 1982.
Tuckerman, Henry T. *Book of the Artists.* New York, 1867.
Turbayne, Murray. *The Myth of Metaphor.* Columbia, S.C., 1970.
Tuve, Rosemond. *Allegorical Imagery: Some Medieval Books and Their Posterity.* Princeton, N.J., 1966.
Twain, Mark. *A Connecticut Yankee in King Arthur's Court.* New York, n.d.
———. *No. 44, The Mysterious Stranger.* Berkeley, 1969.
Vernant, Jean-Pierre. *Die Entstehung des griechischen Denkens.* Frankfurt, 1982.
Vickers, Brian, ed. *Essential Articles for the Study of Francis Bacon.* Hamden, Conn., 1968.
Vitzthum, Richard C. *The American Compromise.* Norman, Okla., 1974.
Wagner, Vern. *The Suspension of Henry Adams.* Detroit, 1969.
Wallace, Karl R. *Francis Bacon on Communication and Rhetoric.* Chapel Hill, N.C., 1943.
———. *Francis Bacon on the Nature of Man.* Urbana, Ill., 1967.
Wallis, R. T. *Neoplatonism.* New York, 1972.
Weinberg, Julius. *Edward Alsworth Ross and the Sociology of Progressivism.* Madison, Wis., 1972.
Whicher, Stephen. *Freedom and Fate.* Philadelphia, 1971.
White, Morton. *Science and Sentiment in America.* New York, 1972.
Wilmerding, John, ed. *The Genius of American Painting.* New York, 1973.
———. *Important Information Inside.* Washington, D.C., 1983.

Wilmerding, John, Linda Ayres, and Earl A. Powell. eds. *An American Perspective: Nineteenth-Century Art from the Collection of Joann and Julian Ganz, Jr.* Hanover, N.H., 1981.
Wollheim, Richard. *On Art and the Mind.* Cambridge, Mass., 1974.
Wright, Conrad. *The Beginning of Unitarianism in America.* Boston, 1955.
Young, Frederic Harold. *The Philosophy of Henry James, Sr.* New York, 1951.

Articles

Aaron, Daniel. "Henry Adams: The Public and Private View." *Hudson Review* 5 (Winter 1953): 608–14.
Albright, Adam Emory. "Memories of Thomas Eakins." *Harper's Bazaar*, August 1947.
Allen, Gay Wilson. "James's *Varieties of Religious Experience.*" *Emerson Society Quarterly* 39 (1965): 81–85.
Allport, Gordon W. "The Productive Paradoxes of William James." *The Psychological Review* 50 (January 1943): 95–120.
Baldinger, Wallace S. "The Art of Eakins, Homer, and Ryder." *Art Quarterly* 9 no. 3 (Summer 1946).
Barker, Virgil. "Imagination in Thomas Eakins." *Parnassus* (November 1939): 8.
Baym, Nina. "Thoreau's View of Science." *Journal of the History of Ideas* 26 (1965): 221–34.
Benjamin, S.G.W. "Present Tendencies of American Art." *Harper's New Monthly Magazine*, 58, no. 346 (March 1879): 481–96.
Berger, H. L. "Emerson and Carlyle: The Dissenting Believers." *Emerson Society Quarterly* 38 (1st quarter, 1965): 87–90.
Bloom, Harold. *The Ringers in the Tower: Studies in Romantic Tradition.* Chicago, 1971, pp. 217–33.
Born, Wolfgang. "Bachelor Artist." *Magazine of Arts Digest* 16 (April 1942): 19.
Bouwsma, William J. "From History of Ideas to History of Meaning" *Journal of Interdisciplinary History* 12, no. 2 (Autumn 1981): 289–91.
Bregler, Charles. "Thomas Eakins as a Teacher." *The Arts* March 1931 and October 1931.
Brown, S. G. "Emerson's Platonism." *New England Quarterly* 18 (1945): 325–45.
Brownell, William C. "The Art Schools of Philadelphia." *Scribner's Monthly* 18, no. 5 (September 1879): 745.
———. "The Young Painters of America." *Scribner's Monthly* 20 (May 1880).
Burroughs, Alan. "Thomas Eakins, the Man." *The Arts*, December 1923.
Caffin, Charles H. "Some American Portrait Painters." *The Critic*, January 1904, pp. 31–48.
Cairns, John C. "The Successful Quest of Henry Adams." *South Atlantic Quarterly* 57 (Spring 1958): 168–93.
Capek, Milic. "The Reappearance of the Self in the Last Century." *The Philosophical Review* 62 (1953): 526–44.

Chirico, R. F. "Some Reflections on Sound and Silence in the Visual Arts." *Arts Magazine* 56 (1982): 103.

Crowley, John W. "The Suicide of the Artist." *New England Quarterly* 46, no. 2 (June 1973): 189–204.

Daniels, George H. "The Process of Professionalization." *Isis* 58 (1967).

Davidson, R. "Museum Accessions: European and American Paintings and Drawings." *Antiques* 99 (May 1971): 676.

Davis, F. "Talking about Sale-Rooms." *Country Life* 149 (1971): 1158–59.

Davis, M.R. "Emerson's 'Reason' and the Scottish Philosophers" *N. E. D.* 17 (1944): 209–28.

Dekay, Charles. "Movements in American Painting." *The Magazine of Art* 10 (1887).

Dreiss, J. "George Bellows." Review of George Bellows: The Boxing Pictures," exhibit at the National Gallery of Art, Washington D.C. *Arts Magazine* 57, no. 4 (December 1982): 15.

Dunstan, B. "Looking at Paintings." *American Artist* 44 (1980): 74–75.

Eisey, George McKee. "The First Education of Henry Adams." *New England Quarterly* 14 (1941): 679–84.

Feld, S. P. "Loan Collection." *Metropolitan Museum of Art Bulletin*, no. 23 (April 1965): 294.

Fleck, Richard. "Thoreau as Mythologist." *Research Studies* 40 (1972): 195–206.

Gombrich, Ernst. "A Classical Quotation in Michelangelo." *Journal of the Warburg and Courtauld Institutes* 1 (1973): 1.

Goode, William J. "Encroachment, Charlatanism and the Emerging Professions." *American Sociological Review* 25 (1960): 902.

Goodrich, L. "Thomas Eakins, Realist." *The Arts*, October 1929.

Harbert, Earl N. "The Education of Henry Adams." *Journal of Narrative Technique* 4 (1974): 3–18.

Hayne, Barrie, and Morrison, K. "Henry Adams." *American Literary Realism* 8 (Summer 1975): 180–88.

Hopkins, Vivian C. "Emerson and Bacon." *American Literature* 29 (January 1958): 408–30.

———. "The Influence of Goethe on Emerson's Aesthetic Theory." *Philological Quarterly* 27 (1948): 325–44.

Katt, Leslie. "Thomas Eakins Now." *Arts*, September 1956.

Koretz, Gene H. "Augustine's *Confessions* and *The Education of Henry Adams*." *Comparative Literature* 12 (Summer 1960): 193–206.

Lassiter, B. B. "American Paintings in the Reynolds House Collection." *Antiques* 98 (1970): 763.

McBride, Henry. "Modern Art." *The Dial*, February 1922, pp. 652–54.

MacQueen, John. "Allegory." *The Critical Idiom* 14 (1970).

Mastai, M.L.D. "American Drawings, Pastels, and Watercolors." *Connoisseur* 161 (February 1966): 138.

Meldrum, Ronald M. "The Epistolary Concerns of Henry Adams." *Research Studies* 37 (1969): 227–34.

Meyers, Robert. "Meaning and Metaphysics in James." *Philosophy and Phenomenological Research* 31 (1971): 369–80.

Michaels, Walter Ben. "Walden's False Bottoms." *Glyph* 1 (1977): 132–49.

Miller, Ross. "Autobiography as Fact and Fiction." *Centennial Review* 16 (1972): 221–32.

Miller, Ross Lincoln. "Henry Adams: Making It Over Again." *Centennial Review* 18 (1974): 288–305.

Parker, B. N. "Old Cupboard Door by W. Harnett." *Boston Museum Bulletin* 38 (1940): 17–18.

Pearlman, B. B. "Eakins Comes of Age." *The Art Digest*, February 15, 1955.

Porte, Joel. "Emerson, Thoreau, and the Double Consciousness." *New England Quarterly* 41 (1968): 40–50.

———. "The Problem of Emerson," In *Uses of Literature*, edited by Monroe Engel, pp. 83–114. Cambridge, Mass., 1973.

Ratcliff, C. "Reality of Appearance: Whitney Museum of American Art, N.Y." *Art International* 14 (1970): 94.

Richardson, E. P. "Grandma's Hearthstone Acquired." *Detroit Institute of Arts Bulletin* 31 (1951–52): 9–11.

Sartain, William. "Thomas Eakins." *The Art World*, January 1918.

Schnakenberg, Henry B. "Thomas Eakins." *The Arts*, January 1931.

Schwartz, N. "American Paintings at Parke-Bernet." *Arts Magazine* 45, no. 6 (April 1971): 9.

Smith, J. C. "The Enigma of Thomas Eakins." *The American Artist*, November 1956.

Stark, Cruce. "The Development of a Historical Stance." *Clio* 4 (1975): 383–97.

———. "The Historical Irrelevance of Heroes." *American Literature* 46, no. 2 (May 1974): 170–81.

Tanner, Tony. "The Lost American—The Despair of Henry Adams." *Modern Age* 5 (1962): 299–310.

Taylor, Francis Henry. "Thomas Eakins, Positivist." *Parnassus*, March 1930.

Taylor, Horace. "Thoreau's Scientific Interests as Seen in His Journal." *McNeese Review* 14 (1963) 45–59.

Vandersee, Charles. "Henry Adams." *American Literary Realism* 8 (Winter 1975): 18–34.

Wasser, Henry. "The Education of Henry Adams: Fifty Years." *Midcontinent American Studies* 10 (1969): 85–87.

Weisberg, G. P. "Sleight-of-Hand Man." *Artnews* 82 (1982): 88–92.

White, Lynn. "Dynamo and Virgin Reconsidered." *American Scholar* 27 (1958): 183–94.

Wilmerding, John. "The American Object." In *An American Perspective: Nineteenth Century Art From the Collection of Jo Ann and J. Gant, Jr.* Edited by John Wilmerding, Linda Ayres, and Earl A. Powell. Hanover, N.H., 1981.

INDEX